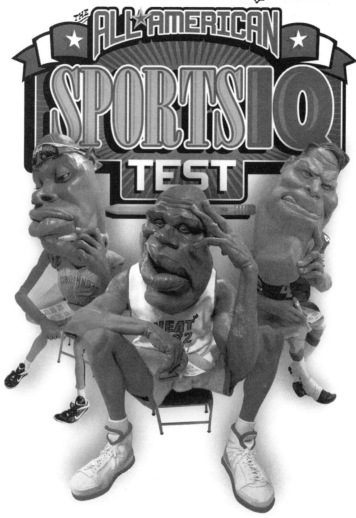

THE ALL★AMERICAN SPORTSIQ TEST

Published by

SportingNews
BOOKS

Compiled by Ron Smith

Ron Smith, who compiled *The All-American Sports IQ Test*, is a senior editor for the Sporting News.

Contributing editors: Dave Sloan, Corrie Anderson, David Bukovich, Matt Crossman, Jessica Daues, Tom Dienhart, Tricia Garner, Tom Gatto, Dan Graf, Joe Hoppel, Kathy Sheldon, Kyle Veltrop.

Research: Sarah Gietschier. **Copyediting:** Corrie Anderson, Chris Bergeron, David Bukovich, Jessica Daues, Katie Koss, Shawn Reid.

Cover illustrations: Richard Heroldt. **Cover design:** Chad Painter, Chris Callan. **Page design:** Michael Behrens, Chad Painter. **Prepress specialists:** Vern Kasal, Steve Romer.

The answers for *The All-American Sports IQ Test* are up to date through July 2004.

ISBN: 0-89204-735-6   10 9 8 7 6 5 4 3 2 1

Contents

Where's Yogi?   4-5

Chapter 1
Baseball   7

Chapter 2
College Mascots   23

Chapter 3
Pro Football   41

Chapter 4
Faces From the Past   59

Chapter 5
Pro Basketball   75

Chapter 6
Pro Team Logos   95

Chapter 7
Hockey   111

Chapter 8
Sports Movies   129

Chapter 9
College Football   151

Chapter 10
Game Faces   171

Chapter 11
College Basketball   185

Chapter 12
Baseball Silhouettes   201

Chapter 13
Pro Sports   213

Four's a Crowd   232-233

Chapter 14
All Sports   235

Answers   256

Photo Credits   287

Where's Yogi?

Can you find Yogi Berra in this crowd? His location is revealed on page 257.

Mystery Guest

Can you name the athlete and the sport?

1 You often can find me three-putting on the green. Or hooking a drive that wasn't supposed to go that way. Or watching a shot dribble off my tee. I love the game of golf, but it sure doesn't love me.

2 I am much better remembered for my feats with another kind of ball. Before I arrived, my college never had a reason to dance. But, thanks to me and another Person, we finally got that chance. The year was 1984, but some spoilsports from Richmond promptly showed us the door.

3 I am a big man, but that never kept me grounded. I'm quicker and more agile than I look. I always loved taking a leap, but I never was averse to going around or through anyone who got in my way.

4 I found firsthand that the City of Brotherly Love wasn't always so lovely. I had some great times there, but I also had some bad ones. I just couldn't rebound from the negativity. Toward the end of my stay, things turned ugly. So when I departed into the Suns-set, everything became as simple as M-V-P.

5 I struck gold twice (it could have been three—thanks, Bob Knight), but unfortunately my career often is criticized because it did not have a ring to it. I swore the Sun was going to shine on me in 1993, but, alas, my good buddy Mike and his boys said, "Bull."

6 I'm no sellout, but I don't mind selling. I've done commercials for deodorant, food and shoes, just to name a few. I went one-on-one with Godzilla and got on a horse for a little polo. But I never claimed to be a role model and slammed the point home when I told people to raise their own kids.

7 My propensity for cleaning my plate—as well as the glass—earned me a moniker: "The Round Mound of Rebound." But because I'm considered one of the 50 best NBA players ever, maybe the nickname that fits me better is, "Sir."

8 I have stayed close to the game since retiring, and even have a sweet little studio gig. I break down the game, make people laugh and weigh myself to see if I'm getting too big. But I have a special knack for making explosive comments, which makes it appropriate that I work for TNT.

CHAPTER 1
BASEBALL

First to Last

Warming up

The leadoff man and starting pitcher are provided for the first game in the history of 14 expansion teams. Name the teams and seasons.

1. Lou Piniella, Wally Bunker.

2. Eric Young, David Nied.

3. Eddie Yost, Eli Grba.

4. Maury Wills, Mudcat Grant.

5. Scott Pose, Charlie Hough.

6. Bob Aspromonte, Bobby Shantz.

7. John Scott, Bill Singer.

8. Quinton McCracken, Wilson Alvarez.

9. Richie Ashburn, Roger Craig.

10. Rafael Robles, Dick Selma.

11. Devon White, Andy Benes.

12. Coot Veal, Dick Donovan.

13. Dave Collins, Diego Segui.

14. Tommy Harper, Marty Pattin.

Lou Piniella, the current manager of one of baseball's newest expansion teams, once was the leadoff man in the first game played by another expansion franchise.

Getting serious

The Baseball Writers Association of America selected its first MVPs in 1931 (A.L. and N.L.), first Rookie of the Year in 1947 (combined leagues) and first Cy Young winner in 1956 (combined leagues). Of the

DID YOU KNOW...

➤ That the 1994 MVPs, Houston's *Jeff Bagwell* in the National League and Chicago's *Frank Thomas* in the American League, were born on the same day—May 27, 1968?

Thomas   Bagwell

➤ That *Danny Ainge* hit two home runs in 211 major league games and 665 at-bats for the Toronto Blue Jays before abandoning baseball in 1981 for a career in the NBA?

four winners, only one failed to gain Hall of Fame election. Name him.

2 On a high-to-low chart of baseball's 3,000-hit men, who would be listed last?

3 Name the former New York Mets catcher who, in 1962, hit into a triple play in his last major league at-bat.

4 Name the Hall of Fame slugger who hit his 521st career home run in his last major league at-bat.

5 In 1959, the Boston Red Sox became the last major league team to break the color barrier. Name the player who served as a Boston pinch runner in the historic July 21 game at Chicago.

6 In May 1966, this St. Louis player hit the Cardinals' last home run at Sportsman's Park and the Cardinals' first homer at new Busch Memorial Stadium. Name him.

7 If you rank the Hall of Fame's five-man charter class according to vote totals, this former great finishes last—but certainly not least.

8 Name the last major league franchise to relocate from one city to another.

9 Name the last position mentioned in Abbott and Costello's "Who's on First?" comedy sketch. Hint: The player's name is "I Don't Care."

10 This 300-game career winner also is the last pitcher to get a hit in an All-Star Game, doubling off Blue Moon Odom in the 1969 classic at Washington's RFK Stadium. Name him.

The Drama Club

Warming up

1 In retrospect, it seems only fitting this sore-legged out-fielder is credited with the first World Series home run at Yankee Stadium. His dramatic Game 1 blow in 1923 gave the New York Giants a 5-4 win over their cross-town rivals.

2 It didn't decide a World Series or All-Star Game, but this home run provided a dramatic end to a 1984 regular-season marathon between the Chicago White Sox and Milwaukee Brewers—in the bottom of the 25th inning. Name the player who decided the 7-6 game with one dramatic swing after 8 hours, 6 minutes and an overnight suspension of play.

3 One of the most memorable home runs in Giants history gave the Atlanta Braves an uncontested West Division title in 1982. The Giants finished only third but experienced great joy when a three-run homer by this second baseman in the regular-season finale secured a 5-3 victory over the hated Dodgers and kept them from forcing a division playoff.

4 Try out this scenario: Bottom of the ninth, Game 1 of the World Series, teams locked in a scoreless tie. The batter hits a dramatic walkoff home run against one of the top righthanders in the National League. Name the hitter who delivered this dramatic blast in the 1949 fall classic.

5 In a 1971 All-Star Game best remembered for Reggie Jackson's 520-foot home run that struck a Tiger Stadium light tower, the American League also got homers from two more-renowned sluggers. Both hit their 500th career homers later that season. Name them.

6 Most "500th" home runs are remembered for their long-term significance. But the one hit in 1987 will be remembered for its dramatic effects. Name the player who joined the elite 500 Club with a three-run, ninth-inning shot that gave his team a stunning 8-6 victory.

7 In 1989, this duo hit back-to-back home runs as the first two hitters for the American League, an All-Star Game first. Name the hitters who connected off National League starter Rick Reuschel of San Francisco.

8 This outfielder hit one home run in his brief 222-game career with the New York Yankees. But what a homer it was! The June 24, 1962, blow at Tiger Stadium ended a 7-hour marathon in the 22nd inning and gave the Yankees a 9-7 victory over Detroit.

Former Tigers great Ty Cobb was one of five charter members of baseball's first Hall of Fame class.

DID YOU KNOW ...

9 Three players have hit three home runs in a League Championship Series game. Name two of them.

10 Hank Aaron hit his 755th and final major league home run on July 20, 1976, for the Milwaukee Brewers. Name the California Angels righthander who was Aaron's final victim.

Getting serious

The following list represents some of the most memorable home runs in baseball history. We supply the hitter and event. You provide the pitcher and year.

1. Joe Carter, ninth inning, Game 6 of World Series.

2. Bill Mazeroski, ninth inning, Game 7 of World Series.

3. Tony Perez, 15th inning, All-Star Game.

4. Bucky Dent, seventh inning, one-game playoff to determine American League East Division champion.

5. Ted Williams, ninth inning, All-Star Game.

6. Jack Clark, ninth inning, Game 6 of National League Championship Series.

7. Johnny Callison, ninth inning, All-Star Game.

8. Bobby Thomson, ninth inning, Game 3 of National League pennant playoff series.

9. Hank Aaron, fourth inning, record-breaking homer No. 715.

10. Reggie Jackson, third inning, All-Star Game.

11. Kirk Gibson, ninth inning, Game 1 of World Series.

12. Roger Maris, fourth inning, record-breaking homer No. 61.

13. Stan Musial, 12th inning, All-Star Game.

Bill Mazeroski circles the bases after his World Series-ending home run.

By the Numbers

3 / **7** / **7**

Through 2003, the players who have won the most Gold Gloves:

1. Brooks Robinson, 3B   16
       Jim Kaat, P   16

3. Ozzie Smith, SS   13
       Greg Maddux, P   13

5. Roberto Clemente, OF   12
       Willie Mays, OF   12

7. Keith Hernandez, 1B   11

14. Dave Henderson, ninth inning, Game 5 of American League Championship Series.

15. Rick Monday, ninth inning, Game 5 of National League Championship Series.

16. Mark McGwire, fourth inning, record-breaking homer No. 62.

17. Reggie Jackson, fourth, fifth and eighth innings, Game 6 of World Series.

18. Red Schoendienst, 14th inning, All-Star Game.

19. Barry Bonds, first inning, record-breaking homer No. 71.

20. Chris Chambliss, ninth inning, Game 5 of American League Championship Series.

—And the Winner Is...—

Warming up

1 Nine pitchers have earned the double honor of league MVP and Cy Young winner. Two did it in the same magical season. Who are they?

2 Name the three second basemen who have won American League MVP awards.

3 What is the highest loss total ever posted by a Cy Young winner?

4 Name four of the five Los Angeles Dodgers who won consecutive Rookie of the Year awards from 1992-96.

5 Name the two players who captured Rookie of the Year and MVP honors in the same season.

6 What two managers have earned Manager of the Year citations in both leagues?

7 What position player won an American League MVP award with a .269 batting average?

8 Who enjoys triple distinction as a former Rookie of the Year, MVP and Manager of the Year?

9 Two others can claim double distinction as MVP and Manager of the Year winners. Who are they?

DID YOU KNOW ...

►That Lefty Gomez, Robin Roberts and *Don Drysdale* each started a baseball-record five All-Star Games?

►That *Ernie Banks* holds the major league record (424) for consecutive games played at the start of a career?

10 What two teams have garnered the most Cy Youngs since the award was introduced in 1956?

Former Yankees owner Jacob Ruppert (right) had a special affection for his MVP-winning second baseman.

Getting serious

Contained within the following line are the initials of 29 American League MVPs. The J and D at the start of the line form the initials of the first player, and the D combines with the A that follows as the initials of the second player, and so on. How many can you get?

JDARCRMMVBPRFRHNFLGBRJJCYBSCGB

Contained within the following line are the initials of 33 National League MVPs. How many can you get?

JRSMSSKBBEBGFFRCJMMCHADDPRCKMWSGHS

Contained within the following line are the initials of 26 American League and National League Cy Young Award winners. How many can you get?

RJDDDMMDEWFJPMMFVBGMSSBWSCH

Rookie Watch

Warming up

1 The Baseball Writers' first Rookie of the Year later won a Most Valuable Player award and election to the baseball Hall of Fame. Who was this celebrated trailblazer?

2 The American League has not had a rookie 20-game winner in 50 years. Name the New York Yankees righthander who recorded a 20-6 mark and won A.L. Rookie of the Year honors in 1954.

3 Name the Philadelphia Phillies' rookie righthander who set the bar high when he posted 28 wins in 1911.

4 In 1963, the Houston Colt .45s started a September 27 game against New York with an all-rookie lineup that averaged 19 years and 4 months old. Amazingly, five members of that starting nine went on to play 12 or more seasons in the major leagues. Name three of them.

Boston rookie lefthander Bill Rohr forever will be linked with Yankees catcher Elston Howard because of a memorable 1967 moment.

5 This colorful Rookie of the Year posted a 19-9 record for a fifth-place team, led all A.L. starters with a 2.34 ERA and started the All-Star Game. He would win only 10 more games over the remainder of his injury-plagued career. Who was he?

6 St. Louis outfielder Vince Coleman obliterated a rookie record in 1985 when he became only the fourth major leaguer to top

The 1998 debut of a talented
rookie was overshadowed by
Mark McGwire, who hit his
then-record 62nd home run.

100 steals in a season. Name the three players who
topped the century mark before Coleman and the two
who beat his 110 rookie total.

7 Bill Rohr and Elston Howard forever will be linked
in the memories of some Boston Red Sox and New
York Yankees fans. How was Rohr, a 21-year-old lefthander when he made his major league debut for the
Red Sox on April 14, 1967, connected to the Yankees'
veteran catcher?

8 Name the single-season rookie home run record-hold-
ers in each league.

9 For rookie managers, it doesn't get much better than
this: a 109-53 record, a pennant and a five-game
World Series romp. Not bad for someone trying to replace
a legend. Name the manager.

10 On September 8, 1998, the game in which Mark
McGwire hit his record-breaking 62nd home run

against the Chicago Cubs, this Cardinals outfielder appeared as a pinch hitter in his first major league game. Identify the talented rookie.

Getting serious

Fill out a starting lineup using baseball Hall of Famers who also were named either A.L. or N.L. Rookie of the Year winners by the Baseball Writers Association of America. For extra credit, provide the three possible choices at first base and the one alternate choice at three other positions.

1B—_____,_____,_____.

2B—_____,_____.

3B—_____.

SS—_____,_____.

C —_____,_____.

OF—_____.

OF—_____.

OF—_____.

P—_____.

—Common Links—

Warming up

The following groups are linked by milestone performances or memorable baseball moments. Identify their connections.

1. Nolan Ryan-Rickey Henderson.

2. Nolan Ryan-Rickey Henderson II.

3. Dave Stewart-Fernando Valenzuela.

4. Tom Seaver-Rod Carew.

5. Joel Youngblood-Ferguson Jenkins-Steve Carlton.

6. Tony Tarasco-Jeff Maier-Derek Jeter.

7. Ozzie Smith-Tom Niedenfuer-Jack Clark.

8. Dale Long-Don Mattingly-Ken Griffey Jr.

Number, Please

Warming up

We provide teams and three retired numbers. You identify the people who wore those uniforms.

1. Cubs: 10, 14, 26.
2. Dodgers: 1, 20, 32.
3. Yankees: 9, 15, 44.
4. Braves: 3, 21, 44.
5. Cardinals: 6, 14, 45.
6. Brewers: 4, 19, 34.
7. Red Sox: 1, 8, 9.
8. Orioles: 5, 22, 33.
9. Pirates: 4, 8, 21.
10. Giants: 24, 27, 44.
11. Twins: 6, 14, 34.
12. Royals: 5, 10, 20.

Getting serious

Identify the significance of the following number sequences.

1. 16, 21, 24, 29, 54, 59, 60, 61, 70, 73.
2. 100, 56, 130, 108, 66, 80, 87, 41, 93, 77.
3. 66, 63, 50, 64, 49, 40.
4. 2.54, 1.88, 1.74, 2.04, 1.73.
5. 4,256, 755, 2,297, 511, 478.
6. 1941, 1930; 1968, 1934.
7. 73, 36, 67, 198.
8. 116-36, 111-43, 114-48, 116-46.
9. 43 inches, 65 pounds, ⅛.
10. 56 runs, 91 hits, 16 doubles, 4 triples, 15 home runs, 55 RBIs.

DID YOU KNOW...

➤That former infielder John Kennedy played for the Washington Senators in 1962 and 1963 when former president John Kennedy was in the White House? And in addition to a name, the two men shared a birthday—May 29.

➤That Gary and *Daryle Ward are* the only father and son to have hit for the cycle in major league baseball? Daryle joined his former big-league father in that select circle when he hit for the cycle in a May 27, 2004, game for Pittsburgh.

Getting serious

Provide the common link for each of the following groups of names.

1 Babe Ruth, Lou Gehrig, Jimmie Foxx, Al Simmons, Joe Cronin.

2 Frank Robinson, Don Sutton, Lou Brock, Mike Schmidt, Frank White.

3 Alvin Dark, Sam Jethroe, Earl Williams, Bob Horner, David Justice, Rafael Furcal.

4 Jose Canseco, Alex Rodriguez, Barry Bonds.

5 Nellie Fox, Dick Allen, Frank Thomas.

6 Gil Hodges, Yogi Berra, Dave Johnson, Bobby Valentine.

7 Maury Wills, Gary Sutherland, Rusty Staub, Mack Jones, Bob Bailey, John Bateman, Coco Laboy, Don Hahn, Mudcat Grant.

Alex Rodriguez still was playing for Seattle when he took his place among a select group of players.

8 George Brett, Julio Franco, Edgar Martinez, John Olerud, Paul O'Neill, Alex Rodriguez, Frank Thomas, Bernie Williams, Nomar Garciaparra.

9 Jim Frey, Bob Lemon, Harvey Kuenn, Paul Owens, Dick Williams, Whitey Herzog, John McNamara, Whitey Herzog, Tony La Russa, Roger Craig.

10 Ted Williams, Johnny Callison, Stan Musial.

Glove Connections

Warming up

1 I was a former teammate of Robin Roberts and Dwight Gooden, Nellie Fox and Lenny Dykstra. I am remembered fondly in Houston, Montreal, Detroit and New York, where I collected the bulk of my 2,716 career hits. Who am I?

2 I was a teammate of Early Wynn in his final major league season, and I was released by the New York Yankees the day before Deion Sanders made his big-league debut. Who am I?

3 My career connects Hoyt Wilhelm and Robb Nen, outstanding relievers and former bullpen buddies I learned from and counseled. Who am I?

4 I am relieved to tell you that I never gave up home runs to Frank Robinson or Nomar Garciaparra, probably because both were teammates during my Hall of Fame career. Who am I?

5 I am a 300-game winner who began his career on the same staff with Warren Spahn and finished it working out of a bullpen that included David Wells. Who am I?

6 Name the two pitchers who surrendered home runs to Babe Ruth in his 60-homer 1927 season and hits to Joe DiMaggio during his 56-game hitting streak in 1941. Both are Hall of Famers.

7 Two of the pitchers who were victimized by Rickey Henderson stolen bases in 1982 (his record 130-steal season) also allowed Mark McGwire home runs in 1998 (his record 70-homer campaign). Neither is in the Hall of Fame.

8 Name the only American League pitcher to surrender homers to both Mark McGwire and Sammy Sosa during their record 1998 home run race. This White Sox lefthander also was victimized for three of the four home runs hit by Seattle's Mike Cameron during a May 2, 2002, game at Comiskey Park.

The careers of relief aces Hoyt Wilhelm (above) and Robb Nen (below) can be linked by a common teammate.

9 This long-running baseball legend, who once traded fastballs with Dizzy Dean in celebrated barnstorming games, faced future Hall of Famer Carl Yastrzemski in major league action. Name him.

10 Identify this star-struck baseball legend: He played on teams with Babe Ruth and Lou Gehrig, romanced and married a celebrated actress and managed teams that included Jackie Robinson, Willie Mays, Ernie Banks, Billy Williams and Cesar Cedeno.

Getting serious

Name the team for which the following groups of players were teammates.

1. 1982: Dave Kingman, Rusty Staub, Jesse Orosco, Mike Scott.

2. 1975: Buck Martinez, Harmon Killebrew, Vada Pinson, Nelson Briles.

3. 1928: Ty Cobb, Tris Speaker, Eddie Collins, Al Simmons.

4. 1976: Reggie Jackson, Ken Holtzman, Lee May, Tommy Harper.

5. 1977: Bert Campaneris, Willie Horton, Gaylord Perry, Bert Blyleven.

6. 1986: George Foster, Steve Carlton, Tom Seaver, Floyd Bannister.

7. 1964: Duke Snider, Harvey Kuenn, Orlando Cepeda, Billy Pierce.

8. 1983: Joe Morgan, Pete Rose, Tony Perez, Tug McGraw.

9. 1962: Richie Ashburn, Gil Hodges, Don Zimmer, Clem Labine.

10. 1971: Luis Aparicio, Sparky Lyle, Cecil Cooper, Reggie Smith.

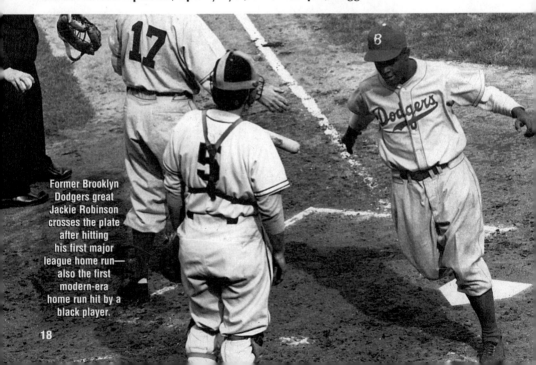

Former Brooklyn Dodgers great Jackie Robinson crosses the plate after hitting his first major league home run—also the first modern-era home run hit by a black player.

By the Numbers

➤The 500-Homer Race

The first 10 members of baseball's 500-homer club with the date and place they reached the milestone:

Babe Ruth
8-11-29
Cleveland

Jimmie Foxx
9-24-40
Philadelphia

Mel Ott
8-1-45
New York

Ted Williams
6-17-60
Cleveland

Willie Mays
9-13-65
Houston

Mickey Mantle
5-14-67
New York

Eddie Mathews
7-14-67
San Francisco

Hank Aaron
7-14-68
Atlanta

Ernie Banks
5-12-70
Chicago

Harmon Killebrew
8-10-71
Minnesota

Warming up

1 Babe Ruth topped the 50-home run plateau four times in the 1920s for the New York Yankees. Who was the second major leaguer to hit 50 homers in a season?

2 In 1932, Yankees great Lou Gehrig became the first 20th century major league player to hit four home runs in a game. Name the first player to join Gehrig in that exclusive club.

3 Jackie Robinson, the first black player in modern major league history, also holds distinction as the first to hit a big-league home run. Name the second black player to hit a big-league homer, the first to hit one in the American League.

4 Ron Blomberg made history on April 6, 1973, when he drew a bases-loaded first-inning walk off Boston ace Luis Tiant while serving as baseball's first designated hitter. Name the Red Sox player who also served as a DH that day, forever relegated to second billing behind Blomberg.

5 Jimmie Foxx became the first three-time winner of the Baseball Writers Association of America annual MVP award in 1938. Who was the second major leaguer to win the award three times?

In 1932, Yankees first baseman Lou Gehrig became the first 20th century player to hit four home runs in one game.

6 Who batted second in the Yankees' Murderers Row lineup of 1927?

7 Name the runner who was stationed at second base in Game 1 of the 1988 World Series when Dodgers pinch hitter Kirk Gibson hit a dramatic walk-off home run off Oakland relief ace Dennis Eckersley.

8 This team posted a 102-60 record and still finished a distant 14 games behind its first-place rival. Identify the second-place team and the season.

9 On April 30, 1969, Cincinnati righthander Jim Maloney pitched a 10-0 no-hitter against the Houston Astros. Name the Houston pitcher who fired a no-hitter the next day against the Reds.

10 Name the second team to win three World Series.

Getting serious

Each of the following names, numbers and baseball groupings are memorable for significant "secondary" distinctions. Identify those distinctions.

1. 47, 54, 66, 64.

2. New York Mets, New York Yankees, San Francisco Giants, New York Yankees.

3. Nellie Fox, Joe Morgan, Frank Frisch, Charlie Gehringer, Rogers Hornsby.

4. 1941, 1943, 1947, 1949, 1952, 1953, 1956, 1977, 1978.

5. Tommie Aaron, Bert Abbey.

6. Ty Cobb, Babe Ruth, Walter Johnson, John Franco.

7. Milwaukee, Kansas City, St. Louis.

8. Morgan Bulkeley, Ban Johnson, Nap Lajoie, Connie Mack, John McGraw, Tris Speaker, George Wright, Cy Young.

9. Gary Sutherland, Charlie Neal, Tommy Harper, Joe Amalfitano, Bret Barberie, Eric Young, Edwin Diaz, Roberto Pena.

10. What?

The great Rogers Hornsby is a featured member of a special baseball club.

Initial Reaction

Warming up

The following initials represent the all-time leader in victories for each of the 26 baseball franchises that existed before expansion to Colorado, Arizona, Florida and Tampa Bay. Your challenge is to provide a name and team for each. Note: Two pitchers are tied for the wins lead of one team.

1. E.P.	7. E.R.	12. B.G.	18. C.M.	24. E.S.
2. B.F.	8. H.D.	13. T.S.	19. W.F.	25. T.L.
3. S.C.	9. J.S.	14. R.J.	20. J.N.	26. J.P.
4. W.S.	10. R.C. and	15. D.S.	21. W.C.	
5. P.S.	C.Y.	16. S.R.	22. W.J.	
6. C.R.	11. C.H.	17. C.F.	23. D.S.	

Getting serious

The following initials represent the leading all-time home run hitter for each of the 30 existing baseball franchises. Your challenge is to provide a name and a team for each.

1. J.G.	7. F.T.	13. T.W.	19. A.K.	25. S.S.
2. J.B.	8. W.M.	14. N.C.	20. L.W.	26. C.D.
3. J.B.	9. J.T.	15. W.S.	21. G.B.	27. T.S.
4. D.S.	10. L.G.	16. B.R.	22. C.R.	28. F.M.
5. H.A.	11. D.S.	17. M.S.	23. D.L.	29. K.G.
6. V.G.	12. R.Y.	18. H.K.	24. M.M.	30. S.M.

The following checklist might be helpful in solving the above puzzles:

American League
Anaheim Angels
Baltimore Orioles
Boston Red Sox
Chicago White Sox
Cleveland Indians
Detroit Tigers
Kansas City Royals
Minnesota Twins
New York Yankees
Oakland Athletics
Seattle Mariners
Tampa Bay Devil Rays
Texas Rangers
Toronto Blue Jays

National League
Arizona Diamondbacks
Atlanta Braves
Chicago Cubs
Cincinnati Reds
Colorado Rockies
Florida Marlins
Houston Astros
Los Angeles Dodgers
Milwaukee Brewers
Montreal Expos
New York Mets
Philadelphia Phillies
Pittsburgh Pirates
St. Louis Cardinals
San Diego Padres
San Francisco Giants

Can you name the athlete and the sport?

1 I grew up in Brooklyn but didn't root for the Dodgers. No, the Giants were my team. Imagine my joy—not to mention all the bragging I could do while playing stickball—after Bobby Thomson hit the Shot Heard 'Round the World.

2 I could brag for other reasons, too. I was a pretty fair player in my own right, good enough to enter a brave new world at age 20, where I found myself playing against Willie, the Duke and a lot of other guys from that New York rivalry. At an age where most guys are barely out of high school, I was a major leaguer with the same club my older brother had played for a few years earlier. And I quickly developed a reputation as a swinger.

3 Like my beloved Giants, my team eventually picked up stakes in search of greener pastures. Instead of heading west, though, we went southeast. The owners got a peach of a deal and the players got a new pad—from which I launched 36 homers in my first season, by far a career high. That didn't help us in the standings, though.

4 Months before man landed on the moon, I took a journey of my own—back west, this time, to a team that was struggling after a successful decade. Success, it seemed, just wasn't in my Cards. My previous team won a division championship that season, and the guy I was traded for had a good year—no bull.

5 I'm still remembered fondly in the midwest. I caught a little, played first and third and put together one of the best seasons in franchise history. I led the league in average, hits and RBIs that year and was rewarded for my effort. Can you spell MVP?

6 That was the highlight of my career—at least my first one. When I returned to New York, I was in for a surprise. The Mets made me their skipper—while I was still playing. Soon, though, I was a full-time manager, learning and suffering on the job.

7 I guess you could say I was run out of town three times before my second career made full circle. After revisiting all of my old stomping grounds, I finally was fitted for a pinstripe suit and handed a team to die for. Things have a funny way of working out sometimes, especially when you have a boss who really, really, really, really cares.

8 Folks figured that boss had made another harebrained decision when he hired me. But we showed 'em— three rings in my first four seasons as zoomaster. And just like that I became a legendary strategist and motivator, no longer just an average Joe.

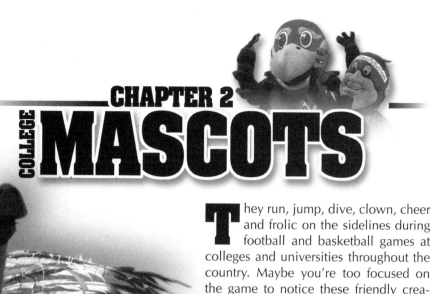

CHAPTER 2

COLLEGE MASCOTS

They run, jump, dive, clown, cheer and frolic on the sidelines during football and basketball games at colleges and universities throughout the country. Maybe you're too focused on the game to notice these friendly creatures, but they're never far away, representing their schools with enthusiasm and adding to the colorful festivities.

Some mascots are live animals beloved by the fans they represent. Others are costumed entertainers who can whip up crowd frenzy or generate smiles when spirits are fading. Still others are inanimate symbols of pride and prosperity.

Test your powers of observation and see if all those college games you've witnessed can help you pass the great mascot test that follows. Identify the school each of the numbered mascots represent. If you're really good, provide the mascot's name as well.

Cheers!

①

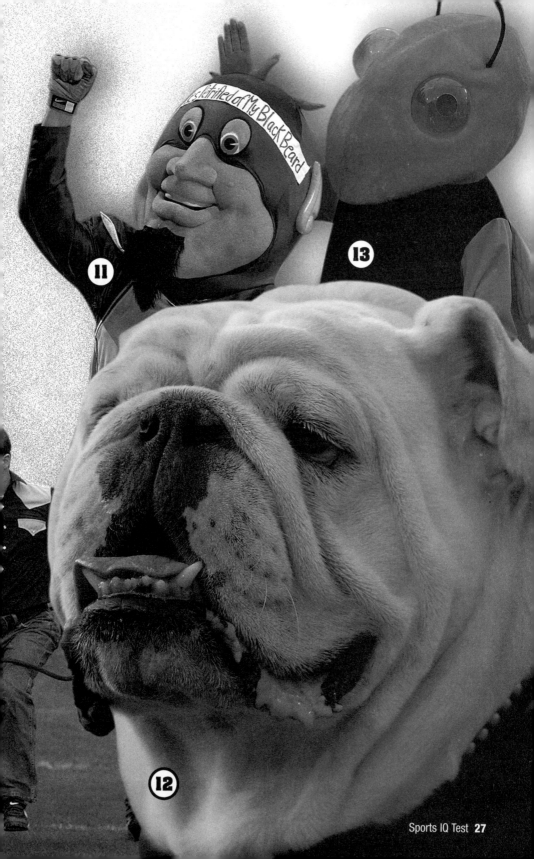

GOT AIR ?

55

38

Mystery Guest

Can you name the athlete and the sport?

1 I'm the baby in a family full of athletes and, in fact, all three of my brothers were pretty good at the game. My dad always seemed to like my big brother best, and I spent most of my life following in his rather large footsteps.

2 I was a surfer boy from California, but nobody ever accused me of being laid back. In my new Midwest home, they could have called me "Wild Thing"—for my attitude on and off the field as well as for my defensive work on it. Yeah, I admit I was a real swinger.

3 That's in no small part because of my good friend Charlie. He was my mentor, the guy who helped me hit my stride. Me and Mac always felt Lausy, but that wasn't a bad thing for people in our profession.

4 Over my 21-year career, I was called a lot of things—intense, clutch, hot-tempered, a gamer. But I never backed off. I did, however, lose a lot of games to injury, one of which was pretty embarrassing. It happened on my sport's biggest stage, but I've put all that behind me now.

5 As a 13-time All-Star, I was treated like royalty in my home city. My position changed over the years, but I ended up first in the hearts of my fans. My best position was in the box, where I seldom failed to hit the jackpot.

6 My team eventually retired my number, but that number wasn't even my favorite. There are all sorts of others I liked better—such as 3,000, 300, 600, 100 or 200. Those all are great, but 400 always will be my absolute favorite.

7 My only ring was the result of a good, old-fashioned civil war. I guess you could say we left our opponents in Misery. It's safe to say I wasn't just your average, everyday player—or your typical Hall of Famer, for that matter. Perhaps that's because of my style of play and the fact I gave old Teddy a run for his money.

8 I played professionally in three decades, and they gave me a crown in each. But there are lots of other reasons why you'll remember me. Historians always will be pining for those film clips of one of my most unforgettable moments, that 1983 home run—yes, look it up, it's in the books—at Yankee Stadium off Goose Gossage.

—Year in Review

The following events and performances all occurred in the same calendar year. Identify the year.

1 ◆ The New York Jets pull off an American Football League coup by signing a pair of high-profile college quarterbacks to long-term contracts—Alabama's Joe Namath and Notre Dame's John Huarte.

◆ The Buffalo Bills defeat San Diego, 23-0, and capture their second straight AFL championship.

◆ Chicago rookie Gale Sayers scores a single-game-record-tying six touchdowns—one on a pass, one on a punt return and four on the ground—in a 61-20 win over San Francisco.

◆ Kansas City fullback Mack Lee Hill dies at age 25 after going into convulsions after an operation to repair a ruptured knee ligament.

It was a very good year for the New York Jets when they signed Alabama quarterback Joe Namath.

2 ◆ Dallas defeats Denver, 27-10, in the Super Bowl at the New Orleans Superdome.

◆ The Buffalo Bills, looking to rebuild, trade record-setting running back O.J. Simpson to San Francisco for five draft picks.

◆ Joe Namath, the star of Super Bowl 3, announces his retirement.

◆ A coaching milestone: Oakland's

DID YOU KNOW...

➤ That 15 future Hall of Famers participated in the 1958 NFL championship game between the Baltimore Colts and New York Giants? That game often is touted as the greatest ever played. The total includes both players and coaches.

➤ That New York Giants linebacker *Lawrence Taylor* was the last defensive player to win NFL MVP honors? In addition to Taylor in 1986, defensive MVPs have included Colts end Gino Marchetti (1958), Lions linebacker Joe Schmidt (1960) and Vikings tackle Alan Page (1971).

Chicago running back Gale Sayers was a touchdown-scoring machine during one incredible game.

John Madden earns his 100th career win as the Raiders down rival Kansas City, 20-10.

3 ◆ In a clandestine operation that leaves Baltimore city officials in a state of shock, Colts owner Robert Irsay cleans out his team's training facility in the dead of night and spirits his club to a new home in Indianapolis.

◆ United States Football League teams snatch two plums away from the NFL—Heisman Trophy-winning running back Mike Rozier from Nebraska and quarterback Steve Young from BYU.

◆ Miami quarterback Dan Marino fires four touchdown passes in a season-closing 28-21 win over Dallas, extending his one-season NFL record to 48.

◆ Walter Payton moves past Jim Brown and becomes the NFL's all-time leading rusher when he picks up 6 yards in the third quarter of a 20-7 win over New Orleans.

4◆ Three Don Chandler field goals and Paul Hornung's 13-yard third-quarter touchdown run help the Green Bay Packers to a 23-12 championship game win over Cleveland at Lambeau Field.

◆ The rival NFL and AFL announce a merger agreement that eventually will result in a 26-team, 25-city circuit and a common draft.

◆ Cleveland great Jim Brown, the NFL's all-time leading rusher, announces his retirement.

◆ The NFL awards an expansion franchise to New Orleans on All Saints Day.

5◆ Mark Brunell passes for 245 yards and two touchdowns and Natrone Means rushes for 140 yards as the Jacksonville Jaguars stun 13-3 Denver, 30-27, in the Broncos' playoff opener.

◆ In a milestone-filled season, quarterback Dan Marino becomes the NFL's first 50,000-yard passer, Jerry Rice becomes its first 1,000-catch receiver and Barry Sanders becomes the first player to top 1,000 yards rushing in each of his first eight years.

◆ Former commissioner Pete Rozelle, who presided over the growth of the NFL into a multi-billion dollar entity, dies at age 70.

◆ Two of the top quarterbacks of the last decade, Jim Kelly and Bernie Kosar, announce their retirements.

6◆ The defending Super Bowl-champion Washington Redskins struggle to a 7-9 season and fail to make the playoffs.

◆ Tom Landry's Dallas Cowboys post a 3-13 record, Chuck Noll's Pittsburgh Steelers finish 5-11 and Don Shula's Miami Dolphins check in at 6-10.

◆ Seattle's Steve Largent breaks Charlie Joiner's career pass-receiving record when he tops 12,146 yards in a game against San Diego.

◆ Art Rooney, founder and sole owner of the NFL's Pittsburgh Steelers for 55 years, dies of a stroke in Pittsburgh at age 87.

Natrone Means ran for 140 yards and the Jacksonville Jaguars stunned the favored Denver Broncos in an NFL playoff thriller.

DID YOU KNOW...

➤That NFL head coaches *Jim Mora Jr.* (Atlanta) and *Mike Mularkey* (Buffalo) were born on the same day? Mora was born November 19, 1961, in Los Angeles, while Mularkey was born the same day in Fort Lauderdale, Fla.

Mora / Mularkey

➤That *O.J. Simpson* has posted the most lopsided victory margins in balloting for the Heisman Trophy and winning an NFL rushing title? In 1968, USC's Simpson outpolled Purdue's Leroy Keyes by 1,750 votes in the Heisman voting. In 1973, Buffalo's Simpson rushed for 2,003 yards, 859 more than Green Bay runner-up John Brockington.

7 ◆ Commissioner Bert Bell's contract is extended for 12 years.

◆ Philadelphia's Adrian Burk joins Sid Luckman as the only NFL quarterbacks to throw seven touchdown passes in a game—the Eagles' 49-21 win over the Washington Redskins.

◆ San Francisco running back Joe Perry claims his second straight rushing championship with 1,049 yards—31 more than his previous season's career best.

◆ Cleveland 56, Detroit 10 in the NFL championship game at Cleveland's Municipal Stadium.

8 ◆ Dennis Byrd, a 6-5, 277-pound defensive lineman for the New York Jets, is partially paralyzed during a game against the Kansas City Chiefs.

◆ Steve Largent, retired since 1989, watches helplessly as Washington's Art Monk breaks his career receptions record, Jerry Rice eclipses his record for career touchdown passes and James Lofton passes him for first place in career receiving yards.

◆ Chicago Bears middle linebacker Mike Singletary, a 10-time Pro Bowl selection, announces his retirement.

◆ The Washington Redskins pound Buffalo, 37-24, in the Super Bowl at the Metrodome in Minneapolis.

9 ◆ New Orleans kicker Tom Dempsey drills a 63-yard field goal, the longest in NFL history, on the final play of the game and gives the Saints a 19-17 win over Detroit.

◆ Vince Lombardi, the man who led the Green Bay Packers into prominence in the 1960s, dies of cancer at age 57.

◆ Keith Jackson, Howard Cosell and Don Meredith describe the Cleveland Browns' 31-21 victory over the New York Jets in ABC-TV's first *Monday Night Football* telecast.

◆ Kansas City owner Lamar Hunt is elected president of the AFC, and George Halas, owner of the Chicago Bears, is elected to head the NFC.

Chicago Bears great Walter Payton (right) performed his ball-carrying magic for three head coaches.

10 ◆ NFL commissioner Bert Bell dies of a heart attack suffered while watching an Eagles-Steelers game at Philadelphia's Franklin Field.

◆ The new American Football League, boasting eight teams, selects 425 players in its first college draft.

◆ Cleveland's Jim Brown becomes the second player in NFL history to win three straight rushing titles when he pounds out 1,329 yards on 290 carries.

◆ Colts 31, Giants 16 in the NFL championship game at Baltimore's Memorial Stadium.

Common Links

Warming up

1 What NFL quarterback and head coach were together for the longest period of time?

2 These players never were teammates, although they posted Hall of Fame-worthy numbers for the same team. They rank No. 1 and No. 2 on the all-time rushing list for *Monday Night Football* games.

3 This Hall of Fame offensive lineman was a primary blocker for two of the NFL's top four career rushers—one in college, one in the professional ranks.

4 This quarterback spent his entire NFL career playing for one team and one coach. He passed for 35,467 career yards and 237 touchdowns and played in four Super Bowls.

5 Name the quarterback who spent 13 seasons under the always astute guidance of Dallas Cowboys coach Tom Landry.

6 Name the player who caught Green Bay quarterback Brett Favre's first NFL completion in 1992.

7 Name the quarterback who holds the record for most touchdown passes in one stadium.

8 Over 13 NFL seasons (1975-87), Walter Payton ran for 16,726 yards and scored 125 touchdowns for the Chicago Bears. Name the three Chicago coaches who benefited from Payton's talent.

9 Talk about being overshadowed! Who were the starting quarterbacks for the 1973 Buffalo Bills

DID YOU KNOW...

➤ That *Ricky Watters* is the only player to have 1,000-yard rushing seasons for three different NFL teams? Watters did it with the San Francisco 49ers in 1992, the Philadelphia Eagles in 1995, 1996 and 1997, and the Seattle Seahawks in 1998, 1999 and 2000.

➤ That on September 13, 1992, the Buffalo Bills and San Francisco 49ers played the first NFL game in which neither team was forced to punt?

Former Denver great John Elway had a not-so-obvious career link with such players as Cornelius Bennett and Marshall Faulk.

when O.J. Simpson ran for a record 2,003 yards, and the 1984 Los Angeles Rams when Eric Dickerson ran for a record 2,105 yards?

10 Name the brothers who combined to catch 83 touchdown passes from quarterbacks who have thrown for more than 95,000 combined yards.

Getting serious

Provide the common link for each of the following groups.

1. Quarterbacks Michael Vick, Ken Stabler, Steve Young, Mark Brunell, Bobby Douglass.

2. Phillip Buchanon, Bryant McKinnie, Ed Reed, Mike Rumph, Jeremy Shockey.

3. John Elway, Cornelius Bennett, Andre Rison, Marshall Faulk, Jeff George.

3 11 7 By the Numbers

Players who have led the NFL in career pass receptions between Don Hutson, who retired with 488 in 1945, and Jerry Rice, the current record holder with 1,519. The first number is the year the player set the record. The second is the record total:

Billy Howton
1963
503

Raymond Berry
1964
631

Don Maynard
1972
633

Charley Taylor
1975
649

Charlie Joiner
1984
750

Steve Largent
1987
819

Art Monk
1992
940

4. Bills, Browns, Bengals, Titans, Jaguars, Texans, Chargers, Eagles, Vikings, Lions, Falcons, Saints, Panthers, Seahawks, Cardinals.

5. Kickers Jim Bakken, Chris Boniol, Billy Cundiff, Rich Karlis.

6. Joe Abbey, Jim Zyntell.

7. Running backs Steve Van Buren, Joe Perry, Jim Brown, Walter Payton, Emmitt Smith.

8. George Wilson, Jimmy Johnson.

9. Chuck Howley, Jake Scott, Ottis Anderson, Larry Brown, Desmond Howard.

10. Quarterbacks Sid Luckman, Adrian Burk, Y.A. Tittle, George Blanda, Joe Kapp.

Jacks and Johns

Warming up

Supply "John" or "Jack" names to each of the following.

1. The Assassin.

2. Moose.

3. Tooz.

4. Chris Berman's sidekick.

5. Bear Bryant's only Heisman winner.

6. Lawrence Taylor's linebacker mate in Super Bowl 25.

7. Vincent Edward.

8. Walter Payton's first NFL coach.

9. Two Amigos.

10. A "Henry" sandwich.

The defensive lineman known as Tooz wreaked havoc for the Raiders in the 1970s.

DID YOU KNOW...

➤That Jim Kelly and *Andre Reed* hold the NFL record for most passes completed between one quarter-back and receiver? The former Buffalo stars hooked up for 663 completions from 1986-96.

➤That four players have finished an NFL season with exactly 1,000 rushing yards? Willie Ellison did it with the Rams in 1971, *Mercury Morris* with the Dolphins in 1972, Greg Pruitt with the Browns in 1976 and Ricky Williams with the Saints in 2000.

Getting serious

Keeping in mind the category, supply names for the following descriptions.

1 Two quarterbacks: One played 16 seasons, reached five Super Bowls and won two; the other played 15 years, passed for 24,410 yards and never played in a postseason game.

2 Two coaches: One led his new team to a Super Bowl championship; the other lost the next Super Bowl in his second year with his team.

3 Two kickers: They played in their only career Super Bowls in consecutive years. One, who would play 17 NFL seasons, kicked one field goal for the losing team in Super Bowl 30; the other, who would play 10 seasons, kicked two field goals for the winning team in Super Bowl 31.

4 Two receivers: One's claim to fame was a Super Bowl-winning catch that kept the Cincinnati Bengals from winning their first championship; the other is a Hall of Famer who often is remembered for a dropped Super Bowl pass.

5 Two coaches: One led the Oakland Raiders to their first Super Bowl, a loss; the other led them to their second Super Bowl, a victory.

6 Two kick returners: One, a 1951 rookie, returned two punts for touchdowns in the same game—twice; the other, a 1975 second-year player, tied the other's single-season record for return touchdowns with four—three on punts, one on a kickoff, all in different games.

7 Two offensive linemen: One is considered by many the best blocking guard in the Hall of Fame; the other, a Hall of Fame tackle, is remembered for his consistency and stamina over a long NFL career.

8 Two defenders: They were longtime teammates who played the same position for a team that dominated professional football over a prolonged period. One did his best work as an inside man; the other preferred to work outside. Both are Hall of Famers.

9 Two running backs: One won two NFC rushing titles in the 1970s but never played in a Super Bowl. The other never won a rushing championship, but he did win a Super Bowl MVP award in the 1980s.

10 A defensive back and a coach: One played 16 seasons (1961-76) in a Hall of Fame career that never produced a championship; the other coached a team to two Super Bowl championships in the 1990s. Though their careers never touched, they maintain a deep-rooted connection, even in retirement.

A License to Kill

Warming up

Seven teams have produced a 4,000-yard passer, 1,400-yard receiver and 1,000-yard rusher in the same season. Identify the quarterback, receiver and runner for each.

1. 2001 Indianapolis Colts.

2. 2000 San Francisco 49ers.

3. 1999 and 2000 Indianapolis Colts.

4. 1995 Detroit Lions.

5. 1995 Green Bay Packers.

6. 1984 St. Louis Cardinals.

One team has produced a 4,000-yard passer, two 1,000-yard receivers, a 1,000-yard rusher and a 20-touchdown scorer. Name the players.

7. 2001 St. Louis Rams.

Three teams have featured two 1,000-yard rushers in the same backfield. Identify the running backs.

8. 1985 Cleveland Browns.

9. 1976 Pittsburgh Steelers.

10. 1972 Miami Dolphins.

Strong-armed Peyton Manning is the fearless triggerman for Indianapolis' high-powered, big-yardage offense.

Pro Football

Getting serious

Identify the NFL's most prolific quarterback/receiver touchdown combinations, as represented by the following initials.

1. S.Y. to J.R., 85 touchdowns.

2. D.M. to M.C., 79 touchdowns.

3. J.K. to A.R., 65 touchdowns.

4. J.U. to R.B., 63 touchdowns.

5. B.F. to A.F., 57 touchdowns.

6. J.H. to L.A., 56 touchdowns.

7. D.M. to M.D., 55 touchdowns.

8. J.M. to J.R., 55 touchdowns.

9. S.J. to C.T., 53 touchdowns.

10. K.A. to I.C., 51 touchdowns.

‑Missing in Action‑
Warming up

Fill in the missing name for the following exclusive football clubs.

1 Quarterbacks selected in the first round of the 1983 draft: John Elway, _____, Jim Kelly, Tony Eason, Ken O'Brien, Dan Marino.

2 Denver's Three Amigos: Ricky Nattiel, Mark Jackson, _____.

3 Players who have scored 125 or more touchdowns: Jerry Rice, Emmitt Smith, Marcus Allen, _____, Cris Carter, Jim Brown, Walter Payton.

4 Quarterbacks who have passed for more than 45,000 yards: Dan Marino, John Elway, _____, Fran Tarkenton.

5 The Los Angeles Rams' Fearsome Foursome: Deacon Jones, Merlin Olsen, Rosie Grier, _____.

Marcus Allen (32) was a workhorse runner during his Hall of Fame career with the Raiders and Chiefs.

6 Players who have scored 25 touchdowns in a season: Emmitt Smith, Marshall Faulk, _____.

7 Washington's Hogs: Joe Jacoby, George Starke, _____, Fred Dean, Jeff Bostic.

8 Buffalo's Electric Company: Mike Montler/Bruce Jarvis, Joe DeLamielleure, _____, Donnie Green, Dave Foley, Paul Seymour.

9 Players who have caught 1,000 or more passes: Jerry Rice, _____, Tim Brown.

10 Hall of Famers named Brown: Jim Brown, Paul Brown, _____, _____.

Getting serious

Pick out the name or number that does not belong in the following groups.

1 Coaches who have led teams to four or more Super Bowls: Bud Grant, Marv Levy, Dan Reeves, Joe Gibbs, Bill Parcells.

2 Quarterbacks who threw for 30,000 or more yards: Sonny Jurgensen, Len Dawson, Ken Anderson, Steve Young, Jim Kelly.

3 Receivers who caught more than 900 career passes: Steve Largent, Cris Carter, Tim Brown, Art Monk, Andre Reed.

4 Teams that have played in five or more Super Bowls: Dallas, Denver, San Francisco, Green Bay, Miami.

5 Players with 3,000 or more rushing attempts: Emmitt Smith, Walter Payton, Tony Dorsett, Barry Sanders, Marcus Allen.

6 Quarterbacks with 750 or more passing yards in the Super Bowl: John Elway, Kurt Warner, Troy Aikman, Jim Kelly, Terry Bradshaw.

7 Players who lead a franchise in career receptions: Herman Moore, Tony Gonzalez, Don Maynard, Lynn Swann, Isaac Bruce.

8 Teams coached by Bill Parcells: Cowboys, Jets, Giants, Bills, Patriots.

9 Teams for which wide receiver Andre Rison played: Chiefs, Cowboys, Packers, Falcons, Jaguars.

10 Pro Football Hall of Famers: Ernie Nevers, Pete Pihos, Leo Nomellini, Tommy McDonald, Ken Stabler.

Statuesque

Warming up

16 Heisman Trophy winners have been picked No. 1 overall in the pro football draft. We provide the drafting team and college; you provide the name.

1. Buccaneers ... Miami (Fla.).

2. Boston Yanks ... Notre Dame.

3. Rams ... LSU.

4. Bills ... USC.

5. Saints ... South Carolina.

6. Eagles ... Chicago.

7. Lions ... Notre Dame.

8. Patriots ... Stanford.

9. Rams ... Oregon State.

10. Bears ... Michigan.

11. Packers ... Notre Dame.

12. Buccaneers ... Auburn.

13. Lions ... Georgia.

14. Redskins ... Syracuse.

15. Oilers ... Texas.

16. Lions ... Oklahoma.

Barry Sanders' Heisman Trophy-winning style translated well in the NFL, where he topped the rushing charts four times as a member of the Lions.

3 77 7 By the Numbers

NFL quarterbacks who have thrown for more than 40,000 regular-season yards and 4,000 playoff yards (through the 2003 season):

Dan Marino
Career 61,361 Playoff 4,510

John Elway
Career 51,475 Playoff 4,964

Brett Favre
Career 45,646 Playoff 4,686

Joe Montana
Career 40,551 Playoff 4,187

Getting serious

1 Name the first two Heisman Trophy winners elected to the Pro Football Hall of Fame. They were inducted in the same class.

2 Who holds the NFL rushing record among former Heisman Trophy winners?

3 Name the first Heisman Trophy winner to score 100 or more points in an NFL season.

4 Who was the first Heisman Trophy winner to rush for 1,000-plus yards in an NFL season?

5 Who was the first Heisman Trophy winner to pass for 2,000-plus yards and 20-plus touchdowns in an NFL season?

6 Four former Heisman Trophy winners also have won Super Bowl MVP honors. Name them.

7 Name the only Heisman Trophy winner who has thrown more than 300 touchdown passes in his professional career?

8 Name the former Heisman Trophy winner who has played in the NFL and coached teams in both the college and NFL ranks.

9 Barry Sanders led the NFL in rushing four times from 1990-97. Who is the last Heisman Trophy winner before Sanders to top the NFL rushing charts?

10 Who holds the record among Heisman Trophy winners for most touchdowns scored in an NFL season?

—— Sequential ——

Warming up

Fill in the blanks that complete the following pro football sequences.

1 Cliff Battles, Gene Roberts, Tommy Wilson, Jim Brown, Cookie Gilchrist, Willie Ellison, O.J. Simpson, _____, Corey Dillon, _____.

2 John McKay, Leeman Bennett, Ray Perkins, Richard Williamson, _____, Tony Dungy, Jon Gruden.

3 Jeff George, Russell Maryland, Steve Emtman, Drew Bledsoe, Dan Wilkinson, Ki-Jana Carter, _____, Orlando Pace, Peyton Manning, Tim Couch.

4 Chiefs, Raiders, Colts, Vikings, Cowboys, Dolphins, _____.

5 Terrell Davis, John Elway, Kurt Warner, Ray Lewis, _____, Dexter Jackson, Tom Brady.

6 Emmitt Smith, Walter Payton, Barry Sanders, Eric Dickerson, _____, Jim Brown.

7 _____, Bert Bell, Pete Rozelle, Paul Tagliabue.

8 Don Shula, George Halas, Tom Landry, Curly Lambeau, _____.

9 Patriots, Buccaneers, Patriots, Ravens, Rams, _____.

10 Houston Oilers, New York Titans, Buffalo Bills, Boston Patriots, Los Angeles Chargers, Oakland Raiders, Denver Broncos, _____.

Getting serious

We provide a five-year record sequence and decade for an NFL franchise. You provide the team.

1. 1980s-90s: 1-15, 7-9, 11-5, 13-3, 12-4.

2. 1970s: 10-4, 10-3-1, 14-0, 12-2, 11-3.

Former Cowboys great Emmitt Smith is the leader of an exclusive NFL fraternity.

3. 1950s: 10-2, 11-1, 8-4, 11-1, 9-3.

4. 1970s-1980s: 0-14, 2-12, 5-11, 10-6, 5-10-1.

5. 1980s: 8-8, 10-6, 15-1, 14-2, 11-4.

6. 1990s: 13-3, 13-3, 11-5, 12-4, 7-9.

7. 1960s: 11-3, 13-1, 11-2-1, 8-5-1, 10-3-1.

8. 1990s-2000s: 3-13, 13-3, 10-6, 6-10, 10-6.

9. 1970s: 12-2, 10-4, 9-5, 14-2, 12-4.

10. 1990s-2000s: 8-8, 8-8, 8-8, 13-3, 13-3.

——— Super Stars ———
Warming up

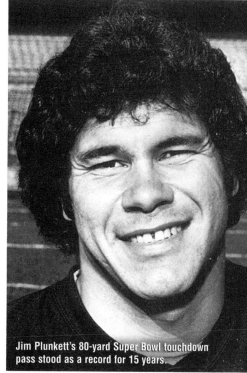

1 Name the Hall of Fame cornerback who scored the first defensive touchdown in Super Bowl history. He did it on a 60-yard interception return.

2 Only one man has scored a Super Bowl touchdown and coached a Super Bowl champion. Name him.

Jim Plunkett's 80-yard Super Bowl touchdown pass stood as a record for 15 years.

3 This quarterback-wide receiver combination clicked for a 75-yard touchdown in one Super Bowl and a 73-yard TD in the next. Name the players.

4 Name the Miami player who returned a Washington kickoff 98 yards for a touchdown in Super Bowl 17—the first scoring kick return in Super Bowl history.

5 This running back romped for a Super Bowl-record 204 yards and two touchdowns in his team's championship-securing victory. But he did not even earn MVP honors. Name him.

6 The record for receiving yardage was set in Super Bowl 23. Name the wideout who caught 11 passes for 215 yards and a touchdown in an MVP performance.

7 Name the player who has competed in the most Super Bowl games.

8 Name the player who has competed in the most Super Bowl games for the winning team.

9 For 15 years, Kenny King's 80-yard touchdown pass from Oakland quarterback Jim Plunkett stood as the longest pass play in Super Bowl history. That changed in Super Bowl 31, when this quarterback and receiver clicked for 81 yards. Name them.

10 Who holds the Super Bowl record for longest run from scrimmage?

Getting serious

Non-quarterbacks have won the Super Bowl MVP award 19 times. We provide the positions, you provide the names.

1. Safety = _____.
2. Safety = _____.
3. Cornerback = _____.
4. Linebacker = _____.
5. Linebacker = _____.

6. Defensive end = _____.
7. Defensive end = _____.
8. Defensive tackle = _____.
9. Running back = _____.
10. Running back = _____.

11. Running back = _____.
12. Running back = _____.
13. Running back = _____.
14. Running back = _____.
15. Running back = _____.

16. Wide receiver = _____.
17. Wide receiver = _____.
18. Wide receiver = _____.
19. Kick returner = _____.

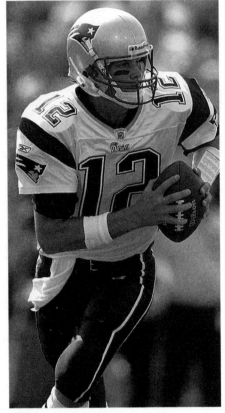

New England quarterback Tom Brady is a two-time Super Bowl MVP.

Initial Reaction

Warming up

The following initials represent the all-time winningest coaches for each of the 32 NFL franchises. Three coaches, the leading career winner for more than one franchise, appear twice. Keep in mind that the history of the Baltimore Ravens (formerly the Cleveland Browns) starts in 1996, and the Browns' legacy now belongs to the expansion Cleveland franchise.

1. S.G.	8. C.L.	15. J.M.	22. J.F.	29. S.W.
2. G.H.	9. D.C.	16. D.S.	23. C.N.	30. J.G.
3. T.L.	10. W.E.	17. H.S.	24. D.R.	31. G.S.
4. D.R.	11. T.D.	18. J.M.	25. W.F.	32. T.C.
5. B.G.	12. J.R.	19. S.O.	26. M.L.	
6. D.S.	13. G.N.	20. C.K.	27. P.B.	
7. M.H.	14. B.B.	21. D.C.	28. D.C.	

Getting serious

The following initials represent the leading career rusher for each of the 32 NFL franchises through the 2003 season. Your challenge is to provide a name and team for each.

1. O.A.	8. F.M.	15. E.S.	22. E.D.	29. J.L.
2. J.T.	9. W.P.	16. S.C.	23. F.T.	30. R.S.
3. C.O.	10. G.R.	17. J.B.	24. C.D.	31. E.G.
4. L.C.	11. W.M.	18. C.W.	25. T.B.	32. G.R.
5. J.P.	12. F.H.	19. M.A.	26. P.L.	
6. T. T.	13. J.W.	20. D.D.	27. E.J.	
7. J.R.	14. B.S.	21. R.H.	28. T.D.	

The following checklist might be helpful in your efforts to solve the above puzzles:

Arizona Cardinals	Green Bay Packers	Oakland Raiders
Atlanta Falcons	Houston Texans	Philadelphia Eagles
Baltimore Ravens	Indianapolis Colts	Pittsburgh Steelers
Buffalo Bills	Jacksonville Jaguars	St. Louis Rams
Carolina Panthers	Kansas City Chiefs	San Diego Chargers
Chicago Bears	Miami Dolphins	San Francisco 49ers
Cincinnati Bengals	Minnesota Vikings	Seattle Seahawks
Cleveland Browns	New England Patriots	Tampa Bay Buccaneers
Dallas Cowboys	New Orleans Saints	Tennessee Titans
Denver Broncos	New York Giants	Washington Redskins
Detroit Lions	New York Jets	

Mystery Guest

Can you name the athlete and the sport?

1 I wasn't poor growing up, but I didn't have $20 to buy my senior high school yearbook. A few years ago, my old principal tracked me down and gave me one.

2 One of the toughest things about my job is the close, hot, steamy quarters I have to work in. To make matters worse, I'm claustrophobic, and with all the gear I have to wear, I can hardly move. Throw in reporters and photographers all over the place, and I feel boxed in too much of the time. If I had to travel around town under such restraints, I'd go nuts.

3 I regularly entertain 100,000 live fans and millions more who watch me on television. But my all-time favorite win was viewed by only a few thousand.

4 One of the first things anyone says about my style—and heck, my personality, too—is that I have plenty of fire, which is probably where I got my nickname.

5 I'm a rare guy in my sport—I didn't have much of a track record before I found success in the big time. I've won 17 times at the Nextel Cup level, but I've never won at the Busch level. Trust me: I'm working on rectifying that little anomaly. But it's not like I wasn't successful at other levels. I've won rookie of the year in seven series and championships in nine.

6 There are two races I really want to win—the Indianapolis 500, which I don't race in anymore but, man, I wish I could, and the Daytona 500. Someday, who knows?

7 The owner of my race team has won two championships in my sport and three in another sport as a coach. He often is asked which of his former players I remind him of, and he usually answers, "Gary Clark." That's because Clark was so intense when he put on his pads on game day, just like I am on race day.

8 I'd love to be the first winner of the Nextel Cup championship. I'd add that to my other firsts: First driver to win the USAC Triple Crown, first rookie to win three Cup races, first driver to win major championships in open-wheel racing and stock car racing. Also, I'm pretty proud of one "last" accomplishment: last driver to win a NASCAR championship in a Pontiac.

FACES FROM THE PAST

The following pages provide a virtual scrapbook of athletes and would-be athletes who went on to attain different levels of success. Some made their mark in sports; others went on to fame and fortune in different professions. Don't let the uniforms fool you. And don't let the youthful features lead you down the wrong path. Look closely at the faces, read the clues carefully and see how many of these celebrity/athletes you can identify.

1. From Florida State to the Silver Screen.

Chapter 4 answers begin on page 263.

3. From Rocky Top to Rockies Top.

2. Is there a doctor in the house?

4. A streaker in baseball clothing.

60

5. The Bear necessities.

6. He just doesn't act like his father.

7. He gets his kicks Daily with comedy.

9. Passion on the parquet.

10. Winged helmets and white houses.

8. If I had a hammer ...

13. A big man by anyone's standard.

12. He kept the NFL in a Miami vise.

11. Still ship-shape in New York.

14. Before L.A. confidential.

15. A Boston-baked superstar.

16. From Harvard to Hollywood.

17. No ordinary Tom, Dick or Harry.

18. Ram tough and flower gentle.

19. From Southern Cal to Duke.

20. A hot shot, even after his playing days.

21. From Heisman hopeful to Hill Street.

22. Life before Octoberfest.

66

23. Sports gave him an anchor.

24. Great success was in the Cards.

25. A success tale of two cities.

26. She really has a nice racket.

27. Yes Sir, a real basket case.

28. 18 plus 42 equals respect.

Mystery Guest

Can you name the athlete and the sport?

1 Born in mining country, I wish I could say I was a diamond in the rough. But it's more like a diamond among diamonds. It's a funny coincidence, though, that I made my fortune with a team of excavators.

2 I was pretty good in high school and always got passing grades. High school is where I learned how to dance—no one ever accused me of having lead feet. My excellence earned me scholarships all over, but instead of heading South, I played just around the bend.

3 With my blue-eyed, blond-haired good looks, I had All-American appeal. But that didn't impress my coach. It would have taken divine intervention to make me his Golden Boy, so I took my place in line and waited for my turn to shine.

4 I finally got it in my junior season—and delivered, big time. It was so exciting! We spun silk from cotton and added to a championship legacy. When we changed cotton to silk again the next year, some people starting calling me Lazarus. That became my career-long M.O.—just when everyone thought I was out for the count, I'd come back out and pound you.

5 When I finally made it to the pros, nobody thought I'd succeed. Can you count to 81? That's the number of teams that passed on me before I was drafted. But I showed 'em. What I lacked in physical ability I more than made up for with grit and desire.

6 My coach, an offensive genius, said I was no Einstein. But no dummy could have succeeded in his complicated system. And succeed I did—I ran four rings around the competition. And I passed every test with the help of my friends. Jerry, Jerry Jerry! He was awesome, but so were Dwight, Roger, John and countless others. Sure, I posted MVP numbers, but I also had a Super supporting cast. Here's the Catch: We were always at our best against America's team.

7 After a dozen great years, injuries took a toll. I still was 16, but I no longer was Young. So I tried the Midwest on for size. The barbecue was great, but I guess Tony Bennett knew what he was talking about—I left my heart in San Francisco.

8 After two good seasons, I called it a career and headed home. Retirement was an adjustment, but it gave me a chance to look back on my Hall of Fame achievements. And I know I still have something to look forward to. I have, after all, always been at my best in the fourth quarter.

CHAPTER 5
PRO BASKETBALL

— Final Thoughts —
Warming up

1 After the Boston Celtics won the NBA Finals in 1986, the league produced a long string of repeat winners. Name the first title team after Boston that failed to defend its championship at least once.

2 Name the first former ABA team to win an NBA championship.

3 Game 4 of the 1987 NBA Finals at Boston Garden is remembered for the dramatic sky-hook that gave the Los Angeles Lakers a stunning 107-106 victory. Who delivered that winning shot?

4 Former Knicks center Willis Reed is a New York legend because of the inspirational boost he supplied to teammates in Game 7 of the 1970 NBA Finals at Madison Square Garden. How many points did the Finals MVP score in that championship-securing victory?

5 Name the two coaches who led teams to ABA and NBA championships.

6 Together, the Boston Celtics (16) and Minneapolis/Los Angeles Lakers (14) have won more NBA championships than all other franchises combined. What team holds the record for most NBA Finals lost?

7 Name the two men who have doubled their pleasure by winning NBA championships as player-coaches.

Larry Bird was a star forward for the 1980-81 champion Celtics. But who was Boston's other starting forward?

➤ That *Fred Roberts* is the only man to be an NBA teammate of both Magic Johnson and Larry Bird in regular-season play? Roberts played for Bird's Celtics from 1986-88 and Johnson's Lakers in 1995-96.

➤ That *Dominique Wilkins* holds the distinction of scoring the most career points without playing in an NBA Finals? Eddie Johnson scored the most career points without playing in an All-Star Game.

Hakeem Olajuwon was the centerpiece for Houston's 1993-94 NBA championship team.

8 What team appeared in the most NBA Finals in the 1970s?

9 Red Auerbach and Phil Jackson share the record with victories in nine NBA Finals. One other coach has reached the Finals eight times, compiling a 4-4 record. Name him.

10 Name the Los Angeles Lakers player who posted his only career triple-double in Game 7 of the 1988 NBA Finals—a victory over Detroit.

Getting serious

We supply four-fifths of the most common starting lineups used by championship teams in the NBA Finals. You supply the missing name.

1 1980-81 Boston Celtics: Center Robert Parish, forward Larry Bird, forward _____, guard Nate Archibald, guard Chris Ford.

2 1993-94 Houston Rockets: Center Hakeem Olajuwon, forward Otis Thorpe, forward Robert

Horry, guard Kenny Smith, guard _____.

3 1984-85 Los Angeles Lakers: Center Kareem Abdul-Jabbar, forward Bob McAdoo, forward James Worthy, guard Magic Johnson, guard _____.

4 1990-91 Chicago Bulls: Center _____, forward Scottie Pippen, forward Horace Grant, guard Michael Jordan, guard John Paxson.

5 2000-01 Los Angeles Lakers: Center Shaquille O'Neal, forward Horace Grant, forward _____, guard Kobe Bryant, guard Derek Fisher.

6 1998-99 San Antonio Spurs: Center David Robinson, forward Tim Duncan, forward _____, guard Avery Johnson, guard Mario Elie.

7 1962-63 Boston Celtics: Center Bill Russell, forward John Havlicek, forward Tom Heinsohn, guard Sam Jones, guard _____.

8 1976-77 Portland Trail Blazers: Center Bill Walton, forward Bob Gross, forward _____, guard Lionel Hollins, guard Johnny Davis.

9 1989-90 Detroit Pistons: Center Bill Laimbeer, forward James Edwards, forward Mark Aguirre, guard Isiah Thomas, guard _____.

10 1957-58 St. Louis Hawks: Center Charlie Share, forward _____, forward Bob Pettit, forward/guard Cliff Hagan, guard Slater Martin.

The Chicago Bulls' six championship winners of the 1990s were built around the incomparable Michael Jordan.

DID YOU KNOW...

–And the Winner Is ...–

Warming up

1 Name the only player who has won back-to-back regular-season MVP awards while playing for different teams.

2 Only three players have won regular-season MVPs for more than one franchise. Name them.

3 Two players won regular-season MVP awards while playing for teams that compiled losing records. Name them.

4 Name the man whose two NBA Coach of the Year citations were separated by a quarter of a century.

5 Name the two players who have won MVP awards and Defensive Player of the Year honors in the same season.

6 Name the last player who was not a first-round draft pick to win Rookie of the Year honors. The player has long been retired.

7 Name the shot-blocking monster who has claimed NBA Defensive Player of the Year honors four times—two more than any other player.

8 Name the three players who have won regular-season MVP, NBA Finals MVP and All-Star Game MVP in the same season.

9 Name the three-time NBA Coach of the Year who won the award for three different teams.

10 Name the last Boston Celtics player to win a scoring title.

Getting serious

We provide the category and initials; you provide the names represented by the initials.

1 Players who have won regular-season and NBA Finals MVP honors in the same season: W.R., K.A., M.M., L.B., E.J., M.J., H.O., S.O., T.D.

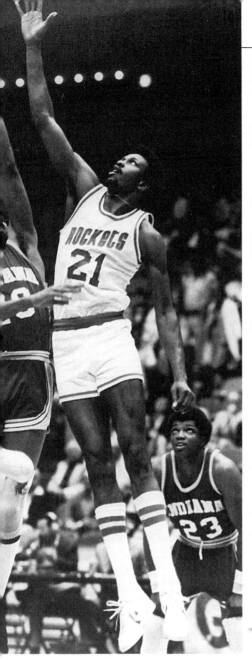

Moses Malone (21) claimed his share of NBA awards during a long career that ended in 1995.

2 Players with eight or more All-Defensive First Team citations: M.J., G.P., S.P., B.J.

3 No. 1 overall draft picks in the 1980s who won Rookie of the Year honors: R.S., P.E., D.R.

4 Two-time winners of the NBA Sixth Man Award: K.M., R.P., D.S.

5 The NBA's first regular-season MVP, NBA Finals MVP, All-Star Game MVP and Rookie of the Year: B.P., J.W., E.M., D.M.

6 Players who have won regular-season MVPs and Rookie of the Year honors in the same season: W.C., W.U.

7 Players named All-NBA First Team 10 or more times: K.M., K.A., E.B., B.C., M.J., B.P., J.W.

8 Members of the 1992-93 NBA All-Rookie First Team: S.O., A.M., C.L., T.G., L.E.

9 The NBA's inaugural All-Defensive First Team in 1968-69: D.D., N.T., B.R., W.F., J.S.

10 Multiple Coach of the Year winners: B.F., G.S., D.N., C.F., P.R., H.B.

—On the Rebound—
Warming up

Each four-letter set represents scrambled initials of the leading career rebounders for the franchises that follow. Unscramble and identify as many as you can.

1. **BOWS—Nets/Magic**

2. **ABRA—Celtics/Suns**

3. **SHOD—Rockets/76ers**

4. **BAKE—Lakers/Bucks**

DID YOU KNOW...

➤That **Larry Bird** is the only person to win NBA Most Valuable Player, Rookie of the Year and Coach of the Year honors?

➤That Shaquille O'Neal is the only player in NBA history to be named NBA Player of the Week after his first week in the league? Giving opponents a preview of things to come, Shaq averaged 25.8 points and 16.4 rebounds in his debut week.

Former Portland star Bill Walton is one of four players to lead the NBA in both blocked shots and rebounds in the same season.

5. JIDD—Nuggets/Mavericks

6. KWUM—Jazz/Wizards

7. SLEP—Kings/Knicks

8. BRPS—Hawks/Heat

9. LJJM—Hornets/Bulls

10. GRKD—Spurs/Timberwolves

11. SLBJ—Pistons/SuperSonics

12. TMND—Warriors/Pacers

Getting serious

Wilt Chamberlain led the NBA in both scoring and rebounding seven times. Name the other two players who captured both crowns in the same season. Hint: Chamberlain was the last to perform the double in 1965-66.

3 11 7 By the Numbers

The chronological order of numbers retired by the Boston Celtics:

1963
Bob Cousy (14)
Ed Macauley (22)
1964
Walter Brown (1)
1966
Tom Heinsohn (15)
Bill Sharman (21)
1967
K.C. Jones (25)
1969
Sam Jones (24)
1972
Bill Russell (6)
1973
Tom Sanders (16)
1978
John Havlicek (17)
1981
Dave Cowens (18)
1982
Jo Jo White (10)
1985
Red Auerbach (2)
1991
Dennis Johnson (3)
1993
Larry Bird (33)
1994
Kevin McHale (32)
1995
Reggie Lewis (35)
1998
Robert Parish (00)

Note: Uniform retirement dates for Jim Loscutoff (LOSCY), Don Nelson (19) and Frank Ramsey (23) are not available.

2 Name the only player to lead the NBA in both rebounding and assists in the same season.

3 Wilt Chamberlain and Bill Russell combined for 22 of the 24 top rebounding games in NBA history. Name one of the two players not named Chamberlain or Russell on that elite list.

4 Wilt Chamberlain led the NBA in rebounding a record 11 times. Who ranks second with seven rebounding titles?

5 This Philadelphia forward earned an NBA rebounding title in 1986-87, becoming the first player 6-6 or shorter to win that honor since 1954. Name the player.

6 Name the only player to capture rebounding titles in both the ABA and NBA.

7 Center Patrick Ewing is the New York Knicks' all-time leading regular-season rebounder with 10,759. How many NBA rebounding titles did Ewing win?

8 Four players have led the NBA in both rebounding and blocked shots in the same season. Los Angeles' Kareem Abdul-Jabbar and Portland's Bill Walton did it in 1975-76 and 1976-77, respectively. Name the two players who have performed this double since 1990.

High-scoring Wilt Chamberlain also was a prolific rebounder.

9 Nobody has averaged more than 20 rebounds per game since 1968-69, when Wilt Chamberlain averaged 21.1 for the Los Angeles Lakers. The closest anyone has come since was the 18.7 figure posted by this rebounding monster in 1991-92.

10 In the March 2, 1962, game in which Wilt Chamberlain scored his record 100 points for the Philadelphia Warriors, how many rebounds did he grab?

Go Figure

Warming up

Figure out the significance of the following number sequences.

1. 37.6, 38.4, 50.4, 44.8, 36.9

2. 19-18; 186-184

3. 36-of-63, 28-of-32, 25, 2

4. 69, 64, 61, 61, 59

5. 1,315-1,133, 1,148-858, 1,110-569

6. 72-10; 9-73

7. 40-1

8. 94 feet X 50 feet

9. 38,387, 23,924, 15,806

10. 1991, 1992, 1993, 1996, 1997, 1998

Getting serious

We provide a team followed by numbers. You provide the names of players who wore those numbers.

1. Warriors: 13, 24, 42

2. Pistons: 4, 11, 16

3. 76ers: 6, 10, 34

4. Trail Blazers: 22, 32

5. Jazz: 7, 12, 32

6. Lakers: 22, 32, 42

7. Rockets: 23, 24, 34

8. Bulls: 4, 23, 33

9. Knicks: 10, 19, 33

10. Spurs: 21, 44

West

Baylor

Feeling a Draft

Warming up

1 In the 2002 NBA Draft, Duke players were selected with the Nos. 2 and 3 overall picks behind No. 1 Yao Ming. Name the Duke first-rounders.

2 Of high schoolers Kevin Garnett, Kobe Bryant, Tracy McGrady and Darius Miles, who was selected with the highest pick in his respective NBA Draft?

3 Lost in the glare of the 1984 NBA Draft that featured Hakeem Olajuwon as the No. 1 overall pick and Michael Jordan as No. 3 was the No. 16 selection of a future NBA record-holder and 10-time All-Star. Name the highly acclaimed guard.

4 The 1956 NBA Draft is remembered for the trade Boston made with St. Louis for No. 3 overall pick Bill Russell. But this memorable deal was not exactly one-sided. The Hawks got two future Hall of Famers in return. Name them.

5 Through 1965, teams participating in the NBA Draft were allowed to trade in first-round picks for "territorial picks," allowing them to pick off players with strong local affiliations. Name the 1959 and 1960 territorial picks who helped define the course of NBA history.

Don Nelson spent 11 seasons in Milwaukee as coach of the Bucks.

DID YOU KNOW ...

➤That the Kings franchise is perfect in NBA Finals play? The team's only Finals appearance came in 1951 when it was based in Rochester, and the then-named Royals defeated the New York Knicks in seven games.

➤That *Karl Malone* is one of only two players to average at least 25 points in 11 consecutive seasons? Malone never fell below that barrier from 1987-98 and joined Jerry West in that exclusive club.

6 This 15-year NBA guard was selected in 1978 with the 14th pick of the second round out of West Texas State. He was a four-time All-Star, a four-time member of the NBA's All-Defensive first team and the point man for an NBA championship team. Name the man who also ranks as the all-time steals and assists leader for the franchise that drafted him.

7 The Milwaukee Bucks have made the No. 1 overall pick in the NBA Draft three times, twice because of good fortune. In 1969 they won a coin flip with Phoenix and drafted No. 1. In 1994, they won the draft lottery. Name the players they selected with those two picks.

8 Orlando's future brightened considerably when the Magic won the No. 1 overall pick in the 1992 and 1993 NBA Drafts—picks that netted them Shaquille O'Neal and Anfernee Hardaway. Name the team that enjoyed similar consecutive-draft fortune in the 1980s and the players it selected.

9 In 1987, the No. 4 (Los Angeles Clippers), No. 12 (Washington) and No. 22 (Boston) picks all were former teammates at Baltimore's Dunbar High School. Name two of the three players, who attended Georgetown, Wake Forest and Northeastern University.

10 Name the only player to be selected in the first round of both the NBA and Major League Baseball drafts.

The Magic picked No. 1 overall in the 1992 and '93 drafts, selections that brought Shaquille O'Neal and Anfernee Hardaway (right) to Orlando.

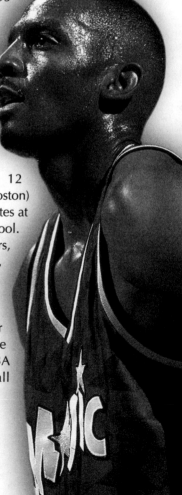

Getting serious

Fill in the missing information (year, player, college or drafting team) for the following No. 1 overall NBA draft picks.

	Year	Player	College	Team
1.	1994	Glenn Robinson	Purdue	_____
2.	____	Derrick Coleman	Syracuse	New Jersey
3.	1997	Tim Duncan	_____	San Antonio
4.	1988	Danny Manning	Kansas	_____
5.	1986	_____	North Carolina	Cleveland
6.	____	Kwame Brown	High school	Washington
7.	1991	Larry Johnson	_____	Charlotte
8.	1989	_____	Louisville	Sacramento
9.	1998	Michael Olowokandi	_____	L.A. Clippers
10.	____	Patrick Ewing	Georgetown	N.Y. Knicks
11.	1981	Mark Aguirre	DePaul	_____
12.	1980	_____	Purdue	Golden State
13.	1996	Allen Iverson	_____	Philadelphia
14.	1978	_____	Minnesota	Portland
15.	1995	Joe Smith	Maryland	_____
16.	____	David Robinson	Navy	San Antonio
17.	2000	Kenyon Martin	_____	New Jersey
18.	1993	Chris Webber	Michigan	_____
19.	____	Ralph Sampson	Virginia	Houston
20.	2002	_____	Shanghai Sharks	Houston

—Alias Smith, Jones and Johnson—

Warming up

1 Identify the player named Smith, Jones or Johnson with the most NBA championship rings.

2 Three Smiths, Joneses or Johnsons have been selected No. 1 overall in the NBA draft. Name them.

3 Name the Smith, Jones or Johnson who was honored with the NBA's first Sixth Man Award in 1982-83.

4 Only one Smith, Jones or Johnson has been honored as the NBA's Coach of the Year. He won it after leading the 1974-75 Kansas City/Omaha Kings to a 44-38 record.

DID YOU KNOW...

➤That two ABA players, Spencer Haywood of Denver and *Dan Issel* of Kentucky, won double distinction as Rookie of the Year and league scoring champion? Haywood led the ABA with a 30-point average in 1969-70 and Issel won the next year with a 29.8 average.

5 This player was a long-time holder of the NBA record for most consecutive games played, a mark that now belongs to A.C. Green. But don't confuse him with the man who holds the Smith-Jones-Johnson record for most NBA seasons played with 17. Name both.

6 This sharp-shooting former Kentucky guard was a key figure for strong Cincinnati Royals teams that also featured Oscar Robertson, Jerry Lucas, Jack Twyman and Wayne Embry in the 1960s.

7 This undrafted guard, a member of the 1999 NBA championship team, is one of two players under 6 feet (Calvin Murphy is the other) to play in more than 1,000 career games.

8 This well-traveled 6-11 forward, one of four brothers who played in the NBA, was one of two former ABA players still active in 1989-90, his final season.

This dapper Kansas City/Omaha Kings boss won NBA Coach of the Year honors in 1974-75.

9 Only Nate Thurmond and Wilt Chamberlain rank ahead of this 6-8 former Alcorn State star on the Warriors franchise's career rebounding list. His career ended in 1992-93, but his reputation as one of the game's best offensive board men lives on.

10 This 13-year NBA guard is best remembered for his yeoman sixth-man efforts for the Detroit Pistons' championship teams in 1989 and '90. His 15-foot jump shot with less than one second remaining gave the Bad Boys a series-clinching Game 5 win over Portland in the 1990 NBA Finals.

Getting serious

We give a year, a team, a scoring average and a last name. You give the first name of the Smith, Jones and/or Johnson who ranked either first or second in scoring average for that team.

	Smith	Jones	Johnson
1. 1982-83 Kansas City Kings			19.8
2. 1977-78 Golden State Warriors	19.7		
3. 2000-01 Portland Trail Blazers	13.6		
4. 1999-00 Charlotte Hornets		20.1	
5. 1981-82 Phoenix Suns			19.5
6. 1964-65 Boston Celtics		25.9	
7. 1985-86 Los Angeles Clippers	23.5		20.3
8. 1989-90 Phoenix Suns			22.5
9. 1990-91 Houston Rockets	17.7		
10. 1966-67 Baltimore Bullets			20.7

——Big Man, Little Man——

Read the following clues and match them with a name and height from the lists that follow.

1 He played 10 NBA seasons and is best remembered for his distinctive look and shot-blocking ability. This high riser is one of the few players to record more blocks (2,086) than points (1,599). He once blocked 15 shots in a game.

2 This fan favorite played 14 NBA seasons and always was ready to help his friends. He still ranks as the career assists leader for an expansion franchise he helped build into a winner, and his career assists-to-turnovers ratio is the best in NBA history. Playing against him was like stirring a hornets' nest.

3 He played 12 NBA seasons and averaged 9.9 points and 5.3 assists, but he's best remembered for winning a slam-dunk contest in 1986 in his hometown of Dallas. Never mind the 4,342 career assists and 922 steals he posted; this guy built his colorful reputation as a human highlight reel.

4 Opponents had to set their sights high to deal with this man, whose size-20 sneakers left an indelible mark during a six-year NBA career in the 1990s. Those who don't remember him as the tallest player in NBA history might recall his starring role with Billy Crystal in a 1998 movie.

5 The only Hall of Famer in this group averaged 17.9 points over an outstanding 13-year NBA career with one team. At one time he held the NBA record for consecutive free throws made with 78.

6 Here's the skinny: This guy has posted six career triple-doubles and is the first NBA player to come off the bench and top 20 points, 20 rebounds and 10 blocks in a single game. The man who delayed his pro career for a two-year church mission in Australia also is a guy who appeared in the movie *Space Jam* with Bugs Bunny, Bill Murray and Michael Jordan.

7 The "Dunking Dutchman" spent his entire 12-year career with the same team. Not surprisingly, he ranks first in franchise history in rebounding and second in points. This guy broke the NBA record for patience when he made his first All-Star Game appearance in 1998, his 10th season.

Muggsy Bogues might have been short in stature, but he was a big man for the Charlotte Hornets.

8 Undrafted in 1998, this hotshot relied on guile and determination to become the second shortest player in NBA history. He can score (28 points in a 2003 game against Minnesota) and make plays (3.6 assists per game in 2003-04). Not bad for a 135-pound weakling out of Eastern Michigan.

9 Talk about persistence, this player out of New Mexico State toiled for eight long years to reach the NBA. He did with Atlanta in 1977, becoming the oldest rookie in league history at age 28. The persistence paid off. He played eight seasons, averaging in double figures twice, and won over all of the skeptics who had pronounced him unfit for a professional career.

10 Go ahead, take your best shot. Odds are this guy will block it. He led the NBA in blocked shots four times in his 11 seasons (all for the same team) and ranks third all-time behind only Hakeem Olajuwon and Kareem Abdul-Jabbar. He swatted away an NBA-record 456 in the 1984-85 campaign. This guy also is a two-time Defensive Player of the Year.

By the Numbers

Players who have won back-to-back MVP awards in the NBA:

Bill Russell
1961-63

Wilt Chamberlain
1966-68

Kareem Abdul-Jabbar
1976-77

Moses Malone
1982-83

Larry Bird
1984-86

Magic Johnson
1989-90

Michael Jordan
1991-92

Tim Duncan
2002-03

Magic Johnson

11 Not getting drafted in 1988 only seemed to inspire this player, the only member of this list to play on an NBA championship team. When he played in his 1,000th game in 2003, he became only the second person under 6 feet to achieve that milestone. If you need to make a point, this former Southern University star just might be your man.

12 His name doesn't appear on any career leaders charts, and he played only two professional seasons—one with Denver in the ABA and the other with the Nuggets in the NBA—but this player left a big impression. He was a passing fancy who made special connections with star forward David Thompson with his pinpoint alley-oop tosses. It was a relationship that traced back to their collegiate days at North Carolina State.

13 His career was not as productive as everyone expected, but at least he can say he was drafted ahead of Michael Jordan. Injuries played havoc with his professional career, sidelining him for more than 400 games over 10 seasons. His best performance came in 1991-92, when he averaged 15 points and 8.1 rebounds for the New Jersey Nets.

14 He has been a good role player for nine NBA seasons on a team with star power. He ranks third on his franchise's shot-blocking list, but his greater claim to fame came off of the court. In 2002 the former Jayhawk with the size-18 sneakers donated a kidney to his sister.

A. 5-3	AA. Shawn Bradley
B. 5-5	BB. Spud Webb
C. 5-6	CC. Rik Smits
D. 5-7	DD. Avery Johnson
E. 5-8	EE. Mark Eaton
F. 5-9	FF. Charlie Criss
G. 5-10	GG. Greg Ostertag
H. 7-1	HH. Calvin Murphy
I. 7-2	II. Gheorghe Muresan
J. 7-3	JJ. Earl Boykins
K. 7-4	KK. Manute Bol
L. 7-5	LL. Monty Towe
M. 7-6	MM. Sam Bowie
N. 7-7	NN. Muggsy Bogues

──── Miscellaneous ────

Warming up

1 Who was the last ABA player to compete in the NBA?

2 In 1974, former Warriors great Nate Thurmond became the first NBA player to perform a quadruple-double—double figures in four statistical categories in a game. Name the three players who have joined Thurmond in that exclusive club.

3 In 1962, Wilt Chamberlain averaged an amazing 50.4 points per game to lead the NBA. Who finished second with a 38.3 average—the highest mark ever posted by somebody not named Chamberlain?

4 Name the Minnesota player who missed a free throw on November 9, 1993, ending his NBA-record streak of 97 consecutive shots made from the foul line.

5 What two franchises played all nine ABA seasons in the same city and with the same name?

6 Name the player who performed an ABA triple in the league's inaugural 1967-68 season—scoring champion, MVP and leader of its championship team.

7 When Michael Jordan won seven straight NBA scoring titles from 1986-87 through 1992-93, two players took turns finishing second. Name the seven-time runners-up.

8 In 1969, this former Rookie of the Year played in a still-standing NBA-record 88 games—the result of a midseason trade from New York to Detroit. Name this 6-11 big man who scored 20,941 career points and grabbed 14,241 rebounds.

9 From 1972-73 through 1992-93, the NBA scoring title was won by either a guard or forward. Name the center who finally broke his position's long drought.

10 If you combine ABA and NBA scoring, what player jumps to No. 5 on the all-time list with 30,026 combined points and a 24.2 average?

Former Warriors big man Nate Thurmond is one of four NBA players to perform a quadruple-double.

Getting serious

Identify the following NBA players and their membership in an exclusive basketball club.

1 A Phi Slamma Jamma original. Averaged 20.4 points over 15 seasons. Played on one NBA championship team and was selected for 10 All-Star Games. A gliding, acrobatic guard.

2 A former first overall draft pick and member of the elite 20,000-point, 10,000-rebound club. Played 15 of 17 seasons with the same team but never won an NBA championship. A statistical giant but he never led the league in a major single-season category.

3 A colorful, fast-talking warrior who scored 23,757 points and grabbed 12,546 rebounds over a 16-year career. Often was perceived as villainous. Might have been the most rugged small forward of his era. An MVP in 1992-93 and an All-Star 11 times but never a champion.

4 A member of two NBA championship teams, one in his 14th and final season. Was a southpaw who averaged 21.1 points, 10.6 rebounds and 3 blocks as his franchise's longtime center of attention. Rookie of the Year in 1990, Defensive Player of the Year in 1992 and MVP in 1995.

5 A jazzy little performer who holds career records in two major statistical categories. Played his entire 19-year career with the same team but never won a championship. A 16th overall draft pick who gets passing grades as one of the game's all-time great guards.

6 One of three players to win three straight league MVP awards. Led his team to three NBA championships. Averaged 24.3 points, 10 rebounds and 6.3 assists over a 13-year career with one team. One of the game's brightest stars in the 1980s.

7 A sharp-shooting lefty who spent 13 golden years in the NBA. Never played for a championship team or won a major league honor, but opponents feared his explosive scoring ability and accuracy from beyond the 3-point arc. A native New Yorker who shot 86.5 percent from the free throw line.

8 He's the standard by which all modern basketball players are judged. A member of six championship teams and owner of the highest career scoring average. The all-everything of professional basketball even though he was not even a first overall draft pick.

9 A high-scoring power forward who completed his 19th season in 2003-04. Big, rugged and consistent—the proud standard bearer for a franchise, even though he never won a championship in his career. Holds the NBA record for most seasons with 2,000 or more points.

10 A leader of five NBA championship teams and the league's one-time career assists leader. His nickname accurately reflects the amazing court savvy and ability that lifted him to elite-of-the-elite status. Career was cut short by illness, but his legendary performances will live forever.

11 Always overshadowed and considered by many an accessory player for six NBA championship teams, this smooth, high-flying forward was a master scorer, rebounder, passer, defender—anything needed to win. A member of the All-Defensive First Team eight times. A seven-time All-Star.

12 This player is best remembered for one of the most famous shots in NCAA Tournament history. Completed his 12th NBA season in 2003-04 but never has lived up to the third overall draft pick status he was accorded in 1992. Has scored more than 10,000 career points.

13 What exclusive club do the above players belong to?

Finger Pointing

Warming up

The following initials represent the leading career point scorer for each of the 29 NBA franchises that played in the 2003-04 season. Your challenge is to provide a name and team for each.

1. D.C.	7. J.H.	13. G.R.	19. P.E.	25. S.A.
2. K.A.	8. K.M.	14. B.D.	20. M.J.	26. R.S.
3. O.R.	9. B.W.	15. D.W.	21. R.M.	27. D.R.
4. H.G.	10. W.C.	16. J.W.	22. W.D.	28. K.G.
5. V.C.	11. H.O.	17. R.B.	23. I.T.	29. N.A.
6. A.E.	12. G.P.	18. E.H.	24. C.D.	

The following checklist might be helpful in solving the above puzzle:

Atlanta Hawks	Miami Heat	Toronto Raptors
Boston Celtics	Milwaukee Bucks	Utah Jazz
Chicago Bulls	Minnesota Timberwolves	Washington Wizards
Cleveland Cavaliers	New Jersey Nets	
Dallas Mavericks	New Orleans Hornets	
Denver Nuggets	New York Knicks	
Detroit Pistons	Orlando Magic	
Golden State Warriors	Philadelphia 76ers	
Houston Rockets	Phoenix Suns	
Indiana Pacers	Portland Trail Blazers	
Los Angeles Clippers	Sacramento Kings	
Los Angeles Lakers	San Antonio Spurs	
Memphis Grizzlies	Seattle SuperSonics	

Getting serious

Using the list of franchise scoring leaders you identified above, answer the following questions:

1 Name the player who holds the career scoring record for a single franchise and, within 1,000, give his point total for that team.

2 Five players have totaled more than 25,000 points for a single franchise. Name them.

3 One franchise scoring leader also ranks second on the career points list for another franchise. Name him.

4 Three of the franchise career leaders also rank 1-2-3 in NBA Finals career points. Name them.

5 Identify the only player among the NBA's top 10 career scorers who is not a franchise points leader.

6 Two players who have scored 70 or more points in a regular-season game are not members of the franchise points leader board. Name them.

7 Name the four-time NBA scoring champion who is not listed among franchise career points leaders. All of his titles came for the same team.

8 Name the only franchise points leader who scored 5,000 or more points for three different franchises.

9 Nine of the 29 franchise leaders played (or have played) for only one team. How many can you name?

10 Name the one franchise points leader who never led his team in scoring average during a single season.

Can you name the athlete and the sport?

1 OK, call me a chip off the old block. It's hard to argue otherwise. I did spend a lot of time with my dad while growing up, but so did a lot of other guys I hung out with. I guess you could call all of our dads "machinists." They were really good with their hands.

2 I had a ball in high school—several in fact, of different shapes and sizes. But I never really had any doubt about what sport I liked best. Moeller High School has produced a lot of great athletes—just ask guys like Woody Hayes, Earle Bruce and John Cooper. But I was different than most. Who needs college, anyway?

3 I've always been the youngest this or the youngest that. It's both a blessing and a curse. You try being the youngest player in an entire league sometime and see how you fare. It has always been like that for me. Even now, as a bona fide veteran, people treat me like some kind of phenom. Sometimes I just want to be left alone.

4 At 19, I heeded Horace Greeley's advice—kind of. I went Northwest, young man, and got into the swing of my new job pretty quickly. Apparently, nobody in my new hometown had ever seen anybody quite like me. I was a huge hit and even my defense rated Gold stars.

5 Some people call me a slacker because I have been hurt a lot, but that hasn't stopped me from producing big numbers. I challenged old Roger a couple of times and helped my team go where it had never gone before. I even learned how to spell M-V-P and collected a couple of records before heading home.

6 Things haven't been quite what I expected since my return to Ohio, but I won't complain. I'm still the center of attention and I've got more than 500 reasons to be thankful. But I just can't stay healthy. If I could, I might have been a contender—for the Top 10 list in my profession.

7 As I look back at my career highlights, I have to rate that 1990 reunion with my dad near the top of the list. And that eight-day blitz wasn't bad, either. I'm no homer, but my teams usually thrive when I become a deep thinker.

8 I'm not through yet and I'm still hoping to catch lightning in a bottle. I want to play on my sport's ultimate stage at least once and I'd like to hear the rumble of another Big Red Machine. But just remember one thing: No matter how old I get, I'll always be 30. And I'll always be Junior in the minds of my fans.

CHAPTER 6
PRO TEAM LOGOS

As sports fans, we are besieged by fish, birds, rockets, fierce animals, fancy letters and numerous other images that trigger instant recognition of teams we follow. Team logos are everywhere we look, from the thousands of pages in various sports publications we read to the advertisements, highlight clips and games we watch every day. Have you been paying attention? See if you can match each of these partial logos to teams that currently play in the NFL, NBA, NHL and MLB.

Chapter 6 answers begin on page 267.

5

8

6

7

9

10

11

12

13

14

15

16

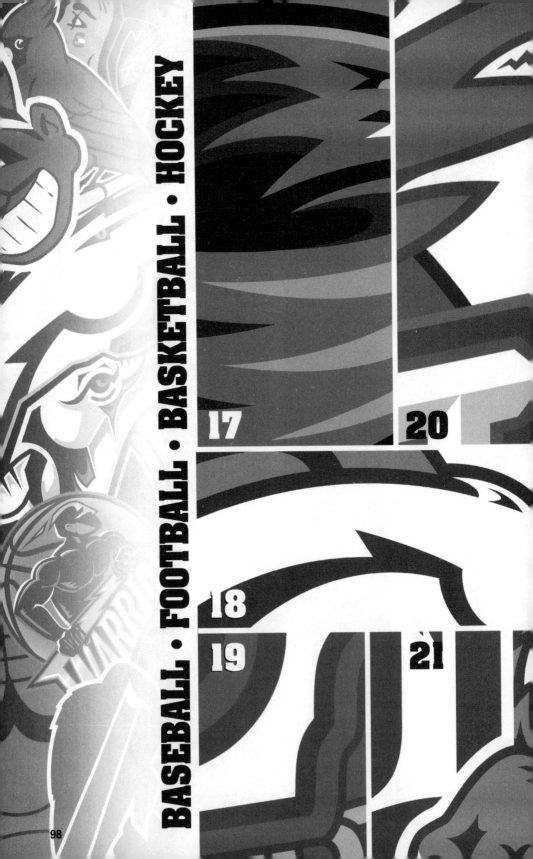

17

20

18

19

21

BASEBALL · FOOTBALL · BASKETBALL · BASKETBALL · HOCKEY

29

31

30 32

BASEBALL • FOOTBALL • BASKETBALL • BASKETBALL • HOCKEY

41

42

43

44

45

46

47

48

BASEBALL · FOOTBALL · BASKETBALL · HOCKEY

49

50

52

51

53

54

55

56

57

BASEBALL · FOOTBALL · BASKETBALL · HOCKEY

58

59

60

61

65

62

66

63

64

67

68

69

70

Mystery Guest

Can you name the athlete and the sport?

1 I'm dead but not forgotten. The venue where I became famous still bears my name, although there's another name attached to it now, too. How tough have I been to replace? Well, since I left 22 seasons ago, seven good men have tried. That's an average of about one every three years. I was there for 25.

2 You probably didn't know that I was once a second-team all-conference selection. But for the first and last time in my life I was overshadowed. I played opposite a guy named Don Hutson. Well, that's the way the old ball bounces. Sometimes you just have to roll with the tide.

3 Believe it or not, I made several early career stops before finding the perfect fit. I even worked for a while in basketball-mad Kentucky, but the state wasn't big enough for me and Adolph Rupp. When I was hired by my alma mater, I promised we'd win a national championship in four years—and delivered.

4 Over the years, I became as famous for my idiosyncrasies and down-home personality as I did for my success. I guess you could say I towered over my troops on the practice field. And game days were not complete without fans and broadcasters pointing out that cat in the hat puffing on a cigarette before going into battle.

5 My guys were incredible on our home field. We lost just two games over my 25 seasons, and at one point had a 57-game winning streak. Ironically, I lost the last game I coached there.

6 You might have seen me in the news recently—at least clips of someone trying to act like me. Everyone was making a big deal about the way I drilled many years ago in Texas. But that's all water over the dam now. My Boys did OK in the long run.

7 I produced a lot of great players over the years, including Bart, Joe and Ozzie. But only one of my guys claimed my sport's biggest trophy—and it wasn't for his accomplishments at the school I am most associated with.

8 I really piled up the wins. In fact, when I retired, I had more than anyone else. Can you count to 323? That's enough counting to make any coach turn crimson. Sure, my win total has since been topped, but how many others have enjoyed these ultimate honors: a postage stamp bearing his image and a museum dedicated to his life and alma mater?

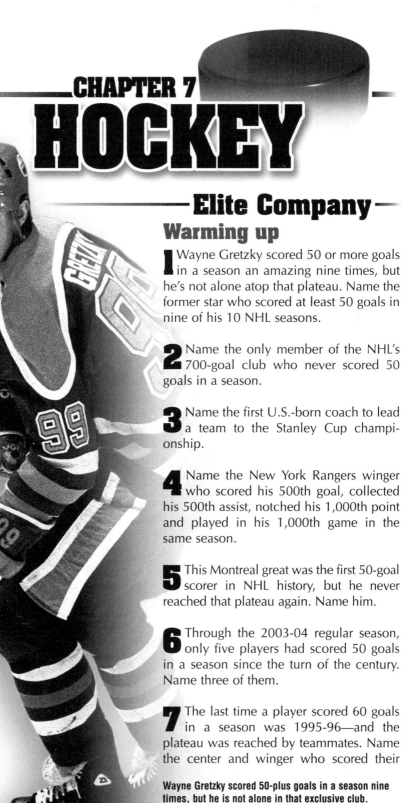

HOCKEY

Elite Company

Warming up

1 Wayne Gretzky scored 50 or more goals in a season an amazing nine times, but he's not alone atop that plateau. Name the former star who scored at least 50 goals in nine of his 10 NHL seasons.

2 Name the only member of the NHL's 700-goal club who never scored 50 goals in a season.

3 Name the first U.S.-born coach to lead a team to the Stanley Cup championship.

4 Name the New York Rangers winger who scored his 500th goal, collected his 500th assist, notched his 1,000th point and played in his 1,000th game in the same season.

5 This Montreal great was the first 50-goal scorer in NHL history, but he never reached that plateau again. Name him.

6 Through the 2003-04 regular season, only five players had scored 50 goals in a season since the turn of the century. Name three of them.

7 The last time a player scored 60 goals in a season was 1995-96—and the plateau was reached by teammates. Name the center and winger who scored their

Wayne Gretzky scored 50-plus goals in a season nine times, but he is not alone in that exclusive club.

DID YOU KNOW...

➤That *Larry Robinson* is the only NHL player who appeared in the playoffs 20 consecutive years? Another defense-man, Ray Bourque, holds the record for most playoff appear-ances with 21.

➤That Hall of Famer Stan Mikita was the first Czechoslovakian-born player in the NHL?

50th goals in the same game and finished the season with 69 and 62, respectively.

8 To say scoring was up in 1992-93 is something of an understatement. Within two, how many players reached the 50-goal plateau that season?

9 In 1995-96, Winnipeg forward Keith Tkachuk scored exactly 50 goals—a first-time membership in that elite club. What was unusual about Tkachuk's 50th goal, scored April 12, 1996, against Los Angeles?

10 Only one goaltender surrendered more than one 500th goal—and he gave up three. Name the great who was in goal when Steve Yzerman, Joe Mullen and Brendan Shanahan notched their career milestones.

Detroit's Steve Yzerman (19) scored his 500th career goal against a goaltender who ranks among the NHL heavyweights.

Getting serious

We provide the season in which a player notched his 500th career goal and the teams he (has) played for during his career. You name the player. Note: The team in italic was the one he was playing for when he reached the milestone.

1. **1985-86:** *Buffalo.*
2. **1988-89:** Toronto, Colorado Rockies, *Calgary.*
3. **1993-94:** Minnesota North Stars, Washington, *Detroit,* Tampa Bay, Florida.
4. **1995-96:** Edmonton, *N.Y. Rangers,* Vancouver, N.Y. Rangers.
5. **1996-97:** Calgary, *St. Louis,* Dallas, Detroit.
6. **1996-97:** St. Louis, Calgary, Pittsburgh, Boston, *Pittsburgh.*
7. **1996-97:** Buffalo, Toronto, *New Jersey,* Boston, Colorado Avalanche, Buffalo, Tampa Bay.
8. **1998-99:** Los Angeles, Pittsburgh, N.Y. Rangers, *Los Angeles,* Detroit.
9. **2001-02:** Hartford, Pittsburgh, *Carolina.*
10. **2001-02:** New Jersey, St. Louis, Hartford, *Detroit.*

Game Winners

Blues goaltender Glenn Hall couldn't stop this classic overtime championship winner.

Warming up

Thirteen Stanley Cup finals series have been decided in seven games. We provide the year and Game 7 score. You provide the winning goaltender.

1. **2004: Tampa Bay 2, Calgary 1.**

2. **2003: New Jersey 3, Anaheim 0.**

3. **2001: Colorado 3, New Jersey 1.**

4. **1994: New York Rangers 3, Vancouver 2.**

5. **1987: Edmonton 3, Philadelphia 1.**

DID YOU KNOW...

➤That Montreal great *Maurice "Rocket" Richard* never won a scoring title? He did, however, have five runner-up finishes.

➤That the Blues, who have never won a Stanley Cup, have watched their former coaches win 14 after leaving St. Louis? *Scotty Bowman* won a combined nine Cups with the Canadiens, Penguins and Red Wings, *Al Arbour* won four with the Islanders and Jacques Demers won one with the Canadiens.

Bowman

Arbour

6. 1971: Montreal 3, Chicago 2.

7. 1965: Montreal 4, Chicago 0.

8. 1964: Toronto 4, Detroit 0.

9. 1955: Detroit 3, Montreal 1.

10. 1954: Detroit 2, Montreal 1 (OT).

11. 1950: Detroit 4, New York Rangers 3 (2 OTs).

12. 1945: Toronto 2, Detroit 1.

13. 1942: Toronto 3, Detroit 1.

Getting serious

We provide the vital information for 10 of the 15 overtime goals that have decided Stanley Cup championships. You supply the goal scorer.

1 Game 7, 1950 Cup finals at Detroit. Second overtime. Red Wings 4, Rangers 3.

2 Game 7, 1954 Cup finals at Detroit. First overtime. Red Wings 2, Canadiens 1.

3 Game 6, 2000 Cup finals at Dallas. Second overtime. Devils 2, Stars 1.

4 Game 6, 1999 Cup finals at Buffalo. Third overtime. Stars 2, Sabres 1.

5 Game 6, 1980 Cup finals at New York. First overtime. Islanders 5, Flyers 4.

6 Game 6, 1966 Cup finals at Detroit. First overtime. Canadiens 3, Red Wings 2.

7 Game 5, 1951 Cup finals at Toronto. First overtime. Maple Leafs 3, Canadiens 2.

8 Game 4, 1970 Cup finals at Boston. First overtime. Bruins 4, Blues 3.

9 Game 4, 1996 Cup finals at Florida. Third overtime. Avalanche 1, Panthers 0.

10 Game 4, 1977 Cup finals at Boston. First overtime. Canadiens 2, Bruins 1.

─Rookies, the Draft─ and Other Things

Warming up

Which name does not belong in the following groups?

1 No. 1 overall NHL draft picks: Guy Lafleur, Doug Wickenheiser, Mike Modano, Eric Lindros, Jaromir Jagr.

2 Calder Trophy (top rookie) winners: Bobby Hull, Frank Mahovlich, Derek Sanderson, Denis Potvin, Pavel Bure.

Former Chicago great Stan Mikita (11) was a multiple winner of the Art Ross Trophy.

3 Players who have won the Art Ross Trophy (scoring leader) four or more times: Wayne Gretzky, Gordie Howe, Phil Esposito, Stan Mikita, Brett Hull.

4 Players who have won the Hart Trophy (MVP) four or more times: Wayne Gretzky, Gordie Howe, Mario Lemieux, Eddie Shore.

5 Players who have won or shared the Vezina Trophy (outstanding goaltender) five or more times: Jacques Plante, Patrick Roy, Bill Durnan, Dominik Hasek, Ken Dryden.

6 Players who were MVP winners in the seven-season World Hockey Association: Bobby Hull, Gordie Howe, Marc Tardif, Mike Bossy, Robbie Ftorek.

7 Men who have won the Jack Adams Award (top coach) two or more times: Pat Burns, Scotty Bowman, Roger Neilson, Jacques Demers, Pat Quinn.

8 James Norris Trophy (top defenseman) winners: Bobby Orr, Rod Langway, Chris Chelios, Chris Pronger, Derian Hatcher.

9 Players who have scored 1,000 or more points: Jean Ratelle, Glenn Anderson, Henri Richard, Pat LaFontaine, Pavel Bure.

No. 1 or No. 2? Eric Lindros was picked high in the 1991 draft, but not by the Philadelphia Flyers.

DID YOU KNOW...

➤That *Eddie Shore* is the only NHL defense-man to be chosen Most Valuable Player four times? The former Boston great won the Hart Trophy in 1932-33, 1934-35, 1935-36 and 1937-38.

➤That Red Kelly, who played for Toronto and Detroit from 1947-67, won more Stanley Cups (8) than any player who never suited up for the Montreal Canadiens?

116

10 Players who have played 20 or more seasons: Marcel Dionne, Mark Messier, Scott Stevens, Phil Housley, Steve Yzerman.

Getting serious

We provide the category and the initials of the players who fit into it. You provide the names.

1 No. 1 overall draft picks who also won the Calder Trophy as rookie of the year: G.P., D.P., B.S., D.H., M.L., B.B.

2 Calder Trophy (top rookies) winners who later won a Hart Memorial Trophy honoring the league's MVP: B.G., B.O., B.T., M.L., P.F.

3 Calder Trophy winners who later won a Vezina Trophy as the league's outstanding goaltender: F.B., T.S., G.W., G.H., T.E., K.D., T.B., E.B., M.B.

4 Calder Trophy winners who later won a Hart Trophy *and* Conn Smythe Trophy, which honors the league's playoff MVP: B.O., B.T., M.L.

5 Rookie brothers and teammates who scored 16 points (eight apiece) in Quebec's 11-7 win over Washington in 1981: A.S., P.S.

6 The only rookies who have scored 50 goals in a season: T.S., M.B., J.N.

7 Five rookies who have topped 100 points in a season: T.S., P.S., D.H., J.J., M.L.

8 Two rookie defense-men who have scored 20 goals in a season: B.L., B.B.

Mark Messier has made NHL stops at Edmonton, New York and Vancouver.

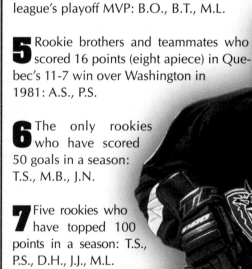

By the Numbers

Players who have scored the most goals for one team (through the 2003-04 season):

Gordie Howe
Red Wings
786

Mario Lemieux
Penguins
683

Steve Yzerman
Red Wings
678

Bobby Hull
Blackhawks
604

Wayne Gretzky
Oilers
583

Mike Bossy
Islanders
573

Marcel Dionne
Kings
550

John Bucyk
Bruins
545

Maurice Richard
Canadiens
544

Joe Sakic
Avalanche
542

9 Most points (21) and goals (14) by a rookie in one playoff series: D.C.

10 The last rookie coach to lead his team to a Stanley Cup championship (1986): J.P.

— The Puck Stops Here —

Warming up

1 A playoff MVP before he won the Calder Trophy as the NHL's top rookie.

2 The active goalie (through 2003-04) who is tied for third all time in wins.

3 A one-season-record 47 wins in 1973-74.

4 The first goalie in NHL history to score a goal.

5 The first goalie to win 400 career games.

6 The first goalie to win 500 career games.

7 The 1985 Vezina Trophy winner who died in an automobile accident later that year.

This talented goaltender set a franchise wins mark for the Chicago Blackhawks.

8 A 1989-90 replacement for injured Grant Fuhr who backstopped Edmonton to a Stanley Cup championship.

9 The man who popularized the goalie mask.

10 The goaltender who lost the most NHL games.

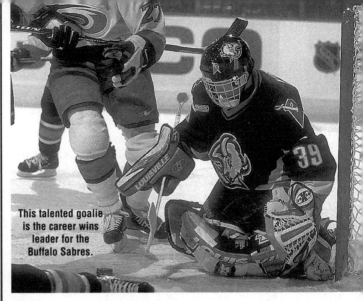

This talented goalie is the career wins leader for the Buffalo Sabres.

Getting serious

Each of the following goaltenders is the career wins leader for one of the 26 National Hockey League franchises that existed before expansion to Nashville, Atlanta, Columbus and Minnesota in the late 1990s and 2000s. Some are obvious; some are tricky. Go ahead, take your best shot.

1. Grant Fuhr
2. Ed Belfour
3. Patrick Lalime
4. Nikolai Khabibulin
5. Patrick Roy
6. Terry Sawchuk
7. Mike Liut
8. Tony Esposito
9. Tom Barrasso
10. Bob Essensa
11. Mike Richter
12. Turk Broda
13. Billy Smith

14. Ron Hextall
15. Martin Brodeur
16. Rogie Vachon
17. Jacques Plante
18. Evgeni Nabokov
19. Dominik Hasek
20. Arturs Irbe
21. Mike Vernon
22. Guy Hebert
23. Tiny Thompson
24. John Vanbiesbrouck
25. Kirk McLean
26. Olaf Kolzig

First Impressions

Warming up

Match the player, goaltender or coach to his "first" feat in the list that follows.

1. Tom Barrasso
2. Denis Potvin
3. Doug Gilmour
4. Kevin Stevens
5. Scott Stevens

6. Ron Tugnutt
7. Terry Sawchuk
8. Gordie Howe
9. Rocket Richard
10. Petr Klima

A. First player to score 1,000 career points.

B. First player to take two penalty shots in the Stanley Cup playoffs (1988 and 1990).

C. Goaltender who was selected with first overall pick of 1967 expansion draft.

D. First player to get 200 assists with three teams.

E. First goaltender to play for eight teams.

F. First man to play 600 games with two teams.

G. First player to score 50 goals in one season.

H. First U.S.-born goaltender to win 300 games.

I. First defenseman to reach the 1,000-point plateau.

J. First player to have 50 goals, 100 points and 200 penalty minutes in the same season (1991-92).

Getting serious

1 I raised eyebrows by scoring 32 goals as a rookie after jumping directly from high school to the NHL in 1981-82. Three seasons later, I became the first U.S.-born player to notch 50 goals in a single season. I never scored 100 points, but I did play 18 years and win a Stanley Cup championship.

2 It's a good thing franchises are inanimate because I would have been totally humiliated in my inaugural season. I was 8-67-5 in 1974-75, the worst mark ever posted by an expansion team. I have improved a lot since then, but not to the point my fans can call me a champion.

Denis Potvin performed an NHL 'first' during his long career with the Islanders.

DID YOU KNOW...

➤That Vic Lynn, a left winger/defenseman who played in the NHL from 1942-43 through 1953-54, is the only man to play for all of the Original Six teams before expansion? In order, Lynn played for the Rangers, Red Wings, Canadiens, Maple Leafs, Bruins and Blackhawks.

➤That *Terry Sawchuk*, Gump Worsley and John Vanbiesbrouck are the only goalies to play 20 or more seasons in the NHL?

In 1993, Pittsburgh's Mario Lemieux (above) and Kevin Stevens became the first teammates to score their 50th goals in the same game.

3 I guess you could say I had a whirlwind debut. I worked my first six NHL games in goal at the end of the regular season and won them all. Then I started all through the playoffs and led my team to victories over Boston, Minnesota and Chicago. The win over the Blackhawks required seven games and made me a Stanley Cup winner before my official rookie season.

4 After scoring the goal that gave my country its first Olympic ice hockey gold medal in 1994, my face was pictured on a postage stamp. But that wasn't enough. So I

worked hard and later became the first player from my country to win the NHL's Art Ross and Hart trophies. I guess you can say I feel an avalanche of popularity whenever I go home.

5 My team won the Stanley Cup in my first season playing center. I won again in my second season. And my fourth, sixth, ninth, 10th, 11th and 12th—eight titles in a dozen years. Then I coached another team to a Cup title in 1994-95. I guess you could call me a winner.

6 Finally! I broke a 21-year stranglehold on the Art Ross Trophy when I scored 52 goals and notched 96 points. I became the first player not named Gretzky, Lemieux or Jagr to win the NHL scoring title since 1979-80, when a Los Angeles King named Marcel Dionne took the honors.

7 The Courtnall brothers, Geoff and Russ, beat us to the punch in 1998-99 when they became the first NHL brothers to each play 1,000 games. We matched them the next season, which still was a worthy feat considering none of our four other brothers could last that long. We were not prolific scorers, but give us an A for effort and durability.

8 I was the first man to coach in five different decades, the first to win 200 games with three different teams, the first to coach four teams in the Stanley Cup finals and the first to lead three teams to championships. I guess you could say I knew what I was doing.

9 I'm the first man to coach eight teams. My Vancouver squad lost once in the Stanley Cup finals. The Flyers played for the Cup the year before I arrived and the Panthers lost in the finals the year after I left. But the real bummer was New York. The Rangers won a championship the year after I departed for Florida.

Jaromir Jagr is one of three players who won NHL scoring titles over a 21-year span.

10 Pittsburgh's Mario Lemieux and Kevin Stevens stole our thunder in 1993 when they became the first NHL teammates to score their 50th goals in the same game. So we approached it from a slightly different angle. In 1994, we became the first players from opposing teams to notch our 50th goals in the same game.

Bobby Hull (9) and his brother terrorized goalies during the 1960s and '70s.

-Public Relations-
Warming up

Name the athlete or celebrity who matches up with the names that follow.

Husband / Wife
1. Wayne Gretzky/_____.
2. Bret Hedican/_____.

Brother / Sister
3. Pascal Rheaume/_____.
4. Tony Granato/_____.

Cousins
5. Shane Churla/_____.
6. Wendel Clark/_____,

_____.
7. Ron Francis/_____.

Uncle / Nephews
8. Ed Kea/_____ and

_____.

Father-in-law / Son-in-law
9. Bobby Clarke/_____.

Brother-in-laws
10. Shayne Corson/_____.

Getting serious

Supply the missing names in the following NHL brother combinations and then, if you want some serious extra credit, rank the brother combinations according to total goals scored:

1. Stastny: Marian, _____, _____.

2. Courtnall: _____, _____.

3. Hunter: Dave, _____, _____.

4. Sutter: Rich, Ron, _____, _____, _____, _____.

5. Hull: Bobby, _____.

6. Richard: Maurice, _____.

7. Mullen: _____, _____.

8. Broten: Aaron, _____, _____.

9. Conacher: Lionel, Roy, _____.

By the Numbers

The seven Montreal Canadiens who played for the most Stanley Cup winners:

Henri Richard	11
Jean Beliveau	10
Yvan Cournoyer	10
Claude Provost	9
Jacques Lemaire	8
Maurice Richard	8
Serge Savard	8

10. Mahovlich: _____, _____.

11. Bure: _____, _____.

12. Dionne: Gilbert, _____.

Coach Speak

Warming up

Match the coach in the first list to the trio of stars he coached at some point during his career.

1. Scotty Bowman

2. Jacques Demers

3. Mike Keenan

4. Roger Neilson

5. Al Arbour

6. Bob Berry

7. Jacques Lemaire

8. John Muckler

9. Bryan Murray

10. Pat Quinn

A. Jari Kurri, Dominik Hasek, Mike Richter

B. Darryl Sittler, Brian Leetch, Eric Lindros

C. Marcel Dionne, Larry Robinson, Mario Lemieux

D. Glenn Hall, Guy Lafleur, Gilbert Perreault

E. Bobby Clarke, Dave Taylor, Pavel Bure

F. Steve Shutt, Scott Stevens, Martin Brodeur

G. Bernie Federko, Steve Yzerman, Patrick Roy

H. Mike Gartner, Dino Ciccarelli, John Vanbiesbrouck

I. Barclay Plager, Bryan Trottier, Billy Smith

J. Denis Savard, Mark Messier, Brett Hull

Jacques Demers has coached several of the game's great players.

Getting serious

We provide an unbroken line of coaches spanning a decade or more, you provide the team.

1 Emile Francis, Ron Stewart, John Ferguson, Jean-Guy Talbot, Fred Shero, Craig Patrick, Herb Brooks.

2 Harry Neale, Roger Neilson, Harry Neale, Bill Laforge, Harry Neale, Tom Watt, Bob McCammon.

3 Bob Pulford, Bob Murdoch, Mike Keenan, Darryl Sutter, Craig Hartsburg, Dirk Graham.

4 Bobby Kromm, Ted Lindsay, Wayne Maxner, Billy Dea, Nick Polano, Harry Neale, Brad Park, Dan Belisle, Jacques Demers.

5 Floyd Smith, Punch Imlach, Joe Crozier, Mike Nykoluk, Dan Maloney, John Brophy, George Armstrong, Doug Carpenter, Tom Watt, Pat Burns.

Well-traveled Mike Keenan (standing) has left his coaching mark on seven NHL teams.

6 Bob Johnson, Terry Crisp, Doug Risebrough, Guy Charron, Dave King, Pierre Page, Brian Sutter.

7 Roger Neilson, Jim Roberts, Scotty Bowman, Jim Schoenfeld, Scotty Bowman, Craig Ramsay, Ted Sator, Rick Dudley.

8 Don Cherry, Fred Creighton, Harry Sinden, Gerry Cheevers, Harry Sinden, Butch Goring, Terry O'Reilly, Mike Milbury.

9 Pat Quinn, Bob McCammon, Mike Keenan, Paul Holmgren, Bill Dineen, Terry Simpson, Terry Murray.

10 Eddie Johnston, Lou Angotti, Bob Berry, Pierre Creamer, Gene Ubriaco, Craig Patrick, Bob Johnson, Scotty Bowman.

—Best of Teams, Worst of Teams—

Warming up

Match the team below to the fact that describes that team in the list that follows.

1. 1983-84 Edmonton Oilers.

2. 1976-77 Montreal Canadiens.

3. 1992-93 San Jose Sharks.

4. 1995-96 Detroit Red Wings.

5. 1979-80 Philadelphia Flyers.

6. 1974-75 Washington Capitals.

7. 1928-29 Montreal Canadiens.

8. 1992-93 Pittsburgh Penguins.

9. 1986-87 Edmonton Oilers.

10. 1980-81 Winnipeg Jets.

A. Posted a single-season NHL record 62 wins.

B. Posted a single-season NHL record 22 shutouts, all by George Hainsworth.

C. Lost an NHL record 71 games.

D. Suffered through an NHL record 30 game winless streak.

E. Scored an NHL single-season record 446 goals.

F. Posted an NHL record 132 points (60-8-12).

G. Managed a single-season low 21 points (based on a 70-game schedule).

H. Scored a single-game playoff record 13 goals against the Los Angeles Kings.

I. Won a one-season record 17 straight games.

J. Posted an NHL record 35-game unbeaten streak.

Getting serious

1 The National Hockey League, which was formed before the 1917-18 season, went American in 1924 with the addition of what still-existing franchise?

2 What was the first American-based NHL team to win a Stanley Cup?

3 In addition to the Canadiens, two other teams have represented Montreal in the NHL. Can you supply the nickname of one of those teams?

4 Name four of the six expansion teams that doubled the size of the NHL before the 1967-68 season.

5 Name the four World Hockey Association teams that were absorbed by the NHL prior to the 1979-80 season.

6 Of those four former WHA franchises, three were based in Canada and two of those have since been relocated to the United States. What are the names of the two relocated teams today?

7 Name the only team other than Montreal to win four straight Stanley Cup championships.

8 Name the first Stanley Cup championship team that was not in existence before 1940.

9 Can you supply one of the two nicknames used by Toronto before the team became known as the Maple Leafs?

10 The New York Rangers played their inaugural game in 1926-27, but they were not the first NHL team based in New York. What was the appropriate nickname of the team that relocated to New York in 1925-26 from the Canadian city of Hamilton.

Goal Oriented

Warming up

The following initials represent the all-time top goal scorers for each of the 26 National Hockey League franchises that existed before expansion to Nashville, Atlanta, Columbus and Minnesota in the late 1990s and 2000s. Your challenge is to provide a name and team for each.

1. J.B.	7. M.R.	13. V.L.	19. R.G.	25. T.F.
2. W.G.	8. B.H.	14. D.H.	20. S.M.	26. J.M.
3. R.F.	9. M.M.	15. M.L.	21. G.H.	
4. B.B.	10. M.B.	16. P.B.	22. A.Y.	
5. O.N.	11. P.K.	17. T.L.	23. G.P.	
6. M.D.	12. D.S.	18. B.H.	24. J.S.	

The following checklist might be helpful in solving the above puzzle:

Anaheim Mighty Ducks	New Jersey Devils
Boston Bruins	New York Islanders
Buffalo Sabres	New York Rangers
Calgary Flames	Ottawa Senators
Carolina Hurricanes	Philadelphia Flyers
Chicago Blackhawks	Phoenix Coyotes
Colorado Avalanche	Pittsburgh Penguins
Dallas Stars	St. Louis Blues
Detroit Red Wings	San Jose Sharks
Edmonton Oilers	Tampa Bay Lightning
Florida Panthers	Toronto Maple Leafs
Los Angeles Kings	Vancouver Canucks
Montreal Canadiens	Washington Capitals

Getting serious

1 Only seven of the 26 franchises listed above have all-time point leaders who are not their all-time leading goal scorers. See how many you can name.

2 Name the two 700-goal scorers who are not career leaders for any NHL franchise.

3 This center/left winger ranks third all-time in career assists and second all-time in points, but he ranks no higher than third for any franchise in goals, assists or points. Name this six-time Stanley Cup champion.

4 Of the NHL's Big Six franchises (Montreal, Boston, New York Rangers, Detroit, Toronto and Chicago), one has a career scoring leader with fewer than 400 goals and 1,000 points. Name him.

5 One NHL franchise can boast three 500-goal scorers. Name the team and the players.

6 Of the NHL's 14 players with 600 or more career goals, only one played in fewer than 1,000 games. Name him.

7 Only one other player has reached the 600-goal plateau in fewer than 1,200 games. Name him.

8 Boston great Phil Esposito produced the first four 60-plus-goal seasons in a five-year span from 1970-71 through 1974-75. Name the first player not named Esposito to score 60 goals in a season.

9 Name the only three players who have scored more than 80 goals in an NHL season.

10 No defenseman has scored 50 goals in a single season. Name the one who came closest in 1985-86 when he totaled 48.

Former Boston great Phil Esposito was the NHL's first 60-goal scorer.

Mystery Guest

Can you name the athlete and the sport?

1 You might not know this, but I'm a serious Cubs fan. Have been for most of my life. That probably gives away my Chicago roots, which remained solid through high school. That's when I opted for an Army life.

2 I guess you could say I continued my education in Knight school. I benefited a lot from military discipline and even learned how to shoot. Trust me, I wasn't the world's greatest marksman, but I was good enough to become a captain—in more ways than one. The Army teaches young men to become leaders and I guess they did a good job with me.

3 The world has its share of one-name superstars. Well, I guess you could call me a one-letter star. I do not consider myself a BMOC, however. I leave that distinction to the men I work with. All I want out of life is for everyone I'm around to be happy and successful. Some say I've achieved that goal many times over.

4 Go ahead, take your best shot. But you better make sure it really is your best. Really, I only demand discipline and hard work. I thrived in Hoosierland and my Army buddies got the Point. Now I'm really smokin' on Tobacco Road.

5 I've got quite a family now. I love my girls more than anything, but I've got a different kind of relationship with my boys. Call it mutual respect. They trust me and are loyal. I give them my heart. Any way you look at it, this is a win-win situation.

6 When push comes to shove, my boys really know how to put up their dukes. They always seem capable of unleashing that devil from within. The rewards just keep dribbling in—you know, championship trophies, individual honors, personal adulation, stuff like that. Does it feel drafty in here to you? Most of my boys think it does, and they're usually right.

7 I don't know about others, but I think my job is as simple as A-C-C. I've been doing it now for almost a quarter of a century and as I get older, the clubs I'm joining are getting a little more snobbish. Sometimes I wonder what else I have to prove, but then, like Cubs fans, I always look forward to next year.

8 OK, here's my Final Four thoughts for you to chew on: 1. 694-240; 2. Three national championships; 3. 64-17 in the NCAAs; 4. Eight 30-win seasons. I'll take those numbers to court anytime.

CHAPTER 8
SPORTS MOVIES

They live in our memories, tributes to both the lighter and more serious sides of the sports we follow. Who can resist a good sports movie, whether we're fantasizing over the emergence of Shoeless Joe Jackson and his former Chicago White Sox teammates from an Iowa cornfield (below) or reliving the dream of the 1980 Miracle on Ice or the horse racing exploits of the great Seabiscuit? The following pages focus on trivia from more than 30 sports movies—many of them classics, all of them permanent pieces of our national sports psyche. Open a box of popcorn, buckle your seatbelt and see how many of the questions you can answer.

1. Like Shoeless Joe and many of the other characters who play on the Field of Dreams, I really did exist. Go ahead, look me up in the Baseball Encyclopedia. I thought it was cool the way movie viewers were introduced to me by the scoreboard at Boston's Fenway Park.

2. Based on real-life author J.D. Salinger, I am the reclusive author sought out by Ray Kinsella. It's unlikely you've ever read The Boat Rocker—because, like me, it was fictional. Can you remember my movie name and the actor who portrayed me?

3. A diamond in the rough? That describes me, the patch of farmland carved into a movie set for Field of Dreams. If you want to visit me, where would you go?

4. I was the movie on the theater marquee when Ray Kinsella discovered he had somehow been transported back to 1972.

1. OK, I'm a fictional high school with a fictional nickname. But the events loosely portrayed with my help in the movie Hoosiers really happened. Do you remember my name and nickname?

2. I might be a town drunk, but that doesn't mean I don't know my basketball. My one-word name tells you everything you need to know. And if you ever get into a late-game coaching pickle and need a bucket, follow this advice: Run the old Picket Fence.

3. My real name is Maris

The 1942 movie *The Pride of the Yankees* featured actor Gary Cooper (right) as New York great Lou Gehrig and Yankees catcher Bill Dickey (left) as himself. Can you identify the Yankees second baseman (center) and 1942 American League MVP who dropped in on the set during filming?

Valainis and I was the only actor on the team who had not played high school basketball. Ironically, I was chosen to portray the star player and I even hit the championship-winning shot. What was my character's name?

4. You probably remember Gene Hackman's character, coach Norman Dale. But other than Barbara Hershey, can anyone remember my name—coach Dale's reluctant love interest? First name will do. Get both and I'll be impressed.

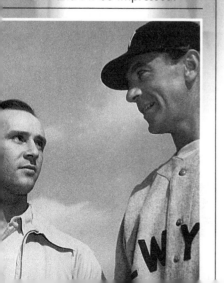

1. OK, I drink a little and I have a foul mouth. But behind that facade is a big heart. Remember, I was a former major league home run champion, or so the script reads. I just don't understand how I ended up in Rockford, managing a girls baseball team. Surely you remember my name.

2. Our movie names were Dottie and Kit, two baseball-savvy sisters who became top players in the World War II-inspired All American Girls Professional Baseball League. Maybe you remember the scene in which we were recruited at our rural home by a fast-quipping scout. What were we doing when he approached us?

3. My name is Mae Mordabito and I played center field for the Peaches. In retrospect, I played just as hard off the field as on, which is why my friends called me (affectionately, of course) All-The-Way-Mae. It took a special actress to capture my character. Can you name her?

4. I'm Doris Murphy, a sharp-tongued clubhouse cutup played by comedienne Rosie O'Donnell. Do you remember my position?

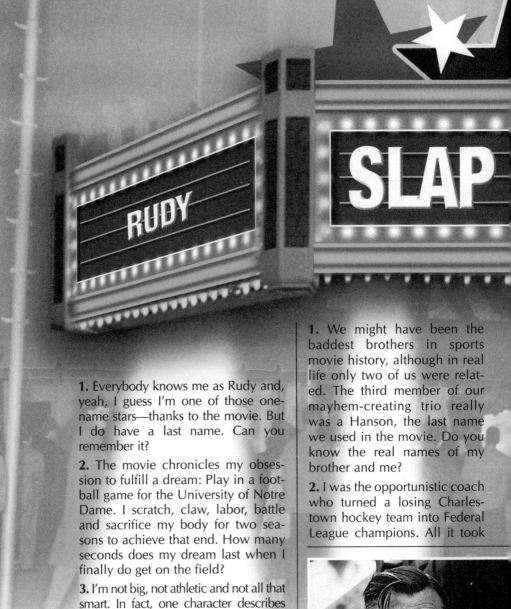

RUDY

SLAP

1. Everybody knows me as Rudy and, yeah, I guess I'm one of those one-name stars—thanks to the movie. But I do have a last name. Can you remember it?

2. The movie chronicles my obsession to fulfill a dream: Play in a football game for the University of Notre Dame. I scratch, claw, labor, battle and sacrifice my body for two seasons to achieve that end. How many seconds does my dream last when I finally do get on the field?

3. I'm not big, not athletic and not all that smart. In fact, one character describes me in the movie as "5-foot-nothin' and you weigh a hundred and nothin', and with hardly a speck of athletic ability." So what actor took the challenge of portraying such an anti-hero?

4. Do you remember my coach in that climactic season? He wasn't really as cold-hearted as he was portrayed in the movie.

1. We might have been the baddest brothers in sports movie history, although in real life only two of us were related. The third member of our mayhem-creating trio really was a Hanson, the last name we used in the movie. Do you know the real names of my brother and me?

2. I was the opportunistic coach who turned a losing Charlestown hockey team into Federal League champions. All it took

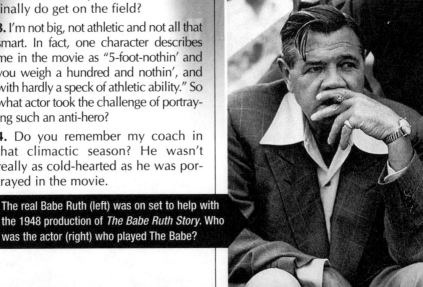

The real Babe Ruth (left) was on set to help with the 1948 production of *The Babe Ruth Story*. Who was the actor (right) who played The Babe?

was a little creative chaos. With Paul Newman playing me in the movie, how could anyone forget my name?

3. Yeah, I'm an inanimate object, but I play a memorable role in the Slap Shot movie. I'm the substance the Hansons wear on their knuckles, under their gloves, in every game.

4. Numbers, numbers, numbers. We were the double-digit IDs on the uniforms of the three Hanson brothers.

1. OK, as Walter Matthau, the actor, I enjoyed tremendous success. But as Morris Buttermaker, the movie character, I was a lazy, down-on-my-luck former minor league player who accepted money to coach a rag-tag Little League team. What was my occupation in the movie?

2. I was the tell-it-like-it-is, in-your-face, super-intense shortstop of the Bears. I didn't take any crap from anyone. Young actor Chris Barnes did a great job portraying me. Do you remember my movie name?

3. When coach Buttermaker tries to talk me into pitching for his team, he tells me his players are not very rough and promises I won't get hurt. My reply: "That's got nothing to do with it. I'm almost 12 and I'll ... I'll be getting a bra soon." What was my movie name?

4. Those Bears weren't that good. We pounded them early in the movie and edged them for the California state title, too. And, besides, our uniforms were much nicer. Do you remember us, the team the Bears played in the championship game?

1. I know you recognize me, Rocky, because I've become an American icon. But do you remember my pooch, the bulldog that came to symbolize my will to succeed? If so, what was his name?

2. If you want to talk about movie animals, don't forget us. We don't get a lot of air time in the movie, but I do think viewers will remember us. We're just a couple of turtles, but Rocky was nice enough to give us names. Do you remember them?

3. Yo, Adrian! I am the actress who got the role as Rocky's love interest, but not until Bette Midler turned it down. Imagine that. We are about as opposite on-screen as two personalities can get. So who am I?

4. I am the only real-life former heavyweight champion who appeared at ringside before the Rocky-Apollo Creed movie fight. There were supposed to have been others, but they didn't show. It worked out well because I live in Philadelphia, where the fictional fight took place. Who am I?

1. My name is Rachel Phelps and I'm the heavy of this movie. I'm a former exotic dancer who just happens to inherit the Cleveland Indians by lucky (wink wink) coincidence. Cleveland? Ughhhhhh! Who can blame a girl for wanting to move her team to a more sexy setting? Do you remember the city to which I wanted to relocate?

2. Sorry Charlie, but when my fastball's working you don't stand a chance. Problem is, I don't always know where my fastballs are going because I don't have what you might call *vision*. The fans like me, though, and give me a nick-name that just happens to

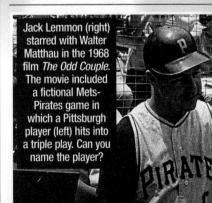

Jack Lemmon (right) starred with Walter Matthau in the 1968 film *The Odd Couple*. The movie included a fictional Mets-Pirates game in which a Pittsburgh player (left) hits into a triple play. Can you name the player?

match a former hit song. Can you recall that moniker?

3. My character name is Harry Doyle and I'm important to the success of this movie even though I don't catch, throw or hit a ball and I really don't have any dialogue with the main characters. Do you remember my role and the actor who portrayed me?

4. I'm tough, strong and intimidating. My name is Haywood and I'm a Yankee slugger who terrorized the Indians leading up to the movie's ultimate showdown. In real life, the actor who portrayed me was a former major league pitcher. Can you recall his name?

1. I'm a lawyer. I'm supposed to be sarcastic, unscrupulous and overbearing. So what happens when I'm hauled into court for a harmless DUI? They force me to do community service by coaching a Minnesota Pee Wee hockey team. Emilio Estevez is my alter ego. Do you remember my movie name?

2. Go ahead and laugh at us because we're the Mighty Ducks. But there really is a method to that madness. We took that name because coach's boss bought us uniforms. Do you recall the name of the man?

3. Every title contender needs a war cry and I just happen to fit the needs of this team. Pucker your lips, flap your feathers and fire out a heart-felt salute to the Mighty Ducks.

4. Movie championship teams need a nemesis and we were happy to provide a foil for the Mighty Ducks. It's only a coincidence that coach was one of us when he was a Pee Wee player some time ago. The Mighty Ducks beat the _____ for the championship—you fill in the blank.

TIN CUP

BRIAN'S

1. The world knows me as Kevin Costner, but for purposes of this movie I was a colorful character nicknamed "Tin Cup." Boy, could I swing a mean golf club. But, boy, could I blow up and do stupid things at the most inopportune times on a golf course. Love almost turned me into a U.S. Open champion. Almost. Do you remember my character name?

2. I'm Tin Cup's driver and, together, we can hit the ball a long way. He treats me with respect. And he even has given me a nickname. What is it?

3. My name is Romeo and I'm Tin Cup's caddie. I'm also his roommate because we share a Winnebago that overlooks our place of employment. What does Tin Cup do for a living—and where?

4. I'm the par 5 18th hole at the U.S. Open. Tin Cup, with a chance to win or force a playoff, is 238 yards from the hole, which is protected by water. Lay up, Tin Cup, lay up. But no, you just can't do that. Well, I'll make you pay! Do you remember how many shots Tin Cup needed to finally get the ball in the hole?

1. Of the actors playing the two lead characters, I'm the superior athlete. Unfortunately, Brian Piccolo, my character, was much less athletic than Gale Sayers, my partner's character. That was problematic for workout scenes in which Sayers, for instance, was supposed to outrun Piccolo. I had to make it look like my partner was faster. Who played the two roles?

2. You probably remember me, Gale Sayers, for my Hall of Fame talent on the football field. But I made history with my dear friend Brian Piccolo in a more

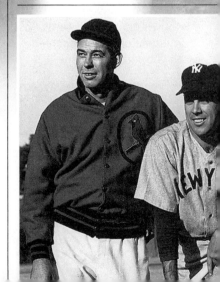

SONG

EIGHT MEN OUT

social context. Do you remember what we did that broke a racial barrier in Chicago?

3. Everybody knows Dick Butkus—everybody who knows anything about football, anyway. Do you remember who played me in the movie?

4. You probably don't know this, but it's interesting and kind of fun. The house purported to be Gale Sayers' home in the movie actually was the house that television viewers had seen many times on a hit 1960s sitcom. Just wiggle your nose and take a wild guess.

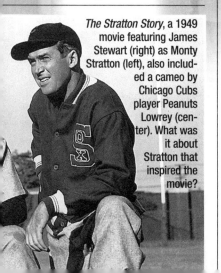

The Stratton Story, a 1949 movie featuring James Stewart (right) as Monty Stratton (left), also included a cameo by Chicago Cubs player Peanuts Lowrey (center). What was it about Stratton that inspired the movie?

1. If you believe everything you saw in the movie, I was the real heavy in the Black Sox scandal. Actor Clifton James made me look like a miserable cheat and cheapskate who drove the Chicago players to fix the 1919 World Series. What was my name and role with the team?

2. Everybody has heard of me, Shoeless Joe Jackson. Yes, I originally agreed to take part in the World Series fix but, no, I didn't actually do anything wrong. It didn't matter. I was suspended from baseball for life. Can you remember who portrayed me in the movie?

3. I'm pitcher Eddie Cicotte and I got a lot of screen time because I was a central figure in the scandal. It was me who signaled to the gamblers that the fix was on. How did I do that?

4. My role was played with dramatic impact by John Anderson, even though we received only about five minutes of screen time in the movie. Still, I was a central figure in the resolution of the Black Sox scandal. Can you name my character.

1. My movie name is Paul Crewe and there's a good reason why Burt Reynolds was selected to play me. Reynolds is a former college football player and his primary role is to organize his fellow prisoners into a competitive football team to play against the guards. So does anybody recall what my occupation was before I went to prison?

2. My name in this movie was Samson, but I attained more enduring fame in later movies as a recurring James Bond villain. I guess you could say I had a sparkling smile. Can you come up with my name in the Bond flicks?

3. I was a Hall of Fame football player—no, not in the movie, but in real life. I was pretty tough on the screen, too, while playing the role of Bogdanski. Can you name me?

4. It's a twisty road from *The Longest Yard* to *Green Acres*, but I made it OK. I'm often asked how I could transform from the conniving and evil Warden Hazen into the lovable Oliver Wendell Douglas. I guess that's why you call it acting. Who am I?

1. It would be way too easy if the answer to this question was Burt Reynolds and Kris Kristofferson, the actors who played us in the movie. So I'm asking you to identify our movie roles—the good-ol'-boy quarterback and his best-friend wide receiver.

2. My real name is Jill Clayburgh and I'm the movie's love interest—for both Burt Reynolds and Kris Kristofferson. What's my character's name/nickname?

3. As the Dallas team captain,

TOUGH

SPACE JAM

Dreamer Tatum, I was convincing because I was a former professional football player. But you might remember me better from the role I played one year earlier as a fighter in a Sylvester Stallone movie that won an Oscar for Best Picture. Do you know my name?

4. As Big Ed Bookman, played by Robert Preston, I was owner of the team that was a central focus to the movie. Where was the team located?

1. OK, I'm Michael Jordan and I never thought I would be playing basketball with a bunch of Looney Tunes. But it really was kind of fun. Bugs, Daffy and the boys were good teammates. Do you remember how they recruited me to coach their team?

2. As Swackhammer, I'm the heavy in this film, a conclusion you might draw quickly when I have my Nerdlucks kidnap all the Looney Tunes stars. But what's a guy to do when he needs big attractions for his new theme park in outer space? I wonder if you recognize my distinctive voice.

3. We're the five unfortunate NBA stars whose talent is stolen by the Monstars. Can you name three of us?

4. I'm the statuesque new Looney Tunes hoopster who gets old Bugs lisping in warp speed. What's my name?

Robert De Niro (left) and Michael Moriarty play teammates on a fictional New York baseball team in the baseball tear-jerker *Bang the Drum Slowly*. What is the team's nickname?

EVERYBODY'S ALL-AMERICAN

RAGING

1. For actor Dennis Quaid, playing me when I was a college football hero was probably the most fun. I was a running back named Gavin Grey and I was a big-time star—a two-time consensus All-American. Do you recall my nickname?

2. I'm the college that Gavin Grey led to a championship in the late 1950s. I'm Southern and proud of it. Too bad this movie wasn't released more recently to coincide with the real NCAA championship my football team won. It would have been great publicity. What school am I?

3. I'm Jessica Lange in real life, Babs Rogers-Grey in the movie. But I was known by a more colorful name in 1956 when I was a beauty queen. What was my title?

4. I am the professional football team that drafted Gavin Grey in the first round. Can you name me?

1. When I signed on to play boxing great Jake La Motta in this movie, it became a personal obsession. Some say I delivered the performance of a lifetime and critics generally loved my work. So did the Oscar voters, who named me best actor for 1980. Who am I.

2. You might be more familiar with my later work as a bumbling lawyer in My Cousin Vinny or in two later Martin Scorsese films, GoodFellas and Casino. At the time I decided to make my movie debut as Joey La Motta in Raging Bull, I was

In a scene from the 1952 movie *The Pride of St. Louis*, Paul Dean (sitting) is helped by brother Dizzy (kneeling right) and other St. Louis players after being hit by a line drive. Who are the actors portraying the Dean brothers?

BULL

NORTH DALLAS FORTY

on the verge of giving up acting. I'm glad I didn't. Who am I?

3. I am the five-word line that an aging Jake quoted while looking into a dressing room mirror late in the movie. I say "quoted" because I originally was spoken by another great actor in a movie that won the Best Picture Oscar in 1954. Do you remember me?

4. I am the substance that Martin Scorsese decided to use to give the appearance of blood in his black-and-white film. Anybody up for ice cream?

1. No, I am not the Dallas Cowboys in this movie. But everybody said I was merely a fictionalized biography of that franchise. What was my city and nickname in the film?

2. I played Phillip Elliott, a character modeled after former Cowboys receiver Pete Gent, and my friend played Seth Maxwell, a character modeled after former Cowboys quarterback Don Meredith. Do you remember our real names?

3. My name is Art Hartman and I'm a backup quarterback. I'm also the player who cost North Dallas a possible conference championship with a misplay in the title game against Chicago. Do you remember how I messed up?

4. I'm sure a lot of people recognized me in the movie. I was playing for the Oakland Raiders when it was released. I stayed true to character as the fiery and unpredictable O.W. Shaddock. What was my real name?

THE ROOKIE

*6

1. My name is Jimmy Morris and I was trapped into fulfilling a promise to the high school team I coached. I had to try out as a professional pitcher. Before doing that, though, I needed to find out just how fast I could throw. So, not having access to a radar gun, I improvised. What did I use to gauge my speed?

2. We played on the real-life high school team coached by Morris, who was portrayed by Dennis Quaid. Do you remember our school nickname and location?

3. I'm the ballpark where Jimmy Morris made his major league debut as a 35-year-old rookie. Coincidentally, I wasn't too far from home for him. What ballpark was I?

4. I'm the first batter Morris faced in his first big-league appearance. What was my name and how many pitches did he need to strike me out?

1. The story chronicled the great home run chase of 1961 featuring Mickey Mantle and Roger Maris, but I'm the player who hit the movie's first home run. Who am I?

2. I am the ballpark where all of the Yankee Stadium sequences were filmed. They disguised me, performed some digital magic and, voila! I was transformed into the House that Ruth Built. What stadium was I really?

3. I felt like a third wheel living in an apartment with two greats like Mantle and Maris, but I

Name the two New York Yankees stars (with bat and glove) who appeared in the 1962 movie *Safe at Home.*

142

REMEMBER THE TITANS

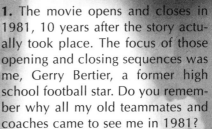

guess you could say I was the rudder that kept things on an even keel during that crazy 1961 season. Do you remember my name?

4. Before this movie, I was just a journeyman actor named Barry Pepper. I got the role of Roger Maris because director Billy Crystal saw me in another movie and thought I had an uncanny resemblance to the real man. Looking at pictures of him, I guess Crystal was right. What movie was Crystal watching when he "discovered" me?

1. The movie opens and closes in 1981, 10 years after the story actually took place. The focus of those opening and closing sequences was me, Gerry Bertier, a former high school football star. Do you remember why all my old teammates and coaches came to see me in 1981?

2. I'm the school, both in the movie and real life, around which the non-fictional storyline was crafted. Can you remember either my city or name?

3. I'm impressed they hired Denzel Washington to play me, the black coach who leads his newly integrated team to a championship. Can you remember my name?

4. I'm the historic landmark that provided a backdrop for one of the movie's inspirational scenes. Coach brought his players to me on an early morning run and then mesmerized them with a stirring speech. What national landmark am I?

1. Don't kid yourself, actors like Rodney Dangerfield, Chevy Chase and Bill Murray are NOT the stars of this movie. I am. I'm the gopher and I create havoc in and around the Bushwood Country Club. If you watch closely on the final credits, you can catch my name. What was it?

2. I'm Judge Smails and I carry a lot of influence in these parts. It was me who kicked this movie into overdrive when I spotted the gopher tracks early on and then watched the flag on the green disappear underground. Do you remember the number on the flag?

3. As Carl Spackler, one of my best movie moments was the Dalai Lama speech. Do you remember what I was holding?

4. I'm the Country Club swimming pool that was swarmed one day by a wild bunch of Caddies. Something unseemly happened in my waters to put a damper on club festivities. Come on now, that really was a floating candy bar. Do you remember what brand?

1. I was the coach of the American hockey team that pulled one of the great sports upsets of all time in the 1980 Winter Olympic Games. My name is Herb Brooks and I was portrayed admirably in the movie by Kurt Russell. Unfortunately, I never got to see the finished product. Why?

2. Any red-blooded American remembers me, Jim Craig, the goalie who backstopped the incredible U.S. upset of the Soviets. I was played by actor Eddie Cahill. Do you remember the motive for my Olympic

CLE

ALI

team tryout?

3. As goalie Jim Craig, my goal-tending abilities were not strong enough to look authentic in the realistic hockey sequences that were filmed. So I had a professional stand-in who was better able to handle the hockey action. Who was that former NHL star?

4. "Do you believe in miracles? Yes!" The memorable 1980 live call, which was used in the movie, was delivered by me, Al Michaels. Who was my booth partner that day, the man who also helped me recreate the movie play-by-play?

1. I studied, worked out and gained 35 pounds for this part. I guess you could call me obsessed. Critics generally agreed that I captured the physical and verbal traits of Muhammad Ali pretty well. Do you know my name?

2. I was Ali's foil, both in real life and in the movie. My name is Howard Cosell and nobody could set off the Champ quite like me. What actor played me in the movie?

3. I'm only in the movie momentarily, but my symbolism is hard to miss. Remember the scene shortly after Ali had knocked out George Foreman? That closeup of Ali, there I was floating behind him. Do you remember me?

4. I'm Jada Pinkett Smith, Will Smith's real wife and Ali's first movie wife. I had a memorably erotic scene with the Champ on the dance floor, at which time he made an interesting comment about my looks. Do you remember what he said?

Co-stars Jeff Richards and Vera-Ellen do a little closeup work while filming the 1953 movie *Big Leaguer*. Name the legendary actor who portrayed a New York Giants tryout camp supervisor.

1. What a sled named "Rosebud" was to Charles Foster Kane, I am to Roy Hobbs. You might view me as just another lightning-charged bat, but I prefer to think of myself as the subtle star of this movie. What was my name?

2. Inspired by Babe Ruth, I'm the portly slugger that young Roy Hobbs struck out on three pitches. My acting name is Joe Don Baker. What's my movie name?

3. Everything was going so well. I was living the good life with the New York Knights and dating the lovely Memo Paris until my unfortunate accident with the outfield fence. Do you recall my name?

4. Love can be dangerous, especially my brand. I'm the gun-crazy femme fatale who takes her best shot at ending Roy Hobbs' baseball dreams—for good.

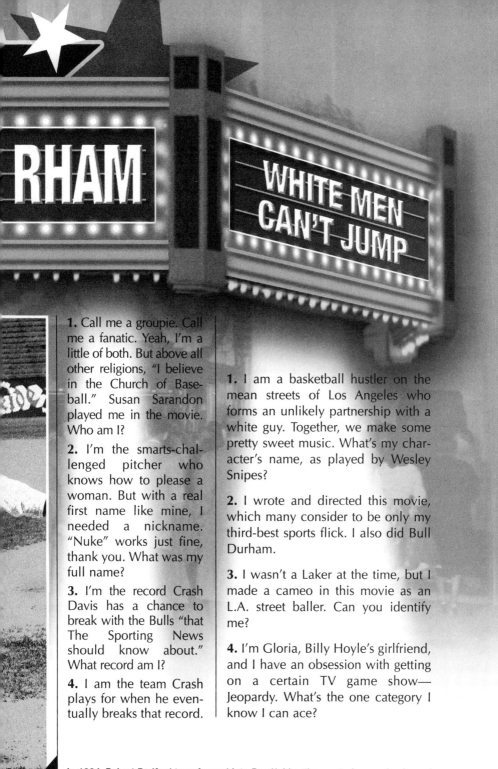

1. Call me a groupie. Call me a fanatic. Yeah, I'm a little of both. But above all other religions, "I believe in the Church of Baseball." Susan Sarandon played me in the movie. Who am I?

2. I'm the smarts-challenged pitcher who knows how to please a woman. But with a real first name like mine, I needed a nickname. "Nuke" works just fine, thank you. What was my full name?

3. I'm the record Crash Davis has a chance to break with the Bulls "that The Sporting News should know about." What record am I?

4. I am the team Crash plays for when he eventually breaks that record.

1. I am a basketball hustler on the mean streets of Los Angeles who forms an unlikely partnership with a white guy. Together, we make some pretty sweet music. What's my character's name, as played by Wesley Snipes?

2. I wrote and directed this movie, which many consider to be only my third-best sports flick. I also did Bull Durham.

3. I wasn't a Laker at the time, but I made a cameo in this movie as an L.A. street baller. Can you identify me?

4. I'm Gloria, Billy Hoyle's girlfriend, and I have an obsession with getting on a certain TV game show—Jeopardy. What's the one category I know I can ace?

In 1984, Robert Redford transformed into Roy Hobbs, the mysterious and aging slugger who leads the New York Knights to great heights. What was the name of the real stadium where action sequences for *The Natural* were filmed?

1. I am the sleepy midwestern college town where this movie takes place. The plot revolves around a rivalry between students and locals that gets out of hand. What city am I?

2. We, the locals, have been given a nickname by the snobish college kids because our city once was the home of a huge quarry that provided the main source of employment. What were we called?

3. My name is Dave and I want to be Italian. I speak with my best Italian accent, I listen to Puccini and Verdi, I eat Italian food and I'm obsessed with bicycle racing and the world-famous Cinzano team. What do I do, like the Italian racers, to cut down wind resistance?

4. You might remember my inspiring training scene in which I race my bicycle to keep up with a fast-moving object. What was I chasing?

1. Well, I'll get you out of the starting gates with an easy one. I'm blind in one eye and I'm too big for the job I do, but I still thrive as Seabiscuit's winning jockey. I'm played by Tobey Maguire. Who am I?

2. In addition to working as a consultant on the movie, I'm the real-life jockey who plays substitute Seabiscuit jockey George Woolf. I'm well qualified for the role because I've ridden winners in all three of horse racing's Triple Crown races. Who am I?

3. I'm the famed thoroughbred who won the 1937 Triple Crown but lost to Seabiscuit in a later match race. You might remember my intense dislike of starting gates.

4. I'm a man of few words and a lot of people have called me dull. But I do have a way with horses, primarily because I believe that "every horse is good for something." That philosophy certainly applied to Seabiscuit, who was good for something very special. What's my name?

1. I'm the smarmy rival agent at SMI who was responsible for firing Jerry Maguire. I did it at Cronin's.

2. I was an outstanding college quarterback preparing to be drafted by an NFL team. When Jerry was fired, my father gave him his word that our relationship was "stronger than oak." But the "oak" snapped like a twig on draft day. What was my name?

3. Played by former Eagle (the band, not the team) Glenn Frey, I'm the Arizona Cardinals general manager who eventually "showed the money" to wide receiver Rod Tidwell.

4. There's debate about whether Jerry Maguire is based on my life as a sports agent. But there's no questioning that I made a cameo in the movie. Who am I?

Tab Hunter played Joe Hardy, a man who would go to any lengths to help his beloved Senators beat the Yankees, in the 1958 musical *Damn Yankees*. Who played the beautiful seductress, Lola?

Mystery Guest

Can you name the athlete and the sport?

1 My dad was my coach in high school, but even he didn't fully recognize my talent. My arm might have been stronger back then than it is today, but Dad made sure I didn't get the chance to use it much.

2 When I first got to college, I sat on the bench behind Michael Jackson. But it wasn't long before he beat it and moved to another position to make room for me. Michael eventually caught on and became a solid pro at his new position, so I might have done him a favor.

3 I didn't play for a top college program, but we had one victory I'll never forget over the No. 1 team in the country. My best play in that game came at the expense of a future teammate—a player who later helped my professional team win a championship.

4 One of the first things anyone says about my playing style is that I have guts. But there was a time in college, after a serious auto-mobile accident, when my lack of guts—I mean that literally—almost cost me my playing career.

5 As a second-round draft pick, I barely played in my first professional season and then was traded to a team to back up a guy nicknamed "Magic." I could have packed it in when I failed my physical with my new team because of a bad hip, but perseverance is one of my best qualities. After watching me play, you might think I never feel pain.

6 When I got my first chance at meaningful playing time, I stepped in and led my new team to a comeback victory. You could say the situation in that game was Taylor-made for me to begin a long string of successes. Comebacks and creative playmaking soon became my trademarks.

7 And don't forget durability. The coach of my new team gave me the starting job after that first win, and I haven't missed a start since. He thought about benching me in our third season together, but we eventually won a championship in our fifth season before he took another job two years later.

8 I talk about retirement more and more these days—after all, I've done a lot. How many other guys have won three MVP awards, brought a title to Titletown after almost 30 years without one and played through every injury imaginable? Some days, going back to Mississippi and riding around on my tractor sounds pretty good. But I'd like to win another Super Bowl first.

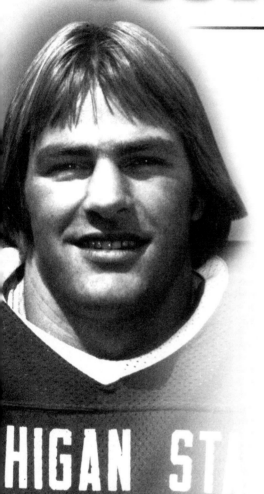

Michigan State wide receiver Kirk Gibson never got to test his football skills in the NFL.

COLLEGE FOOTBALL

Caught in a Draft
Warming up

1 What college has produced the most first-round picks in the history of the NFL draft?

2 What Big 12 power has had at least one player selected in each of the last 67 NFL drafts?

3 Name the Nebraska players who were selected first and second overall in the 1984 NFL draft.

4 What NFL team drafted former Michigan State receiver and 1988 World Series hero Kirk Gibson in the seventh round in 1979?

5 Which of the following star running backs was not an NFL first-round pick: Ron Dayne, Tony Dorsett, Bo Jackson, Herschel Walker or Ricky Williams?

6 Name the 1957 first-round NFL draft picks from Purdue, Syracuse and Ohio State who later earned enshrinement in the Pro Football Hall of Fame.

7 Name the three players who won a Heisman Trophy, were picked No. 1 overall in the NFL draft and later gained election to the College and Pro Football halls of fame.

Jeremy Shockey (88) was a Hurricane with draft appeal, but was the talented tight end a first-round pick?

8 Dave Winfield, a three-sport star at Minnesota, went on to gain election in the Baseball Hall of Fame. What NFL team selected Winfield in the 17th round of the 1973 draft?

9 What college produced the most NFL first-round draft picks in the 1990s?

10 Five Miami (Fla.) players were taken in the first round of the 2002 NFL draft. Which of these former Hurricanes was not in that group: Bryant McKinnie, Clinton Portis, Ed Reed, Mike Rumph or Jeremy Shockey?

Getting serious

Identify the No. 1 overall draft picks produced by each of the following schools.

1. Notre Dame: 1950 _____, 1957 _____, 1972 _____.

2. USC: 1968 _____, 1969
_____, 1977 _____, 1996
_____, 2003 _____.

3. Ohio State: 1979 _____, 1994
_____, 1997 _____.

4. Texas: 1966 _____, 1978
_____, 1982 _____.

5. Stanford: 1954 _____, 1971
_____, 1983 _____.

6. Auburn: 1965 _____, 1986
_____, 1988 _____.

7. Virginia Tech: 1985 _____, 2001
_____.

8. Penn State: 1995 _____, 2000
_____.

9. Oklahoma: 1976 _____, 1980
_____.

10. Miami (Fla.): 1987 _____, 1991 _____.

Heismen

Warming up

1 Name the only Heisman Trophy winner who also won the Division I-A rushing title while playing for a consensus national champion.

2 Name the only teammates to finish 1-2 in the Heisman voting.

3 Only one school has produced Heisman Trophy and Outland Trophy winners in the same season twice. Name it.

4 The same school has produced Heisman winners in consecutive years three times. Larry Kelley and Clint Frank of Yale won in 1936 and '37; Army's Doc Blanchard and Glenn Davis won in 1945 and '46. Name the other instance when one school claimed the Heisman two years in a row.

5 Name the last player to win a Heisman in his junior season.

DID YOU KNOW ...

➤That Penn State holds the record for most consecutive non-losing seasons? The Nittany Lions had their streak of 49 consecutive years with a .500-or-better record snapped in 1988, when the team finished 5-6.

➤That *Jerry Rice* holds the college record for most passes caught in a game? Rice caught 24 passes for Division I-AA Mississippi Valley State in a game against Southern on October 1, 1983. The Division I-A, Division II and Division III records are 23.

6 Who was the last Heisman winner who played in a non-BCS conference?

7 One Heisman Trophy winner can claim distinction as the NCAA's career rushing leader. Another has bragging rights as the all-time single-season rushing champion. Who are they?

8 Name the New York University star who never won a Heisman but will forever be associated with the award because he posed for the statue.

9 Name the 1973 Ohio State offensive tackle who won the Outland Award and finished a surprising second to John Cappelletti in the Heisman voting.

10 This flamboyant Oklahoma linebacker won the first two Butkus Awards and even garnered 395 Heisman votes for a fourth-place finish in 1986.

Penn State's John Cappelletti (22) had to beat out an offensive lineman to win the 1973 Heisman Trophy.

Getting serious

1 Which of these Heisman Trophy-winning running backs did not win a Division I-A rushing title: Earl Campbell, Charles White, George Rogers, Mike Rozier, Ron Dayne?

2 Which of these Heisman winners did not play for a consensus national champion: Angelo Bertelli, Doc Blanchard, Charlie Ward, Gino Torretta, Danny Wuerffel?

3 Which of these Heisman runners-up was not a No. 1 overall NFL draft pick: Ricky Bell, Billy Sims, Marshall Faulk, Ki-Jana Carter, Peyton Manning?

4 Which of these Heisman winners enjoyed the largest margin of victory over the runner-up: Roger Staubach, Jim Plunkett, Earl Campbell, Tim Brown, Barry Sanders?

5 Which of these Heisman winners had the lowest margin of victory in the history of the award: O.J. Simpson, Archie Griffin, Bo Jackson, Ty Detmer, Eric Crouch?

6 Which of the following USC stars did not win a Heisman Trophy: Mike Garrett, O.J. Simpson, Anthony Davis, Charles White, Marcus Allen?

7 Which of these Heisman winners came from a school that produced more than one winner: Doak Walker, Alan Ameche, Jim Plunkett, John Cappelletti, Rashaan Salaam?

8 Which of these Heisman winners passed for the most career years: Doug Flutie, Danny Wuerffel, Ty Detmer, Carson Palmer, Peyton Manning?

9 Which of these Heisman winners ran for the most yards in a single game: Ron Dayne, Tony Dorsett, Barry Sanders, Ricky Williams, Eddie George?

10 Which of these Heisman winners never played a game professionally: Johnny Lujack, Tom Harmon, Steve Owens, John Cappelletti, Charlie Ward?

Ty Detmer used his powerful right arm to earn Heisman Trophy distinction for BYU in 1990.

──Seasonal Offerings──

The following news, events and performances all occurred in the same year. Identify that year.

◆ The NCAA announces freshmen will be eligible to play football and basketball, beginning in the fall.

◆ Nebraska tops second-ranked Alabama 38-6 in the Orange Bowl and claims its second straight national championship.

◆ In the final AP poll released after the New Year's Day bowl games, Big Eight powers Nebraska, Oklahoma and Colorado are ranked 1-2-3.

◆ Southern Cal running back Anthony Davis dazzles Notre Dame with a sensational six-touchdown performance in a 45-23 victory at the Los Angeles Coliseum.

2 ◆ Tailback Herschel Walker, after completing his junior season at Georgia, becomes the highest paid performer in pro football history when he signs a precedent-setting contract with the USFL's New Jersey Generals.

◆ Legendary Alabama boss Bear Bryant, the winningest coach in college football history, dies of a heart attack in Tuscaloosa.

◆ Nebraska's Mike Rozier rushes for 2,148 yards en route to winning a Heisman Trophy.

◆ The Miami Hurricanes lose their opening game at Florida, 28-3, but sweep the rest of their schedule en route to a national championship.

3 ◆ Colorado defeats Notre Dame, 10-9, in the Orange Bowl but is forced to share the national championship with Georgia Tech when UPI voters favor the Yellow Jackets by a single point.

◆ Notre Dame Heisman runner-up Raghib Ismail spurns the NFL and signs the richest contract in CFL history—a four-year deal with Toronto worth a guaranteed $18.2 million.

◆ BYU quarterback Ty Detmer becomes the NCAA's career passing leader (11,606 yards) in a 27-23 loss to UCLA.

◆ Kansas running back Tony Sands finishes his college career in spectacular fashion when he runs for a Division I-A record 396 yards in a 53-29 victory over Missouri.

4 ◆ Ohio State quarterback Rex Kern fires two fourth-quarter touchdown passes, and the Buckeyes claim a national championship with a 27-16 New Year's Day victory over USC in the Rose Bowl.

◆ The NFL's Buffalo Bills sign USC running back O.J. Simpson to a rich four-year contract.

◆ Texas quarterback James Street rallies the No. 1-ranked Longhorns to a 15-14 win over No. 2 Arkansas in a huge Southwest Conference showdown at Fayetteville, Ark.

◆ Oklahoma running back Steve Owens outpoints Purdue quarterback Mike Phipps to win the Heisman Trophy.

5 ◆ The Miami Hurricanes secure their second national championship in five years when quarterback Steve Walsh fires a pair of TD passes in a 20-14 Orange Bowl

Herschel Walker heeded the call of the USFL and left Georgia after his junior season.

DID YOU KNOW...

➤That *Peyton Manning* is the winningest starting quarterback in Division I-A history? Manning won 39 games at Tennessee from 1994-97. Runners-up Ken Dorsey (Miami, 1999-2002) and Rick Leach (Michigan, 1975-78) each won 38.

➤That *Anthony Davis* scored more points against Notre Dame than any player? USC's star running back scored 11 touchdowns and one two-point conversion (68 total points) against the Irish from 1972-74.

win over Oklahoma.

◆ Columbia ends its major college-record 44-game losing streak with a 16-13 win over Princeton at Columbia.

◆ Oklahoma State's Barry Sanders runs for a single-season record 2,628 yards, scores a record 39 touchdowns and caps his incredible season by winning the Heisman Trophy.

◆ Utah quarterback Scott Mitchell throws for a Division I-A single-game record 631 yards in a game against Air Force.

6 ◆ USC holds off a frantic Wisconsin rally and claims a 42-37 victory in the Rose Bowl, a win that secures the national championship.

◆ Former Syracuse All-American running back and Heisman Trophy winner Ernie Davis dies of leukemia at a Cleveland hospital.

◆ Texas claims its sixth straight victory over rival Oklahoma, a 28-7 romp in Dallas, and positions itself for a run at the national title.

◆ Navy quarterback Roger Staubach is a runaway winner in voting for the Heisman Trophy.

7 ◆ Alabama's 14-7 upset of top-ranked Penn State in the Sugar Bowl earns the Crimson Tide half of a national championship. USC claims the other half with a 17-10 Rose Bowl win over Michigan.

◆ Former Iowa State coach Earle Bruce succeeds Woody Hayes at Ohio State.

◆ Indiana cornerback Tim Wilbur scores on a 62-yard return of a fumbled punt, and the Hoosiers shock undefeated BYU, 38-7, in the Holiday Bowl.

◆ USC running back Charles White easily outpoints Nebraska's Billy Sims and wins the Heisman Trophy.

8 ◆ TCU's LaDainian Tomlinson becomes college football's first 400-yard rusher when he bolts for 406 in a game against Texas-El Paso.

◆ Wisconsin running back Ron Dayne pounds out 216 yards in a 41-3 victory over Iowa while passing Texas' Ricky Williams as the NCAA's all-time leading rusher.

◆ Florida State's 30-23 win at Florida caps an 11-0 regular season and sets the stage for a national championship showdown against Virginia Tech in the Sugar Bowl.

◆ Virginia Tech's Frank Beamer wins Coach of the Year honors.

9 ◆ For the third straight season, California takes an unbeaten record into the Rose Bowl and loses to a Big Ten foe. Michigan turns the trick this time, 14-6.

◆ Undefeated Oklahoma, already declared the Associated Press national champion, sees its unbeaten streak end at 31 games when an inspired Kentucky team posts a 13-7 victory in the Sugar Bowl.

◆ Mississippi star Showboat Boykin sets a major college record by scoring seven touchdowns in a 49-7 victory over rival Mississippi State at Starkville.

◆ And the winner is ... Princeton tailback Dick Kazmaier captures the Ivy League's third Heisman Trophy.

10 ◆ Record-setting BYU quarterback Steve Young elects to sign with the Los Angeles Express of the USFL.

◆ Washington State running back Rueben Mayes breaks the Division I-A single-game rushing record with a 357-yard effort in a 50-41 win over Oregon.

◆ Doug Flutie's 48-yard Hail Mary bomb to Gerard Phelan on the final play of the game gives Boston College a stunning 47-45 victory over Miami (Fla.).

◆ BYU quarterback Robbie Bosco, limping noticeably throughout the game, passes for two fourth-quarter touchdowns in a 24-17 Holiday Bowl win over Michigan that cements the Cougars' claim to a national championship.

Kansas running back Tony Sands finished his career with a spectacular 396-yard rushing effort against Missouri.

Bowl Sessions

Warming up

1 Name the coach with the most appearances and victories in the Cotton Bowl.

2 What coach led his team to the Orange Bowl nine times but never appeared in a postseason game at New Orleans or Dallas?

3 Name the first school to appear in the Rose, Sugar, Orange and Cotton bowls.

4 Name the only school that has won each of the Big Four bowls (Rose, Sugar, Orange and Cotton) at least two times.

5 Only three schools have won each of the Big Four bowls plus the recently prestigious Fiesta Bowl. Name them.

6 Only three coaches not named Joe Paterno have led Penn State to a bowl. Name one of them.

7 How many bowl games did Notre Dame coaching legend Knute Rockne win?

Vince Dooley led Georgia to many bowl games and one national title.

8 Through the 2003 bowl season, 10 Division I-A teams had never appeared in a bowl game. Name two of them.

9 What school has won the most bowl games?

10 Name one of the three schools that finished the 2003 bowl season with an NCAA-high 21 losses.

3 11 7 By the Numbers

Schools that have won the most individual awards/trophies* in college football:

1.	Ohio State	28
	Oklahoma	28
3.	Nebraska	23
	Notre Dame	23
5.	Miami (Fla.)	21
6.	Penn State	18
	USC	18
8.	Florida State	17
9.	Texas	13
10.	Michigan	12

* Awards/trophies include the following: Heisman, Maxwell, Outland, Walter Camp, Lombardi, Davey O'Brien, Dick Butkus, Jim Thorpe, Johnny Unitas, Doak Walker, Lou Groza, Bronko Nagurski, Fred Biletnikoff, Chuck Bednarik, Mosi Tatupu, Ray Guy, John Mackey, Dave Rimington, Ted Hendricks.

Getting serious

The first section lists the 10 college coaches who have appeared in the most bowl games. Match the information in the section that follows to the coaches.

1. **Joe Paterno**

2. **Bear Bryant**

3. **Bobby Bowden**

4. **Tom Osborne**

5. **LaVell Edwards**

6. **Lou Holtz**

7. **Vince Dooley**

8. **John Vaught**

9. **Hayden Fry**

10. **Bo Schembechler**

LaVell Edwards kept BYU in the national consciousness for 29 years.

A. I coached in more Orange Bowls than any other man, but I can't brag too much; I was only 4-7 on New Year's Day in Miami.

B. I guess you could say I had a pretty Rosy career, as long as you don't mention my 5-12 bowl record.

C. I'm the only coach to win games in the Rose, Orange, Sugar and Cotton bowls.

D. My 11-8-2 bowl record is only so-so, but I'm the only coach on this list to take four different teams to a postseason classic.

E. I took teams to a bowl 22 times, but only one of those games was played in Miami, New Orleans, Pasadena or Dallas.

F. I never took a team to the Rose Bowl, but nobody can match my 17 combined appearances in the Sugar, Orange and Cotton bowls.

G. I was more of a medium-level bowl guy, but my teams did smell the Roses three times.

H. I don't mean to brag, but my bowl winning percentage is better than anyone else's on this list.

I. My boys never hedged a bet in the 1960s, '70s or '80s, when we played in 20 bowl games, including multiple stops in New Orleans and Dallas.

J. My teams made eight appearances in the Sugar Bowl, a feat matched by only one other coach.

Who's the Boss?

Warming up

These former and current college football coaches all made multiple career stops on their way to the top. Identify the missing school in each coach's career resume.

1. Lou Holtz: William & Mary, N.C. State, _____, Minnesota, Notre Dame, South Carolina.

2. Bear Bryant: Maryland, _____, Texas A&M, Alabama.

3. Bobby Bowden: Samford, _____, Florida State.

4. Bob Devaney: _____, Nebraska.

5. Dennis Franchione: Pittsburg State, Southwest Texas State, _____, Alabama, Texas A&M.

6. Woody Hayes: Denison, _____, Ohio State.

7. Johnny Majors: _____, Pittsburgh, Tennessee.

8. Darrell Royal: Mississippi State, _____, Texas.

9. Bobby Ross: The Citadel, Maryland, _____, Army.

10. Jackie Sherrill: Washington State, _____, Texas A&M, Mississippi State.

Darrell Royal enjoyed his greatest success at Texas, but he cut his coaching teeth during two previous stops.

Getting serious

Name the only Heisman Trophy winner coached by each of the following college football legends.

1. Joe Paterno, 1973.

2. Bear Bryant, 1957.

3. Bud Wilkinson, 1952.

4. Steve Spurrier, 1996.

5. Vince Dooley, 1982.

6. Ara Parseghian, 1964.

7. LaVell Edwards, 1990.

8. Shug Jordan, 1971.

9. Barry Switzer, 1978.

10. Lou Holtz, 1987.

Lou Holtz (left) has made six stops during his long and successful coaching career.

The Name Game

Warming up

Games featuring evenly matched opponents always arouse fan passion on college football Saturdays. On paper at least, the following nickname-inspired matchups would suggest an exciting finish. Name the Division I-A schools that go with the nicknames.

1. Mean Green vs. Demon Deacons.

2. Blue Raiders vs. Red Raiders.

3. Bobcats vs. Nittany Lions.

4. Zips vs. Golden Flashes.

5. Chippewas vs. Seminoles.

6. Badgers vs. Gophers.

7. Buffaloes vs. the Thundering Herd.

8. Terrapins vs. Horned Frogs.

9. Wolfpack vs. Lobos.

10. Owls vs. Owls.

Getting serious

Answer the following questions based on college football consensus championships or co-championships since the Associated Press poll was introduced in 1936.

1 Only one nickname has appeared in the championship circle multiple times. Name the three schools with the same nickname that have won titles.

2 Name the four schools beginning with the letter "A" that have won or shared championships.

3 Name the three teams from the Lone Star State that have won titles.

4 Three champions with colors in their nickname have won titles. Name them.

5 How many different schools with "State" as part of their name have won titles? Name them.

6 Only two schools with a canine nickname have won titles. Name them.

7 Six different schools that begin with the letter "M" have won titles. Name them.

8 Five schools located west of the Rocky Mountains have won titles. Name them.

9 Name the only two champions whose stadiums are accessible by water.

10 Name the four champions whose names begin with either the letter "O" or "N."

Barry Sanders won a Heisman Trophy with a prolific 1988 season, but he's not even the career rushing leader for Oklahoma State.

By the Numbers

College football's top five rushing seasons by freshmen:

Ron Dayne
Wisconsin
1,863/1996

Chance Kretschmer
Nevada
1,732/2001

Herschel Walker
Georgia
1,616/1980

Tony Dorsett
Pittsburgh
1,586/1973

Alex Smith
Indiana
1,475/1994

Dorsett

—Rush, Rush, Rush—

Use the following sets of initials to identify all-time leading rushers for the schools that follow.

Southeastern Conference

H.W.	E.R.	G.R.	B.J.	K.F.	D.M.

1. LSU
2. South Carolina
3. Auburn
4. Georgia
5. Mississippi
6. Florida

Big Ten Conference

A.G.	R.D.	C.W.	A.T.	D.T.

7. Indiana
8. Ohio State
9. Penn State
10. Minnesota
11. Wisconsin

Big 12 Conference

M.R.	T.T.	E.B.	B.S.	T.D.

12. Colorado
13. Nebraska
14. Oklahoma State
15. Oklahoma
16. Iowa State

Pacific-10 Conference

D.N.	W.G.	C.W.	R.M.	K.S.

17. USC
18. Stanford
19. Arizona State
20. Washington State
21. Oregon State

—Famous Pairs—

Warming up

1 What two schools have been paired most often in the Rose Bowl?

2 What two schools have been paired most often in the Orange Bowl?

3 Name the two current members of the Southeastern Conference who have never played (through 2004) in the Orange Bowl.

4 Name the teams that finished atop the inaugural Associated Press (1936) and United Press International polls (1950).

5 What two teams compete in the oldest continuous rivaly west of the Mississippi River?

6 What two Big Ten teams compete annually for Paul Bunyan's axe?

7 What two teams played in the first Rose Bowl game in 1902?

8 Name the only two quarterbacks to run for 1,000 yards and pass for 2,000 yards in the same season.

9 Name the only two teams to boast a 2,000-yard runner, a 2,000-yard passer and a 1,000-yard receiver in the same season. Hint: Both are members of the Big 12 Conference.

10 Name the only two players to score 200 points and pass for 200 points in their careers. Hint: Both were members of the Big Ten Conference.

Getting Serious

Each person in column 1 is closely associated with someone in column 2 because of a famous play, incident, game or career achievement. See if you can make the matches.

Nebraska quarterback Scott Frost has a memorable connection with a former Cornhuskers teammate.

1. Woody Hayes	A. Jack Snow
2. Pete Giftopoulos	B. Kordell Stewart
3. Michael Westbrook	C. Matt Davison
4. Cotton Speyrer	D. Fred Biletnikoff
5. Dicky Moegle	E. Joe Namath
6. Doug Flutie	F. Matt Vogler

Bryant

Hayes

7. John Huarte	G. James Street
8. Scott Frost	H. Ed Smith
9. David Klingler	I. Charlie Bauman
10. Doc Blanchard	J. Gus Dorais
11. Thurman Thomas	K. Ernie Davis
12. Bear Bryant	L. Gerard Phelan
13. Ara Parseghian	M. Jack Mildren
14. Knute Rockne	N. Dan Marino
15. LaDainian Tomlinson	O. Tommy Lewis
16. Steve Tensi	P. Glenn Davis
17. Jay Berwanger	Q. Tony Sands
18. Jim Brown	R. Vinny Testaverde
19. John Brown	S. Duffy Daugherty
20. Jerry Tagge	T. Barry Sanders

Places of the Heart

Warming up

1 Name the oldest facility still in use at the Division I-A level.

2 Where would you go to find the oldest venue at any level?

3 A game played at War Memorial Stadium, Rice-Eccles Stadium, Qualcomm Stadium, University Stadium or Hughes Stadium would feature at least one team from what conference?

4 Utah defeated West Virginia in the 1964 Liberty Bowl game played at Convention Hall in Atlantic City, N.J. What was the historic significance of that contest?

5 What do the venues of the following schools have in common: Air Force, Arkansas, Boise State, Fresno State, Louisville, LSU, Northern Illinois, Penn State and Washington?

6 Name the Division I-A teams that play in the following venues: Rose Bowl, Sun Bowl, Glass Bowl, Orange Bowl, Liberty Bowl and Rubber Bowl.

7 When Washington State played at Houston on September 23, 1966, what was the historic significance of the game?

8 Name the four Division I-A college football stadiums that list official capacities over 100,000.

9 Name the only Division I-A venue to be named after a Heisman Trophy winner.

10 Name the first Division I-A facility to bear the name of an active coach.

Getting serious

Identify the college football venues where you can experience the following sights, sounds and traditions.

1 Parachutists, cannons firing, parades, pushups and scenic views of the Hudson River.

2 The Bucky Wagon, the Chicken Dance, the Budweiser Beer song, the old Fieldhouse and the Fifth Quarter.

3 The Hill, Howard's Rock, Tiger Rag, Orange frenzy and "the most exciting 25 seconds in college football."

4 Mr. Two Bits, Mic-Man, chomping, Nine Inch Nails and Swamp fever.

5 Checkerboard end zones, blinding orange, the Power T, Smokey and Rocky Top.

6 Osceola and Renegade, flaming spears, the Ankle Walk, the Sportsmanship sculpture and The Good, the Bad and the Ugly.

7 Big Bertha, Smokey the Cannon, Bevo, the Wabash Cannonball and burnt orange passion.

8 Uga, the Hedges, Sanford Bridge, the Redcoat Marching Band and silver britches.

9 War Eagle, Toomer's Corner, the Tiger Walk and Aubie.

10 Red, red and more red, the Tunnel Walk, Lil' Red, Herbie and Der Viener Schlinger.

Students and alumni who go to Beaver Stadium will cheer on their team with the help of 100,000-plus other fans.

Mystery Guest

Can you name the athlete and the sport?

1 Not being from these parts, my childhood sports interests were a little unusual. I was a swimmer—a good one with Olympic aspirations. That, fortunately, didn't work out. When I grew up, I discovered my build was more conducive to a different kind of competition.

2 I guess you could say I hit my stride quickly. I really had a ball for the first time in my life in high school and, by college, I was a real demon. Wake me up, I told my friends, when this wonderful dream ends. But, I'm happy to say, it never has.

3 Just look at me now! All those awards I got in college pale in comparison to what has happened to me since. I never was a college champion, but the word "all" became a permanent attachment to my name. I never met an award I couldn't win or a record I couldn't at least challenge.

4 Hey, y'all, come on down and see me some time. You won't be disappointed. We don't get much of a draft here, but fans found me to be a refreshing exception to that. I've enjoyed the sweet taste of victory since my promotion and I've learned how to spell M-V-P. I've become bigger than the average superstar.

5 I score big points with my attitude. I'm also steady as a rock, I know how to rebound from adversity and I get out of the blocks fast. Versatility might be my biggest strength, and I'll always defend against complacency. By my league's standards, I'm a complete player and a tall order for anyone who wants to stop me.

6 Challenges spur me on and there are plenty at the level I play. There's a really big one just across the state. There's another big one in Florida now. We all think we're the best, so toss the ball in the air and let's get it on. There's no crying in my sport, either.

7 I don't know that you would call me dominant as much as relentless. I just keep coming at you. I don't jump through hoops for anyone and when I reach the finals, I'm unbeatable—at least so far. Some people gauge their performances by double-doubles. I gauge mine by 20-20s.

8 Twice a champion and under 30. Not too shabby. And I jump at the chance to help kids and charities in the state where I play. I'm a straight shooter and a good guy. Remember the Alamo!

CHAPTER 10
GAME FACES

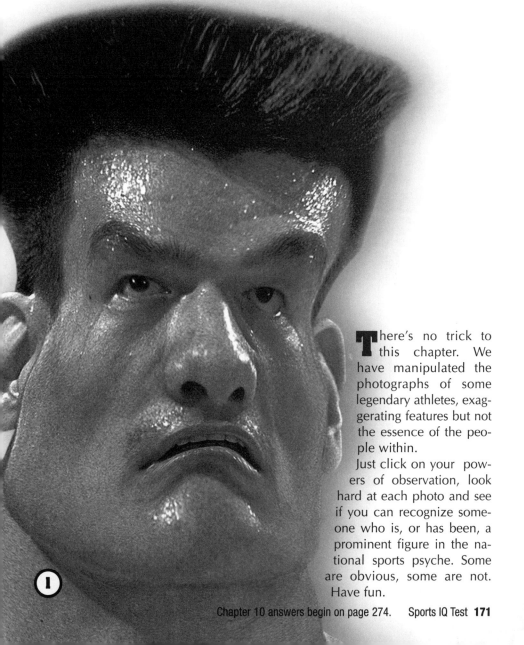

There's no trick to this chapter. We have manipulated the photographs of some legendary athletes, exaggerating features but not the essence of the people within.

Just click on your powers of observation, look hard at each photo and see if you can recognize someone who is, or has been, a prominent figure in the national sports psyche. Some are obvious, some are not. Have fun.

①

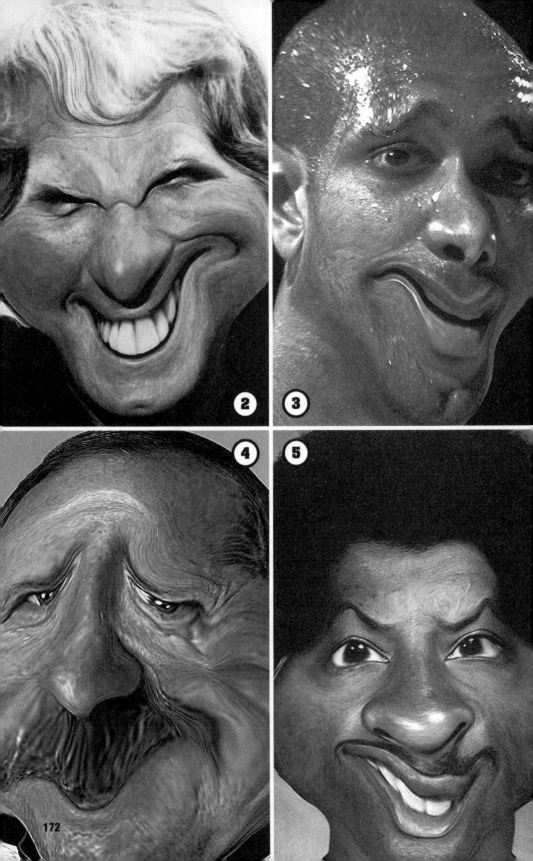

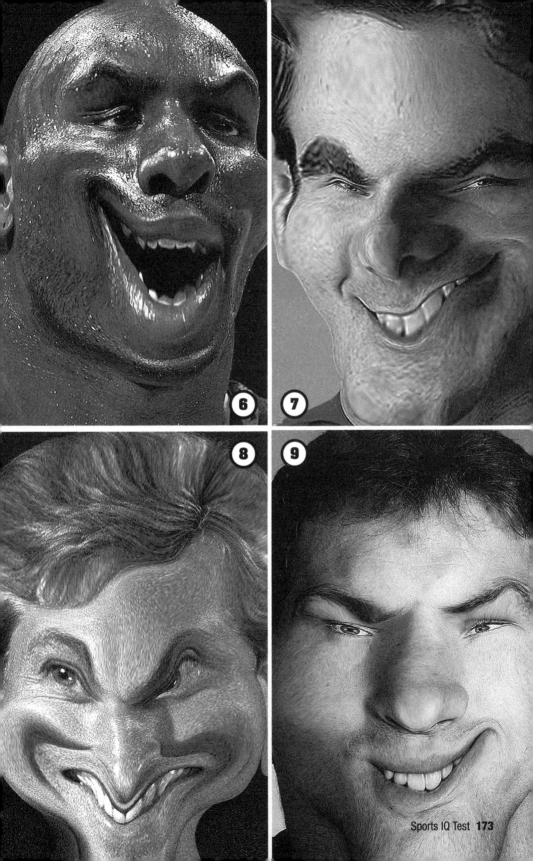

6 7 8 9

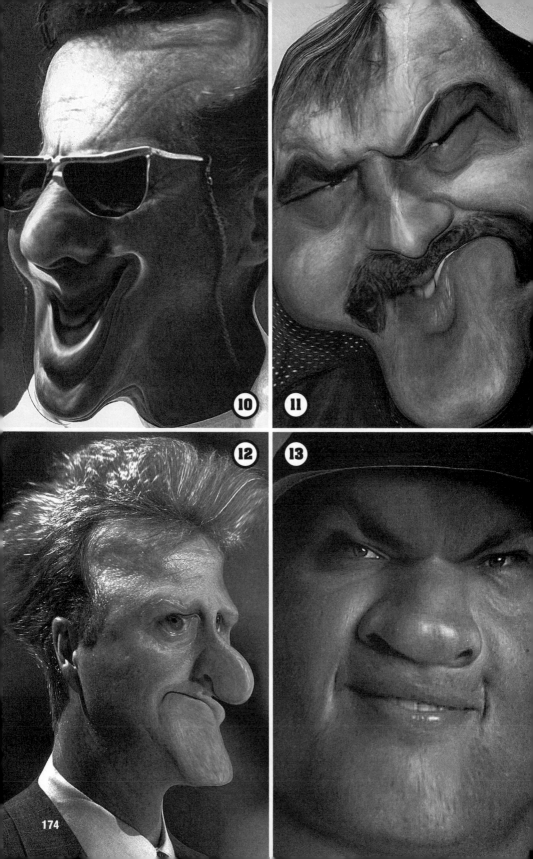

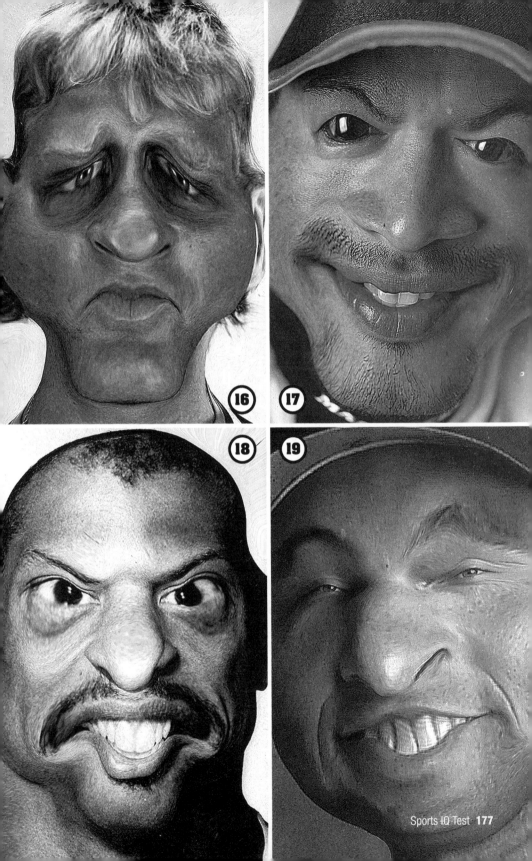

16

17

18

19

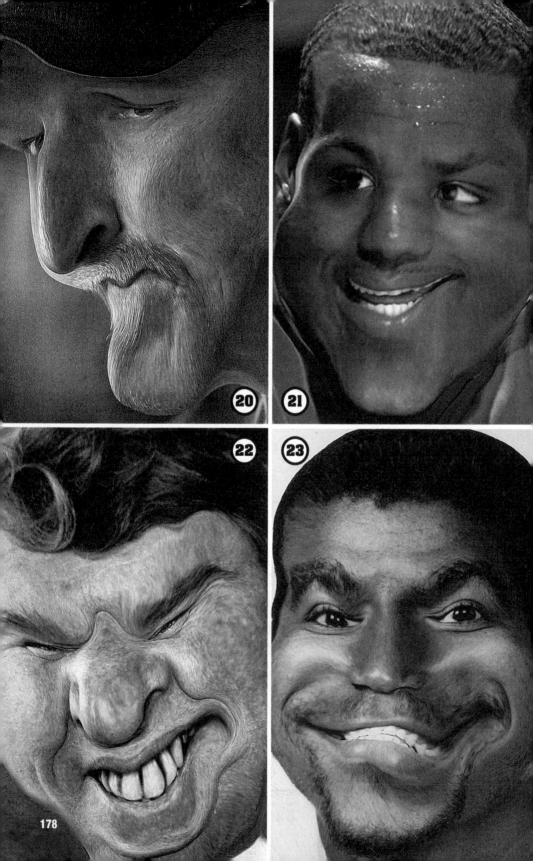

20 21 22 23

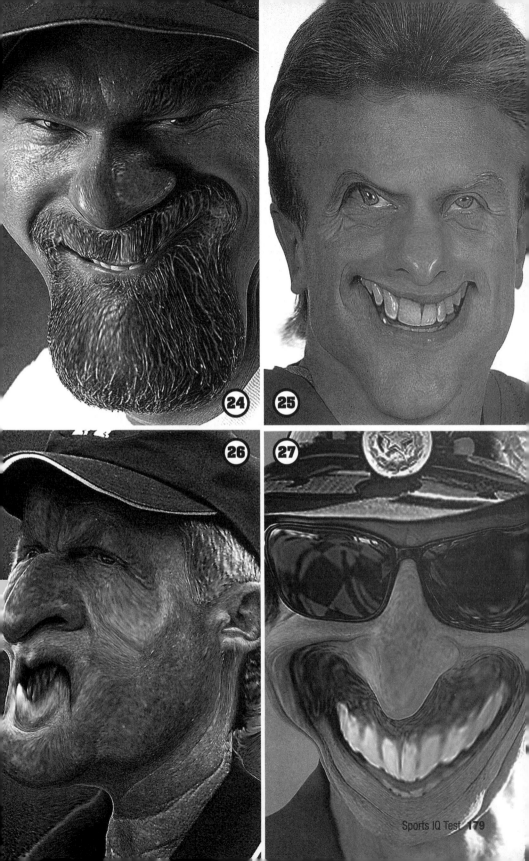

24 **25**

26 **27**

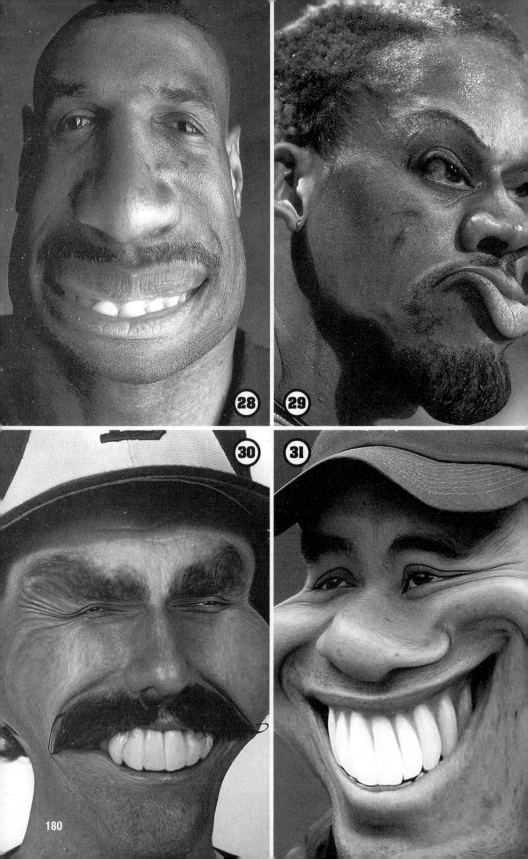

28

29

30

31

Mystery Guest

Can you name the athlete and the sport?

1 The state of Montana hasn't produced many professional athletes, but I cut my teeth playing for a "Little Grizzlies" youth team in the city of Missoula.

2 My father was a coach, and he knew the way to many places—not the least of which was San Jose.

3 After attending high school in the Los Angeles area, I had to decide on a pastoral setting or life in the big city. I chose the farm.

4 I was a big star who received passing grades in college—77 career touchdowns and 9,349 yards—but I never led my team to a bowl game. In fact, my school had a losing record (20-23-1) over my four seasons on the varsity. Along the way, I discovered that father really did know best—or that he knew a lot, anyway. Dad's team got the best of mine twice in four years. Ouch.

5 I wanted to go out in style in my final college game. But, as luck would have it, our archrivals beat the band (and won the big game) in one of the wackiest conclusions ever seen in sports.

6 Opposing teams in my first pro league featured such players as Dwight Gooden, Mike Greenwell and Todd Worrell. I batted .318 as a bush leaguer and played errorless ball in the outfield. Pretty good, eh? Yet I was not destined to wear pinstripes.

7 My real calling, career-wise, got off to a shaky start. I was supposed to get my paychecks on the East Coast, but I finagled a transfer west before ever reporting for work. Then I threw for all of 14 yards in my first NFL game. By the end of my rookie season, I had put up dismal numbers—I completed only 47.5 percent of my passes, had a quarterback rating of 54.9 and was intercepted 14 times while throwing only seven touchdown passes. I got the hang of my job, though, and loved working under pressure. In fact, I was a comeback kid like no other.

8 Owner of many auto dealerships in retirement, I left a football legacy that included a memorable Sunday afternoon drive in northern Ohio. I passed for more than 51,000 yards and exactly 300 touchdowns in my pro career. I amassed 4,030 passing yards in one year and also had season totals of 3,970 and 3,891. I helped my high-horsepower team win back-to-back trophies named in honor of a truly invincible man. I retired on top of the football world, which left me feeling a mile high after years of dealing with a "he can't win the big one" label.

COLLEGE BASKETBALL

— Matchups —

Warming up

Match each of the following to a sports arena or venue where it happened.

1 Where Elvin Hayes scored 39 points and led Houston to a 71-69 win over UCLA, ending the Bruins' 47-game winning streak.

2 Where UCLA suffered two losses, its only missteps in an incredible 90-game span.

3 Where Kentucky's Jack Givens exploded for 41 points in a national championship game win over Duke.

4 The country where the Soviet Union snapped the United States' 63-game Olympic winning streak with a controversial 51-50 victory.

5 Where Bob Knight, upset with a referee's call, picked up a chair and hurled it across the floor, just as the Purdue player was preparing to shoot a technical foul.

6 Where CCNY defeated Bradley twice in 10 days to pull off an unprecedented sweep in the NIT and NCAA championship games.

7 Where Loyola Marymount star Hank Gathers collapsed and died during a game against Portland in the West Coast Conference postseason tournament.

UCLA center Bill Walton's best career performance came in the 1973 NCAA Tournament championship game.

DID YOU KNOW ...

8 Where Isiah Thomas led Indiana to an NCAA championship game win over North Carolina, the same day U.S. President Ronald Reagan had been shot in an assassination attempt.

9 Where Bill Walton connected on 21 of 22 field-goal attempts and scored 44 points while dominating Memphis State in UCLA's 87-66 NCAA championship game win.

10 Where, in the final game coached by UCLA's John Wooden, the Bruins knocked off Louisville in overtime and claimed their 10th NCAA Tournament championship in 12 years.

Getting serious

Two of the three player combinations in each group battled against each other in a national championship game. See if you can identify the title game participants and the winning team.

1 1960: Jerry Lucas-John Havlicek, Oscar Robertston-Paul Hogue, Darrall Imhoff-Bill McClintock.

2 1984: Michael Young-Clyde Drexler, David Wingate-Reggie Williams, Hakeem Olajuwon-Alvin Franklin.

3 1993: Juwan Howard-Jalen Rose, Jamal Mashburn-Travis Ford, Eric Montross-Donald Williams.

4 1991: Larry Johnson-Stacey Augmon, Grant Hill-Thomas Hill, Mark Randall-Adonis Jordan.

5 1969: Lew Alcindor-Sidney Wicks, Rick Mount-Herman Gilliam, Charlie Scott-Bill Bunting.

6 1974: David Thompson-Tom Burleson, Bill Walton-Keith Wilkes, Maurice Lucas-Bo Ellis.

7 1978: Kelly Tripucka-Bill Laimbeer, Kyle Macy-Rick Robey, Jim Spanarkel-Gene Banks.

8 2002: Drew Gooden-Kirk Hinrich, Jared Jeffries-Tom Coverdale, Juan Dixon-Lonny Baxter.

9 1986: Danny Manning-Greg Dreiling, Billy Thompson-Milt Wagner, Johnny Dawkins-David Henderson.

10 1996: Ron Mercer-Antoine Walker, John Wallace-Todd Burgan, Erick Dampier-Darryl Wilson.

-Follow the Leader-
Warming up

Each of the following schools has won one NCAA college basketball championship. Name the championship teams that preceded them into the winner's circle.

1. **UNLV**

2. **Texas Western**

3. **Arizona**

4. **Georgetown**

5. **Marquette**

6. **Ohio State**

7. **Loyola of Chicago**

8. **Maryland**

9. **Villanova**

10. **CCNY**

Getting serious

Each of the following players is the career scoring leader for a school in the Big 12, Big Ten, SEC, ACC or Pac-10 conferences. Name the school.

1. **Johnny Dawkins**

2. **Allan Houston**

3. **Todd Day**

Danny Manning was the talented leader of Kansas teams that prospered in the late 1980s.

DID YOU KNOW...

➤ That LSU players hold the single-season records for scoring average by a senior, junior, sophomore and freshman? Pete Maravich averaged 43.8 points as a sophomore in 1968, 44.2 as a junior in 1969 and 44.5 as a senior in 1970—all class records. *Chris Jackson* set a freshman scoring record in 1989 with a 30.2 mark.

➤ That in 2002, Texas point guard T.J. Ford became the first freshman to lead the nation in assists? Ford led the Longhorns to a Final Four in 2003.

College Basketball

4. Michael Finley
5. Jeff Grayer
6. Litterial Green
7. Rich Yunkus
8. Eddie House
9. Derrick Chievous
10. Roy Marble
11. Dan Issel
12. Phil Ford
13. Terry Teagle
14. Todd Lichti
15. Bob Sura
16. Don MacLean
17. Jeff Malone
18. Bryant Stith
19. Rick Mount
20. Calbert Cheaney
21. Dave Hoppen
22. Gary Payton
23. Deon Thomas
24. Elden Campbell
25. Chuck Person

First Things First

Warming up

1 Name the first team to win NCAA championships in back-to-back seasons.

2 What school was the first to win NCAA and NIT championships?

3 On January 5, 1991, U.S. International's Kevin Bradshaw performed an NCAA first involving games against Division I opponents. What did he do?

4 Name the first freshman to average more than 30 points in a season.

5 Name the first player to reach the 3,000-point plateau in his career.

6 This former La Salle great was the first of two players to top the 2,000 level in both career points and rebounds. Name him.

7 Three teams have won 37 games in a season, athough none went on to win the national championship. Name the first of the three to reach that record win total as championship runner-up in 1986.

8 Name the first team to win 50 or more consecutive games.

U.S. International's Kevin Bradshaw (right) put his name into the NCAA record books in 1991.

9 Name the first of three players to top the 40-point plateau in NCAA championship games.

10 Name the first team to top the 100-point barrier in an NCAA title game.

This high-scoring Purdue star made a dent in the Boilermakers' record books in the late 1960s.

Getting serious

We provide a national championship team and the year it won. You provide the team's leading scorer during the regular season.

1. **North Carolina, 1982**

2. **Indiana, 1976**

3. **Arkansas, 1994**

4. **Michigan State, 1979**

5. **Ohio State, 1960**

6. **Michigan, 1989**

7. **Connecticut, 1999**

8. **UCLA, 1970**

9. **Kentucky, 1949**

10. **Oklahoma A&M, 1946.**

—The Winning Touch—

Warming up

Four of the five players in each group played for a team that won a national championship. Identify the player who did not.

1 Ed Pinckney, Rick Robey, Oscar Robertson, Quinn Buckner, David Thompson.

2 Patrick Ewing, Christian Laettner, John Havlicek, Clyde Lovellette, George Mikan.

3 Darrell Griffith, Elgin Baylor, Michael Jordan, Kyle Macy, Danny Manning.

4 Wayman Tisdale, Isiah Thomas, Gail Goodrich, Steve Alford, K.C. Jones.

5 Phil Ford, Jerry Lucas, Milt Wagner, Scotty Thurman, Mateen Cleaves.

6 Juan Dixon, Lennie Rosenbluth, Cazzie Russell, Mike Bibby, Ed O'Bannon.

7 Pervis Ellison, Tom Gola, Steve Patterson, Butch Lee, Jerry West.

3 11 7

By the Numbers

Career 3,000-point scorers in Division I:

Pete Maravich
LSU
3,667

Freeman Williams
Portland State
3,249

Lionel Simmons
La Salle
3,217

Alphonso Ford
Mississippi Valley
3,165

Harry Kelly
Texas Southern
3,066

Hersey Hawkins
Bradley
3,008

Maravich

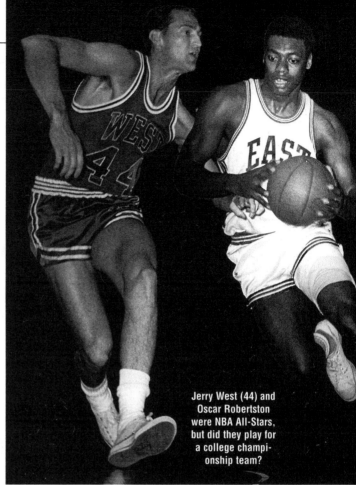

Jerry West (44) and Oscar Robertston were NBA All-Stars, but did they play for a college championship team?

8 Shane Battier, Tony Delk, Matt Doherty, Walter Davis, Walt Hazzard.

9 Glen Rice, Loren Woods, Keith Smart, Alex Groza, David Lattin.

10 Chris Webber, Thurl Bailey, Richard Washington, Tim Stoddard, Larry Siegfried.

Getting serious

The following lists include all of the victims a team has beaten in national championship games. Identify the school that fits each list.

1. Kansas, Kansas, Michigan, North Carolina and Syracuse.

2. Kansas, Georgetown and Michigan.

3. Duke and Georgia Tech.

4. UCLA and Duke.

5. Baylor, Oklahoma A&M, Kansas State, Seattle, Duke, Syracuse and Utah.

6. Seton Hall.

7. Marquette and Houston.

8. St. John's and Oklahoma.

9. Kansas, Michigan and Arizona.

10. Cincinnati.

-And Then There Were Four-
Warming up

1 Only one team in NCAA Tournament history has defeated three No. 1 seeds en route to a national championship. Name it.

2 Only two teams with as many as 13 losses have advanced to a Final Four—and they did it together in 2000. Name those teams.

3 Seven different coaches have taken three different teams to the Sweet 16, but only three of them are active. Name two of those active coaches.

4 Name the only coach since 1951 to lead two different schools to the NCAA Tournament's Elite Eight in consecutive years. Hint: He's one of the possible answers in Question 3.

5 Name the only school that has produced championships in men's basketball and women's basketball in the same year.

6 Name the only player to play in Final Four championship games for two different schools.

7 Three schools have lost in the national championship game two straight years. Name them.

8 Two sets of fathers and sons have played for NCAA championship teams. Can you name them?

9 The state of Texas has been represented in NCAA Tournament play by a record 18 different schools. How many have won the championship?

Kelly Tripucka and his Notre Dame Fighting Irish were participants in the 1978 Final Four.

10 The last time two schools from the same state advanced to the Final Four was 1991. Can you name them?

Getting serious

We give you a year plus the coach and a key player from each of the Final Four teams. You give us the championship game matchup and winner.

1 1990: Bobby Cremins-Kenny Anderson, Jerry Tarkanian-Anderson Hunt, Nolan Richardson-Todd Day, Mike Krzyzewski-Bobby Hurley.

2 1985: John Thompson-Reggie Williams, Lou Carnesecca-Chris Mullin, Rollie Massimino-Dwayne McClain, Dana Kirk-Keith Lee.

3 1978: Bill Foster-Mike Gminski, Digger Phelps-Kelly Tripucka, Joe B. Hall-Kyle Macy, Eddie Sutton-Sidney Moncrief.

DID YOU KNOW...

►That when Notre Dame ended UCLA's 88-game winning streak in 1974, the Irish had to survive five missed Bruins shots during a nail-biting final 21 seconds to escape with a 71-70 win?

►That NBA teams have retired the numbers of more former North Carolina players than those of any other school? Billy Cunningham and **Bobby Jones** (Philadelphia), Brad Daugherty (Cleveland), Walter Davis (Phoenix), Michael Jordan (Chicago) and James Worthy (L.A. Lakers) are former Tar Heels who have been accorded that honor.

4 1966: Vic Bubas-Jack Marin, Adolph Rupp-Pat Riley, Jack Gardner-Jerry Chambers, Don Haskins-Bobby Joe Hill.

5 1976: Gene Bartow-Marques Johnson, Bob Knight-Kent Benson, Johnny Orr-Rickey Green, Tom Young-Phil Sellers.

6 1994: Lute Olson-Damon Stoudamire, Mike Krzyzewski-Grant Hill, Lon Kruger-Andrew Declercq, Nolan Richardson-Scotty Thurman.

7 1962: Fred Taylor-John Havlicek, Ed Jucker-Paul Hogue, John Wooden-Walt Hazzard, Bones McKinney-Billy Packer.

8 1981: Terry Holland-Ralph Sampson, Bob Knight-Randy Wittman, Dale Brown-Durand Macklin, Dean Smith-Sam Perkins.

9 1970: Larry Weise-Bob Lanier, Lou Henson-Jimmy Collins, Joe Williams-Artis Gilmore, John Wooden-Sidney Wicks.

10 1955: Phil Woolpert-Bill Russell, H.B. Lee-Burdette Haldorson, Frank O'Connor-Bill Logan, Ken Loeffler-Tom Gola.

Signal-Callers

Warming up

Each of the coaching names listed below is followed by two players he did not coach. Your job is to rearrange the players so that each coach is paired with players he did coach.

1. **Bob Knight—Larry Kenon, Billy Donovan.**

2. **Jerry Tarkanian—Wayman Tisdale, Jamal Mashburn.**

3. **Gene Bartow—Kent Benson, Bryant Reeves.**

4. **Jim Harrick—Rickey Green, Mike Bibby.**

5. **Gary Williams—Larry Johnson, Andre Emmett.**

6. **Lute Olson—Tyus Edney, Marques Johnson.**

7. **Rick Pitino—Ronnie Lester, Brent Price.**

8. **Eddie Sutton—Jarvis Hayes, Jeff Grayer.**

9. **Billy Tubbs—Sidney Moncrief, Steve Francis.**

10. **Johnny Orr—Dennis Hopson, Melvin Ely.**

Getting serious

Each of the schools in the first section were coached by three current or former coaches in the second. Your job is to match up three coaches with each school, keeping in mind that every school will have at least one coach in common with another school.

1. UCLA

2. Kansas

3. Kentucky

4. Memphis

5. Illinois

6. Florida

7. Kansas State

8. Marquette

9. N.C. State

10. Creighton

A. Joe B. Hall

B. Norm Sloan

C. Jack Hartman

D. Billy Donovan

E. Jim Valvano

F. Dick Harp

G. Gary Cunningham

H. John Calipari

I. Tex Winter

J. Willis Reed

K. Les Robinson

L. Lou Henson

M. Hank Raymonds

Towel-biting Jerry Tarkanian has coached a lot of players during his stints at Long Beach State, UNLV and Fresno State.

Where does John Calipari fit into the coaching puzzle?

N. Gene Bartow

O. Ted Owens

P. Rick Pitino

Q. Lon Kruger

R. Dana Kirk

S. Larry Brown

T. Eddie Sutton

U. Tony Barone

V. Al McGuire

What's in a Name?

Warming up

Match the college coaches in column 1 with their real first names in column 2:

1. Big House Gaines	A. Charles
2. Lefty Driesell	B. Forrest
3. Phog Allen	C. Winfrey
4. Tubby Smith	D. John
5. Piggy Lambert	E. Ward
6. Digger Phelps	F. Clarence
7. Skip Prosser	G. George
8. Wimp Sanderson	H. Orlando
9. Lute Olson	I. Richard
10. Honey Russell	J. Robert

Getting serious

We provide a player, team or college basketball-related phenomena. You provide the nickname.

1. Chris Webber, Ray Jackson, Juwan Howard, Jalen Rose, Jimmy King.

2. Bryant Reeves.

Bryant Reeves (50) was a big load when he played for Oklahoma State.

196

By the Numbers

Longest Division I winning streaks:

UCLA–88
1971-74
Ended by Notre Dame

San Francisco–60
1955-57
Ended by Illinois

UCLA–47
1966-68
Ended by Houston

UNLV–45
1990-91
Ended by Duke

Texas–44
1913-17
Ended by Rice

Seton Hall–43
1939-41
Ended by Long Island

Long Island–43
1935-37
Ended by Stanford

UCLA–41
1968-69
Ended by USC

3. Duke's basketball fans.

4. Big Dog.

5. Keith Wilkes, Dave Meyers, Greg Lee, Henry Bibby, Larry Farmer, Larry Hollyfield, Swen Nater, etc.

6. John Wooden.

7. University Arena in Albuquerque, N.M.

8. Jerry West.

9. The Shark.

10. Hakeem Olajuwon, Clyde Drexler, Michael Young, Benny Anders, etc.

Poll Climbing

Warming up

The *Associated Press* poll has served as a barometer for college basketball success since 1948-49, when Kentucky was declared its first champion. See how many of the following questions you can answer.

1 What midwestern power was the first No. 1 team in the AP's inaugural 1948 poll?

2 Name the last team to carry the No. 1 ranking from the preseason all the way through the championship game without dropping out at any point.

3 This team never was ranked No. 1 during the regular season of its national championship campaign. But it was No. 1 from preseason through final poll the next year—before getting upset by Duke in the Final Four.

4 What team was ranked No. 1 from February 9, 1971, through January 15, 1974—a span of 46 AP polls.

5 This Big Ten school held the No. 1 ranking for 27 straight polls—from December 13, 1960, through March 13, 1962—and it did not win a championship during that span.

6 Name the only school to rank No. 1 in four consecutive AP final polls.

7 What school finished in the AP's final top 10 nine times during the 1990s?

Kansas, which prospered in the 2003 postseason behind the playmaking of guard Aaron Miles (11), is one of college basketball's more consistently ranked teams.

8 Name the two schools that claimed top 10 finishes in the 1990s seven times.

9 What do the following games have in common: North Carolina 97, Duke 73 in February 1998; Missouri 77, Kansas 71 in February 1990; Georgetown 85, St. John's 69 in February 1985?

10 What was UCLA ranked in the preseason poll before its first championship season in 1963-64?

Getting serious

The first column contains the 10 teams that have spent the most weeks ranked No. 1 by the *Associated Press* poll and the first and last years they were accorded that honor. The second column contains the number of weeks spent as No. 1. Match the teams to their column 2 number.

1. Indiana, 1953-93	A. 128
2. Arizona, 1988-2003	B. 96
3. Duke, 1966-2004	C. 84
4. Cincinnati, 1959-2000	D. 80
5. Kansas, 1952-2004	E. 45
6. UCLA, 1964-95	F. 44
7. UNLV, 1983-91	G. 40
8. San Francisco, 1955-77	H. 32
9. Kentucky, 1949-2003	I. 29
10. North Carolina, 1957-2001	J. 28

Mystery Guest

Can you name the athlete and the sport?

1 When I was with the team I played 10-plus seasons for, I worked well with a teammate. Mentioning our last names together in a certain manner was reminiscent of a pop music act. Writers and broadcasters liked to write or say, for instance, "Such and such (insert our names) made sweet music again Tuesday night. ..."

2 My dad, an all-time great in my sport, made a certain devastating offensive technique famous, and I've got better numbers than him and will go into the Hall of Fame the first time I'm eligible. But guess what? My uncle used to slap opponents silly with that same offensive technique, sometimes with the same precision as Dad or me.

3 I've piled up significantly better statistics than my dad, but no one who saw us both play would say I was anywhere near as good as he was. I guess you could call our relationship icy, although we can be downright chummy away from work.

4 One of my nicknames is a hybrid of one of my dad's. I guess I'll never get away from the career comparisons. Maybe that's why I've approached my job a little more casually and always concentrated on carrying a big stick.

5 I'm always viewed as a maverick, sometimes because I can act like the class clown but most of the time because it appears that I'm trying to get away with something. It's fitting, then, that on the most significant play of my career, I was clearly in violation of the rules at that time. Bless my lucky Stars! Guess I got away with one, huh?

6 One reason is because the officiating in my sport is notoriously inconsistent. That can be annoying, but in this case it was like a shot to the heart for my opponents. The play fulfilled one of my goals and gave my team a championship.

7 Later in my career, I joined a bunch of skilled folks with a storied franchise. We won one championship while I was there and I drank from the victory cup again. Hint: That's a burning police car you smell.

8 We were led to that championship by the greatest coach in team sports history. Some of his methods were questionable, but the results are indisputable. Some observers suggest—perhaps tongue-in-cheek, perhaps not—that one of his greatest accomplishments was getting me to work hard on a previously neglected part of my game. But you can't change a reputation overnight. I'm still known primarily as a shooting star.

CHAPTER 12 BASEBALL SILHOUETTES

Baseball players often are recognizable by their throwing, running or batting form, a distinctive swing or unsual physical features and habits. The silhouettes in this chapter come from photographs that catch those distinctions for some of the top players in the game. See if you can identify the players, all still active, pictured on the following pages. Some will jump out at you, others will require more detailed analysis. Test the long-held theory that a picture is worth a thousand words.

1

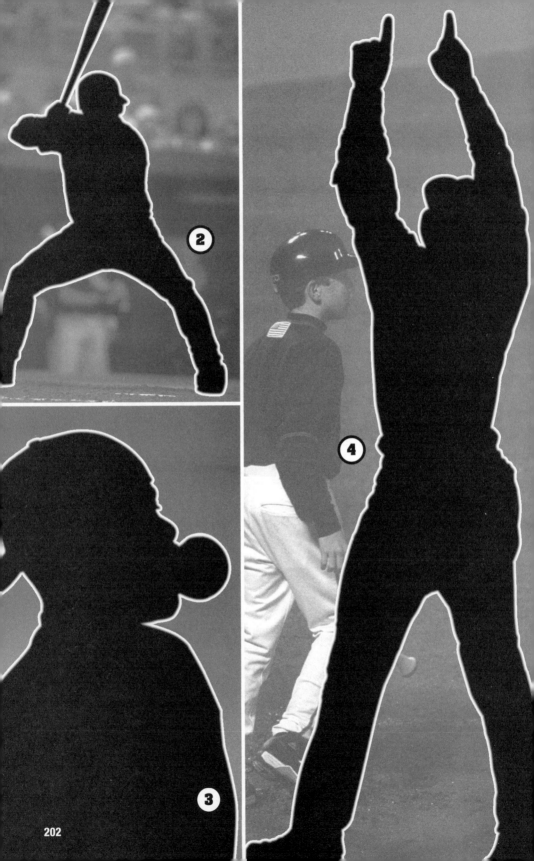

5

6

7

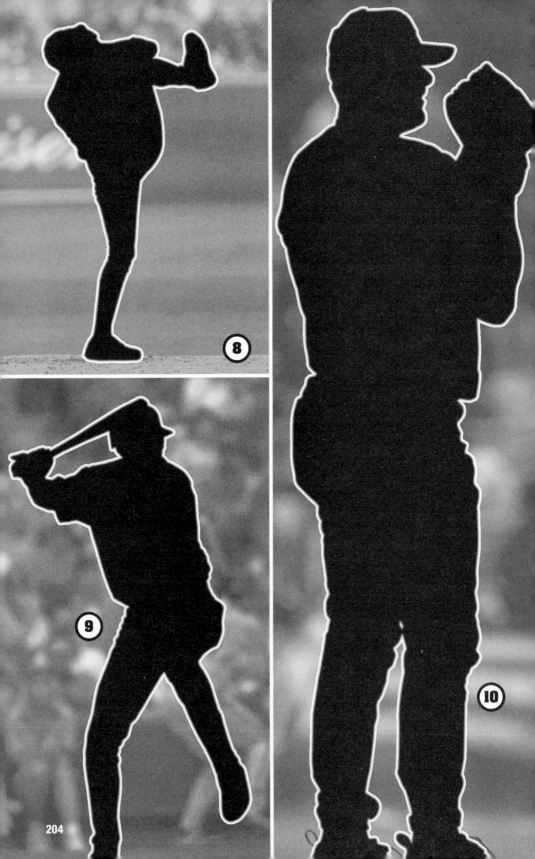

8

9

204

10

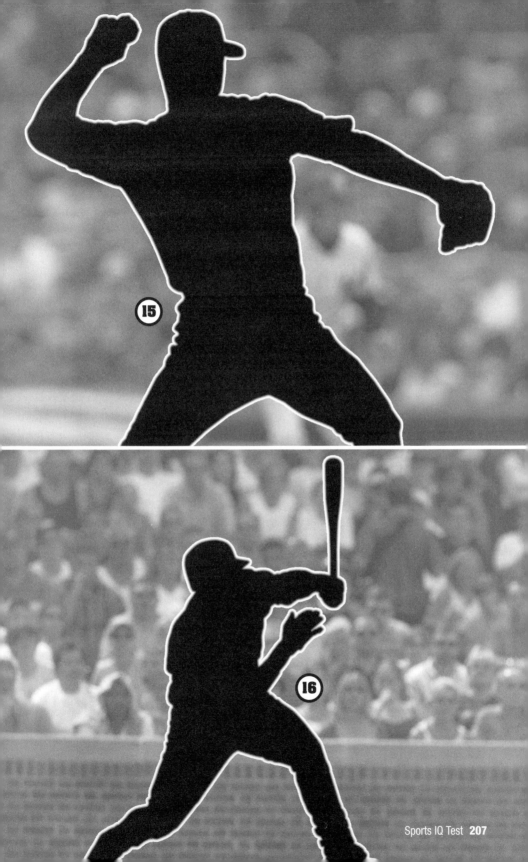

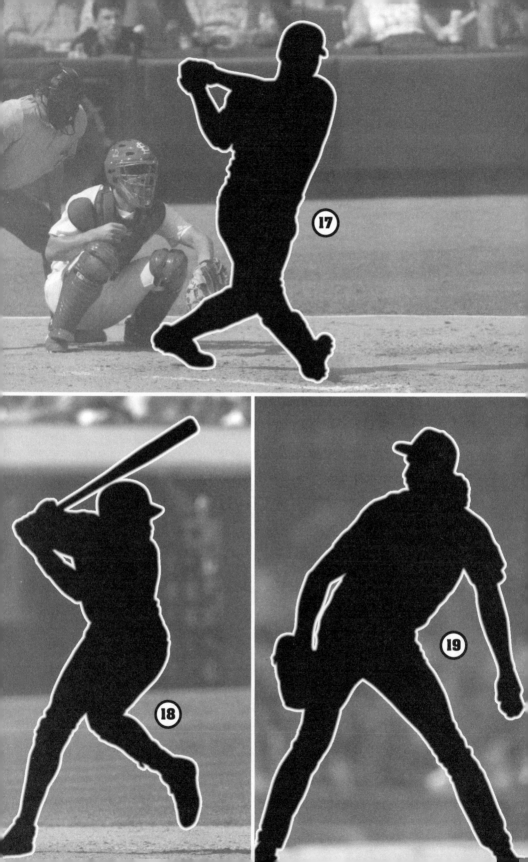

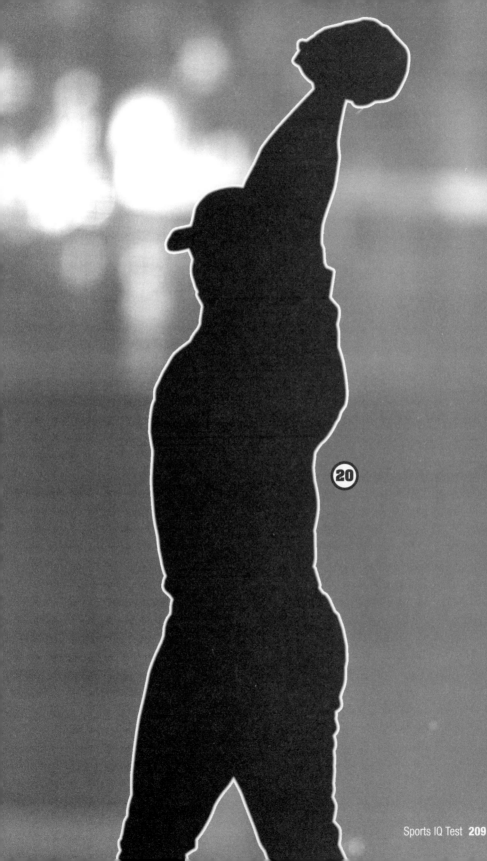

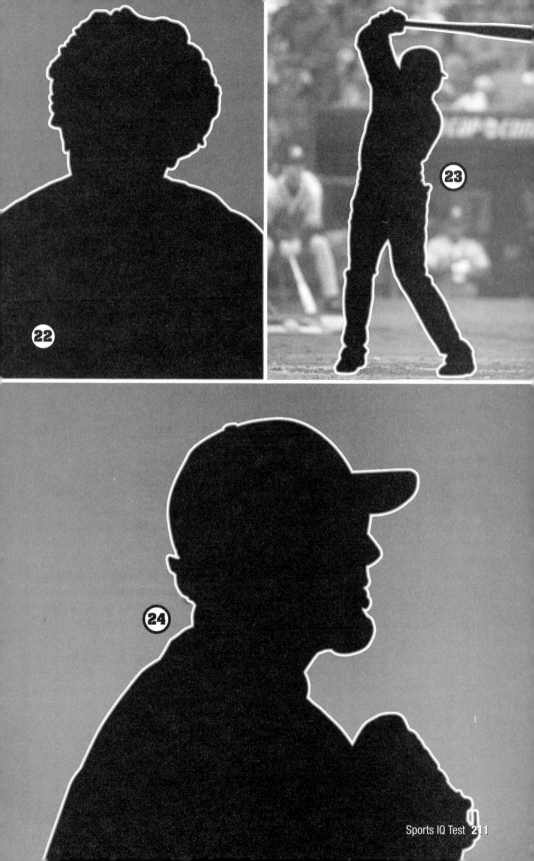

Mystery Guest

Can you name the athlete and the sport?

1 I started attracting attention from scouts when I was just 10. By the time I was old enough to go to my senior prom, I was playing games with my childhood idol. Everybody called me a prodigy. Looking back, I guess they were right.

2 I still was a teen when I discovered oil. And fans quickly made me their center of attention, flocking to sports venues to see me do my thing. I scored big with them. Despite my peace-loving ways, I could swing a mean stick and I always was willing and able to help a hungry teammate.

3 My rise to fame was quick. And like anybody who is capable of making sweet music, I began collecting records. I also began collecting silverware. My hard-charging, fast-shooting, quick-scoring buddies and I enjoyed the sweet taste of victory—four times in five years.

4 By 1988, I was a national icon. But money dictated a change of address and I went Hollywood. Some would call me a missionary, spreading the gospel of my game from California to Arizona, Florida, Georgia, North Carolina, Tennessee and even Texas. It didn't take long for me to settle in and become King of another domain.

5 Team success was elusive in L.A., but I still was able to score big with fans. The net results always were impressive and I exceeded even my most lofty goals. My career was filled with numbers, but I've always been partial to the bigger ones: 92, 99, 215, 885 and 2,795.

6 You might have heard of my wife, too. She's from California and even played an athlete on the silver screen—an Olympic gymnast, in fact. But there's really only one Olympian in this family, at least so far. Maybe one of our five children will change that.

7 MVPs? Scoring titles? All-Star selections? You need a calculator to assess my career by those standards. I've even been called "gentlemanly" by my peers, many of whom I played with while wandering from coast to coast in my final years. I'm proud of my legacy, which is documented on virtually every page of my sport's record book.

8 I'm a governor now, and I have to admit my career was a great one. Technically, it's not over—I've just traded a sweater for a suit. I still howl like a Coyote every autumn when leaves and pucks begin to fall. And there's still that quest for gold … I found a nice chunk of it in the 2002 Salt Lake City Olympics, using a clipboard instead of a stick.

CHAPTER 13
PRO SPORTS

A 10-Year Itch

We provide five memorable moments or events from each decade of the 20th century. You arrange the five items of each group in chronological order.

1900-1909

1 ◆ The Boston Red Sox edge Pittsburgh in baseball's first World Series.

◆ Pirates shortstop Honus Wagner wins his first N.L. batting title with a .381 average.

◆ Fred Merkle's baserunning blunder costs the New York Giants an N.L. pennant.

◆ Baseball's first concrete-and-steel stadium opens in Philadelphia. Shibe Park is named after the Athletics' owner.

◆ Owner John T. Brush and manager John McGraw refuse to let their N.L.-champion Giants play against an inferior team from the upstart A.L. in a "World Series."

1910-1919

2 ◆ Cincinnati's Fred Toney and Chicago's Jim "Hippo" Vaughn hook up in baseball's only double nine-inning no-hitter at Wrigley Field.

◆ The NHL's first season ends when the Toronto Arenas defeat Pacific Coast Hockey Association champion Vancouver in a five-game Stanley Cup playoff.

◆ A new concrete stadium opens for Boston baseball fans. It is named Fenway Park.

Pittsburgh shortstop Honus Wagner won seven N.L. batting titles in the century's first decade.

Chapter 13 answers begin on page 279.

DID YOU KNOW...

➤That *Hugo Bezdek* is the only man to manage a major league baseball team and coach an NFL team? Bezdek managed the Pittsburgh Pirates from 1917-19 and the Cleveland Rams from 1937-38.

➤That Barry Bonds, Lynn Swann, Tom Brady, *Gregg Jefferies* and Jim Fregosi all attended Serra High School in San Mateo, Calif.?

◆ Philadelphia righthander Grover Alexander completes one of the great rookie seasons of all time: 28-13, 2.57 ERA, 366 innings, 227 strikeouts.

◆ Young Red Sox pitcher Babe Ruth hits his first career home run—against the New York Yankees.

1920-29

3 ◆ The National Hockey League expands to six teams with the addition of its first American franchise— the Boston Bruins.

◆ The American Professional Football Association, the future NFL, is founded at a loosely structured meeting in Canton, Ohio.

◆ Babe Ruth completes his 60-home run season and the powerful New York Yankees roll past Pittsburgh in a World Series sweep.

◆ Babe Ruth christens new Yankee Stadium with a home run in a 4-1 victory over Boston.

◆ Washington righthander Walter Johnson becomes the second pitcher to win 400 games.

1930-39

4 ◆ Ty Cobb, Babe Ruth, Christy Mathewson, Honus Wagner and Walter

Red Auerbach and his Boston Celtics dominated the 1960s pro basketball scene.

Johnson are announced as the first electees to baseball's new Hall of Fame.

◆ The Giants defeat the Chicago Bears, 30-13, and claim the NFL championship in the famed "Sneakers Game" at New York's Polo Grounds.

◆ In "Lou Gehrig Day" ceremonies at Yankee Stadium, the Iron Horse bids a sad farewell to baseball.

◆ Chicago Cubs outfielder Hack Wilson hits a then-N.L.-record 56 home runs and drives in a still-standing-record 191 runs.

◆ The American League wins baseball's first All-Star Game, 4-2, at Chicago's Comiskey Park.

1940-49

5 ◆ Joe Fulks leads the Philadelphia Warriors past the Chicago Stags in the first Basketball Association of America (forerunner to the NBA) championship series.

◆ Babe Ruth dies of throat cancer at New York's Memorial Hospital.

◆ Yankee Clipper Joe DiMaggio's 56-game hitting streak ends after several close calls during a game at Cleveland's Municipal Stadium.

◆ Cleveland Rams owner Dan Reeves, after watching his team win its first NFL championship, announces it will relocate before the next season to Los Angeles.

◆ After losing the first three games of the Stanley Cup final and trailing Detroit in the third period of Game 4, the Toronto Maple Leafs come to life and win the series in seven games.

1950-59

6 ◆ Pittsburgh's Harvey Haddix pitches 12 perfect innings against Milwaukee, only to lose in the 13th.

◆ The NBA introduces an innovative new rule: the 24-second clock.

◆ Bobby Thomson's ninth-inning playoff home run gives the New York Giants a 5-4 win over Brooklyn and ends the most dramatic pennant race in history.

◆ New York Yankees center fielder Mickey Mantle wins the American League Triple Crown with a .353 average, 52 home runs and 130 RBIs.

◆ Bobby Layne passes the Detroit Lions to a 17-16 championship game win over Cleveland and their second straight NFL title.

1960-69

7 ◆ The Boston Celtics win their record eighth straight NBA championship, a nice retirement present for coach Red Auerbach.

◆ Los Angeles Dodgers shortstop Maury Wills steals 104 bases, becoming the

DID YOU KNOW ...

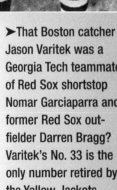

first player in history to top the century mark.

◆ Boston's Ted Williams hits career homer No. 521 in his final big-league at-bat.

◆ The Green Bay Packers defeat Kansas City, 35-10, and win the first Super Bowl.

◆ The Harris County Domed Stadium, more commonly known as the Astrodome, opens in Houston.

1970-79

8◆ The World Hockey Association, a rival to the NHL, introduces its first 10 franchises.

◆ Pittsburgh Pirates star Roberto Clemente dies in a plane crash near San Juan, Puerto Rico.

◆ Pittsburgh's "Family" beats Baltimore in a seven-game World Series.

◆ 2003: a rushing odyssey. Buffalo's O.J. Simpson becomes pro football's first 2,000-yard man.

◆ Philadelphia's "Broad Street Bullies" defeat Buffalo, win their second straight Stanley Cup.

1980-89

9◆ Cincinnati's Pete Rose collects career hit No. 4,192, surpassing Ty Cobb as baseball's all-time hits leader.

◆ In one of the most sensational trades in sports history, the Edmonton Oilers send Wayne Gretzky to the Los Angeles Kings.

◆ Oakland's Rickey Henderson steals 130 bases, surpassing former St. Louis star Lou Brock's single-season mark of 118.

◆ The Los Angeles Lakers capture their fourth NBA championship of the 1980s with a six-game win over the Boston Celtics.

◆ The New York Islanders win their first Stanley Cup with a six-game victory over the Philadelphia Flyers.

1990-99

10◆ St. Louis first baseman Mark McGwire hits 70 home runs, setting a new single-season standard.

◆ The Scottie Pippen- and Michael Jordan-led Chicago Bulls win their first NBA championship, beating the Los Angeles Lakers in five games.

◆ Major league baseball, handcuffed by a general players' strike, cancels the final half month of the regular season and postseason. It marks the first season without a World Series since 1904.

◆ In his final professional game, Denver quarterback John Elway guides the Broncos to their second straight championship with a Super Bowl 33 win over Atlanta.

◆ The Colorado Avalanche win the franchise's first Stanley Cup.

Uniformity

Warming up

So you think you know uniforms? Do the math on the following retired player uniform numbers and see how it all adds up. If you add, subtract, divide and multiply correctly, the answer will help you identify a famous player from the team in parentheses.

1 (Kareem Abdul-Jabbar + Don Mattingly + Lou Brock) ÷ Bobby Orr = (Baltimore Colts)

2 Dick Butkus + John Havlicek + Hank Aaron — (Phil Esposito + Al Kaline) = (Minneapolis Lakers)

3 Wayne Gretzky — Bill Russell — Steve Carlton + Doug Harvey = (Kansas City Chiefs)

4 (Jackie Robinson X Harmon Killebrew) — Jerry West) ÷ Tom Seaver) + Dan Fouts = (New York Giants, NFL)

5 Nolan Ryan + John Elway — Wes Unseld + David Thompson = (Boston Celtics)

6 (Raymond Berry + Mike Bossy) ÷ Yogi Berra = (Philadelphia Warriors, Los Angeles Lakers)

By any calculation, Lou Brock left a memorable imprint on his sport.

DID YOU KNOW...

➤That two-time National League Cy Young winner *Tom Glavine* was a promising hockey prospect who was drafted by the NHL? Glavine, a second-round pick by the Atlanta Braves in baseball's free-agent draft, was a fourth-round pick by the NHL's Los Angeles Kings.

➤That the 2002-03 Detroit Pistons and Detroit Red Wings, both of which played 82-game schedules, won more games than baseball's 2003 Detroit Tigers, who played 162 games? The Pistons won 50, the Red Wings 48 and the Tigers 43.

No. 42 has been universally retired in baseball, a tribute to the former Dodgers player and social pioneer.

7 (Reggie Jackson + Bernie Parent + Thurman Munson) X Sidney Moncrief ÷ Dale Murphy = (Seattle Seahawks)

8 Don Sutton X Babe Ruth X Alex English — Alan Page + Bill Bradley = (New York Giants, NFL)

9 Pete Maravich ÷ Jean Beliveau X (Paul Molitor + Tommy Lasorda) = (Detroit Red Wings)

10 Walt Frazier + Gale Sayers — Marcel Dionne = (Houston Oilers)

Getting serious

The 10 numbers listed below were made famous by players in various team sports. Match the uniform numbers to players on the accompanying checklist (one each from professional baseball, football, basketball and hockey). Note: There is one extra name on the checklist, a player who did not wear any of the numbers.

#	Baseball player	Football player	Basketball player	Hockey player
4				
5				
33				
22				
10				
16				
11				
19				
31				
21				

Checklist:

Sammy Baugh	Kevin Garnett	Joe Montana	Phil Simms
Elgin Baylor	Lou Gehrig	Joe Morgan	Emmitt Smith
Mike Bibby	Tony Gwynn	Eddie Murray	Sammy Sosa
Larry Bird	Paul Hornung	Bobby Orr	Fran Tarkenton
Mike Bossy	Jason Kidd	Jim Palmer	Jim Taylor
George Brett	Guy Lafleur	Mike Piazza	Isiah Thomas
Bobby Clarke	Bob Lanier	Denis Potvin	Johnny Unitas
Brett Favre	Barry Larkin	Willis Reed	Chris Webber
Whitey Ford	Mark Messier	Patrick Roy	Steve Yzerman
Grant Fuhr	Stan Mikita	Deion Sanders	
	Reggie Miller	Ron Santo	

Roots

Warming up

Many of today's professional sports franchises underwent difficult growing pains in the formative and expansion periods of their leagues. See if you can provide the names used by these current franchises in their inaugural seasons in the NFL, NBA, NHL and MLB.

1. Dallas Stars

2. Chicago Bears

3. New York Yankees

4. Sacramento Kings

5. Toronto Maple Leafs

6. Baltimore Orioles

7. Tennessee Titans

8. Philadelphia 76ers

9. Phoenix Coyotes

10. St. Louis Rams

DID YOU KNOW...

➤That baseball Hall of Famer *Frank Robinson* was a high school teammate of basketball Hall of Famer *Bill Russell?* Robinson played guard and Russell played center for Oakland's McClymonds High, which won the Northern California state basketball championship. Robinson also played on the same high school baseball team with future major leaguer Curt Flood.

Russell   Robinson

➤That when the Seattle Mariners won 116 games in 2001, they surpassed the victory total of the NFL's Seattle Seahawks over the franchise's first 15 seasons? The Seahawks won 112 games from 1976 through 1990.

Jack Twyman played for the Cincinnati Royals, one of three forerunners to the Sacramento Kings. But there was another location before Cincinnati.

Getting serious

The following teams were members of rival leagues that challenged MLB, the NFL, the NBA and the NHL at various periods of their existence. Identify the league in which they competed.

1. Spirits of St. Louis.

2. Chicago Fire.

By the Numbers

Players who have logged the most seasons in the Big Four professional sports:

Nolan Ryan
MLB
27

George Blanda
NFL
26

Gordie Howe
NHL
26

Tommy John
MLB
26

Deacon McGuire
MLB
26

3. Baltimore Blades.

4. Los Angeles Express.

5. Indianapolis Hoosiers.

6. Memphis Sounds.

7. Miami Seahawks.

8. New York Titans.

9. Toronto Toros.

10. Los Angeles Xtreme.

——Mixed Results——

Warming up

1 The best records in NBA, NFL and baseball history are represented by the winning percentages .763, .878 and 1.000. Identify the teams that compiled those percentages.

2 The 1970 Baltimore Orioles and Baltimore Colts gave their city an unusual double—World Series and Super Bowl winners. But only one of those teams also boasted its league MVP. Name the player.

3 Eight coaches—three in baseball, three in the NHL and one each in the NFL and NBA—have coached or managed two different teams to championships. But only one has guided three teams to the victory circle. Name him.

4 Name the two Heisman Trophy winners (1985 and 1993) who went on to make their greatest professional impact in a different sport.

5 Name five NHL, NBA and MLB players who have won MVP awards with more than one team. There are eight to choose from.

Sparky Anderson guided two different teams to World Series championships. But one professional coach performed a trifecta.

DID YOU KNOW...

➤That Canadian-based teams won as many World Series in the 1990s as Stanley Cups? Baseball's Toronto Blue Jays won consecutive fall classics in 1992 and '93. Two Canadian-based teams won the Stanley Cup: Edmonton in 1990 and Montreal in 1993.

➤That the 2002-03 season was magic for five athletes who joined their sports' 500 clubs? NHL stars Joe Sakic (Colorado), Joe Nieuwendyk (New Jersey) and *Jaromir Jagr* (Washington) all notched their 500th career goals. Baseball's *Sammy Sosa* (Chicago Cubs) and Rafael Palmeiro (Texas) hit their 500th career home runs in the most productive "500 season" in history.

Sosa

Jagr

Kicker Gary Anderson sits atop the NFL's career scoring list.

6 Name the players who hold the NHL, NBA, NFL and MLB records for games played.

7 Philadelphia teams produced two Rookie of the Year winners in 1997. Can you name those top NBA and baseball rookies?

8 Baseball's Rickey Henderson, the NHL's Wayne Gretzky, the NBA's Kareem Abdul-Jabbar and the NFL's Gary Anderson were the career scoring leaders (runs in baseball) through the 2003 seasons. Put those players in order of total points/runs.

9 The last three NFL, NBA and NHL MVPs from New York-based teams have been claimed by Buffalo players. Can you name them?

10 Through the 2004 NBA Finals, what U.S. state has claimed the most titles (NHL, NBA, NFL and MLB combined) since the turn of the century?

Getting serious

We provide the categories and initials, you provide the names.

1 Coaches or managers who won multiple championships in the 1980s: T.L., T.F., B.W., J.G., P.R., K.J., A.A., G.S.

2 Players for Los Angeles teams who have won league MVP and All-Star Game (Pro Bowl in football) MVP awards in the same season: S.G., R.G., W.G., M.J., S.O.

3 Leading career scorers (points in the NHL, NBA and NFL; runs in baseball) for Boston area teams: R.B., G.C., L.B., C.Y.

4 Coaches or managers of the last five Canadian-based teams to win championships: J.D., C.G., J.M., T.C., G.S.

5 Players who have led their league in scoring (RBIs in baseball) five or more times: M.J., W.G., W.C., B.R., G.H., M.L., L.G., P.E., D.H., J.J.

6 Future stars selected No. 1 overall in the four 1987 drafts: K.G., V.T., D.R., P.T.

7 MVPs in the 2000 World Series, Super Bowl, NBA Finals and Stanley Cup play-offs: D.J., K.W., S.O., S.S.

8 The first coaches with 100 or more wins who are listed in the alphabetical rosters that appear in the encyclopedia for each of the four sports: G.A., F.A., R.A., S.A.

9 The players who hold the consecutive-games ironman record in each of the four sports: J.M., C.R., A.G., D.J.

10 The No. 1 overall draft picks for each of the sports in 2002: M.V., Y.M., R.N., B.B.

── Nicknames ──

Warming up

Nicknames transcend time and sport. Identify the current and former players who are associated with the following titles.

1. Mr. Cub, Mr. Goalie, Mr. October, Mr. Hockey.

2. The Big Train, Big Dog, Big Bird, The Big Unit.

3. The Pearl, The Flower, Silk, Twinkle Toes.

4. White Shoes, Le Grande Orange, The Golden Jet, Greyhound.

Fans remember former Montreal great Bernie Geoffrion by his more colorful nickname.

5. Kong, Manimal, Cujo, The Beast.

6. Moose, Bambi, Ducky, Snake.

7. Shoeless Joe, Broadway Joe, Jumpin' Joe, Mean Joe.

8. The Hawk, The Stork, The Worm, The Cobra.

9. Boom Boom, Bye-Bye, Choo Choo, Say Hey.

10. The Russian Rocket, The Reading Rifle, The Commerce Comet, The Tyler Rose.

Getting serious

The following nicknames are common to professional (NFL, NBA, NHL and MLB) teams that played in a particular city. Identify the city, but avoid falling into easy traps.

1. Stags, Packers, Cubs, Tigers, Zephyrs, Bulls, Cardinals, Bears.

2. Falcons, Lions, Panthers, Cougars, Tigers, Heralds, Pistons, Wolverines.

3. Hawks, Bombers, Rams, Blues, Cardinals, Eagles, Browns.

First baseman George McQuinn was a big hit for a team known as the Browns.

4. Rebels, Browns, Tigers, Naps, Indians, Bulldogs, Barons.

5. Kings, Cowboys, Athletics, Chiefs, Scouts.

6. Bruins, Bulldogs, Braves, Celtics, Patriots, Pilgrims.

7. Giants, Americans, Highlanders, Jets, Nets, Rangers, Mets, Islanders.

8. Arenas, Huskies, St. Patricks, Raptors, Blue Jays, Maple Leafs.

9. Warriors, Quakers, Eagles, Athletics, Flyers, 76ers.

10. Lions, Robins, Tigers, Americans, Dodgers.

Rich Man, Joe Man

Warming up

1 Five players named Joe have won National League and American League MVP awards. Name four.

2 This 14-year NBA star scored 20,497 points and enjoyed his most success with Golden State and Sacramento. But he got his only championship ring in his final season with another West Coast team. Name him.

3 Elmer Lach centered a Montreal line in the early 1940s that included Rocket Richard and another winger who went on to even greater fame. The third member of the Canadiens' famed Punch Line was not exactly a "Joe," but he was close.

4 Who was the NFL's career rushing champion before Jim Brown?

5 In 1964, this player became the only "Rich" man to win one of baseball's three major awards—the MVP, Cy Young or Rookie of the Year. Name him.

6 Name the last Joe or Rich(ard) inducted into the pro football Hall of Fame.

7 Through the 2003-04 season, this man ranked third among active goaltenders in career victories. Name this above-average Joe.

8 What "secondary" distinction do these former NFL quarterbacks have in common: Richie Lucas (1960-61), Joe Theismann (1974-85), Joe Hamilton (2000)?

9 Who is the career goal-scoring leader for the Quebec Nordiques/Colorado Avalanche franchise, which began NHL play in 1979-80?

10 The Lakers won their first Los Angeles-based NBA championship in 1972 when they defeated the New York Knicks in five games. Who was the leading scorer for that Lakers team?

Elmer Lach (right) centered a 1940s Canadiens line that included a 'Rich' (left) and an almost 'Joe.'

Getting serious

"Rich" and "Joe" are important considerations when attempting to discern the following identities.

1. The NFL's first 4,000-yard passer.

2. The Chicago Bulls' top 2003 draft pick.

3. The "Pocket Rocket."

4. NFL record-holder for most pass completions in a season.

5. "No. 1" in the hearts of Phillies fans.

6. No. 1 villain of Phillies fans and Mitch Williams.

7. A starter for two NBA championship teams in the 1970s.

8. Batting champion, MVP, Manager of the Year.

9. 40,551 yards passing, 273 touchdowns.

10. Virginia birthplace of Hall of Fame quarterback Fran Tarkenton.

Mitch Williams is no Rich or Joe, but he forever will be linked by Philadelphia fans to someone who was.

By the Numbers

States that have produced the most championship winners (NBA, NFL, NHL and MLB) over the last decade (1995-2004):

Texas–5
3 NBA, 1 NHL, 1 NFL

California–4
3 NBA, 1 MLB

Colorado–4
2 NFL, 2 NHL

Florida–4
2 MLB, 1 NFL, 1 NHL

Michigan–4
3 NHL, 1 NBA

New York–4
4 MLB

Illinois–3
3 NBA

New Jersey–3
3 NHL

Massachusetts–2
2 NFL

─Relatively Speaking─
Warming up

1 This righthander, who recorded 96 saves while pitching 12 seasons (1972-83) for the Giants, Astros and Blue Jays, was upstaged and overshadowed by his older sister, a celebrated tennis champion. Name this brother-sister act.

2 Punishment, both giving and receiving, was a father-son job description for this two-sport family. Dad reached championship heights in the 1970s with his fists. Junior was a multiple champion in the 1990s on the football field. Name them.

3 Dinner-table bragging rights in this two-sport family belongs to the wife, who has won multiple titles and earned membership in her sport's Hall of Fame. The husband, however, is not defenseless. He can always flash his 1986 World Series championship ring.

4 Brother and sister could stage an interesting one-on-one basketball show at this family's reunions. But neither could match up in a baseball competition against their brother, who spent five major league seasons with the California Angels. Name this talented trio.

5 Father, a quarterback, helped Notre Dame win a national football championship in 1949 before playing professionally in the NFL and AFL. Son helped the Fighting Irish reach the NCAA Tournament's Final Four in 1978 before averaging 17.2 points over a successful 10-year NBA career. Name this illustrious father and son.

6 This longtime major leaguer can hit and field balls better than his wife, but he would quickly concede he's no match for her overall athleticism. The husband is best known for his 11-team migration over a 15-year big-league career. The wife was a key member of the 1984 women's gymnastics team that won a silver medal in the Los Angeles Olympic Games.

7 Father was a Golden Domer who made his mark professionally as a wide receiver for the Los Angeles Rams. Son is a Gold Glover who attended the University of Arizona and has spent 11 of his 12 major league seasons on the West Coast.

8 One brother gained Hall of Fame status in the National Basketball Association. The other, an offensive lineman, had an unspectacular three-year career with the Dallas Cowboys. Both are UCLA products, but the former is remembered as one of the great athletes in school history. Name both.

9 He was one of the most feared and respected pitchers in baseball history. She was a driving force of women's basketball, one of the best all-around players of her era. Identify this Hall of Fame couple.

10 Father, a former Ivy Leaguer, rumbled for 6,083 yards over a 12-year NFL career with the Dallas Cowboys, Washington Redskins and Cleveland Browns. Son is a six-time NBA All-Star in his 10th professional season. Identify them.

Getting serious

Name the current or former athlete that matches up to the names that follow.

Father-in law/Son-in law

1. Digger Phelps/_____.
2. John Brodie/_____.
3. Ralph Branca/_____.
4. Lou Boudreau/_____.
5. Howie Morenz/_____.
6. Jack McKeon/_____.
7. Jack Ramsay/_____.

Father/Son

8. Man o'War/_____.
9. Peter Marshall/_____.
10. Ronnie Lott/_____.

Grandfather/Grandson

11. Wally Post/_____.
12. Ray Boone/_____, _____.
13. Sid Abel/_____.

Uncle/Nephew

14. Dwight Gooden/_____.
15. Dennis Hull/_____.

Brothers

16. Dale Carter/_____.

Cousins

17. Bert Campaneris/_____.

The son-in-law of former Cleveland player/ manager Lou Boudreau (right) had All-Star talent.

Calling the Shots

Warming up

Answer the following questions regarding MLB, the NFL, the NBA and the NHL, keeping in mind that pro football seasons are defined by the calendar year in which games were played, not the date of the Super Bowl.

1 Identify the last two-year period that produced repeat champions in more than one sport. Name the championship coaches.

2 Twelve coaches have guided MLB, NFL, NBA or NHL teams to three or more straight titles. But only one has taken teams to three consecutive championships on three different occasions. Name him.

3 Only three baseball managers have won three or more consecutive championships. All did it with the New York Yankees. Name them.

4 Who holds the record for coaching/managing the most consecutive championship teams?

5 Who was the last NFL coach/manager to lead a team to three straight championships?

6 Name the last coach/manager to lead his team to four or more straight titles.

7 Larry Brown became a first-time NBA championship winner with the 2003-04 Detroit Pistons. Before Brown, who was the last coach to win his first title and not go on to win another.

8 Add the championship totals for the top five coaches in each of the four groups. Which group has the most?

9 Who has coached/managed the most championship winners among coaches in the four groups?

10 Name the last coach/manager to lead a team to championships during his first two seasons.

Digger Phelps (left) found success in basketball, but his son-in-law has thrived in a different sport.

Vince Lombardi (top) and Alex Hannum led teams to titles in the same season.

Getting serious

Identify the seasons in which the following groups of managers/coaches directed championship winners. Note: Each grouping reflects the year in which pro football's champion played its regular season, not the date of the Super Bowl game.

1. Tony La Russa, George Seifert, Chuck Daly, Terry Crisp.

2. Chuck Tanner, Chuck Noll, Lenny Wilkens, Scotty Bowman.

3. Gil Hodges, Hank Stram, Bill Russell, Claude Ruel.

4. Dave Johnson, Bill Parcells, K.C. Jones, Jean Perron.

5. Fred Haney, George Wilson, Red Auerbach, Toe Blake.

6. Cito Gaston, Jimmy Johnson, Phil Jackson, Jacques Demers.

7. Alvin Dark, Chuck Noll, Tommy Heinsohn, Fred Shero.

8. Red Schoendienst, Vince Lombardi, Alex Hannum, Punch Imlach.

9. Lou Boudreau, Greasy Neale, Buddy Jeannette, Hap Day.

10. Joe Torre, Dick Vermeil, Gregg Popovich, Ken Hitchcock.

City Slickers

Warming up

This quiz covers the time span 1960 through 2003. Football champions reflect the year in which the regular season was played, not the Super Bowl. The New England Patriots are considered a Boston team. The New Jersey Devils and Anaheim Angels are considered separate entities from New York and Los Angeles.

1 What city has produced more championship teams than any other in this 44-year period?

2 Name the next three cities in order of championships produced.

3 Detroit, New York, Boston and Montreal all produced title teams in this year.

4 New York, Philadelphia, Los Angeles and Baltimore all reached championship heights in this year.

5 What two cities produced the most title teams in a single decade?

6 Baltimore's five championships were produced in four decades. In which decade did Baltimore teams fail to win?

7 Two other cities won five championships, four each in the same decade. Name those two cities.

8 Name five of the nine cities that celebrated only one championship during the period.

9 Only two cities have celebrated championships in each of the four sports. Name them.

10 Name the four cities that have celebrated two championships in the same year.

Getting serious

We provide the city and decade(s) from 1960 to the present, you provide the number of championships that teams representing the city captured in the NFL, NBA, NHL and major league baseball during that span. Note: Football champions reflect the year in which the regular season was played, not the Super Bowl.

1. Boston, 1960s and 1970s.

2. Pittsburgh, 1970s.

3. Los Angeles, 1970s and 1980s.

4. Detroit, 1960s and 1990s.

5. Philadelphia, 1960s, 1970s and 1980s.

6. Montreal + New York in the 1960s.

7. San Francisco + Oakland in the 1980s.

8. Denver + Dallas in the 1990s — Kansas City from 1960-present.

9. Boston + Phoenix + Tampa in the 2000s — Los Angeles.

10. Cleveland, 1960s and 1980s.

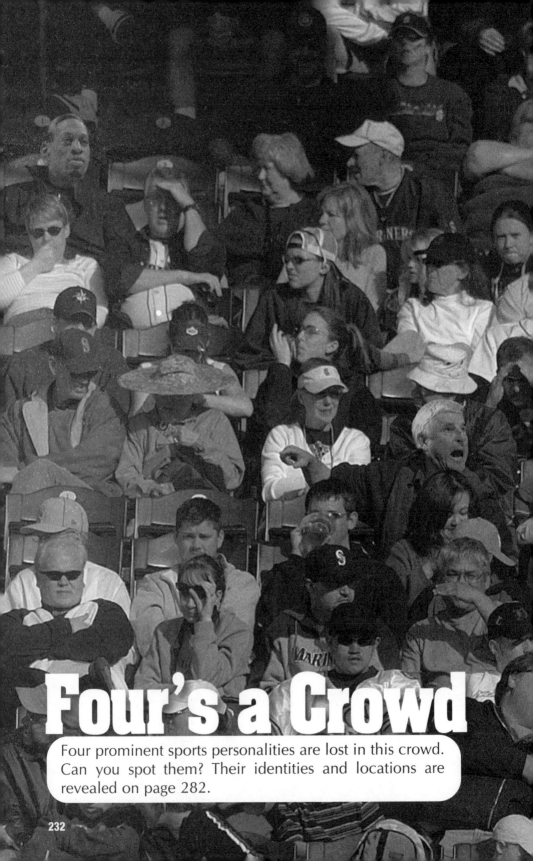

Four's a Crowd

Four prominent sports personalities are lost in this crowd. Can you spot them? Their identities and locations are revealed on page 282.

Mystery Guest

Can you name the athlete and the sport?

1 Despite my reputation, I'm really just a family man, as in several, as in you can't even keep things straight with a family tree diagram. Talk about confusing. One of my sons easily could ask, "Is that guy over there a boss or an uncle?" He's both. See what I mean?

2 My dad did what I did, and so do my two sons, at least sort of. One of them is pretty successful; the other is less so. The latter is the one who looks the most like I did.

3 My oldest daughter also has great drive as well as a strong business sense. She was the one who helped guide the younger boy as he grew up. I was on the road a lot in those days, so he was the one who stood up for her at her wedding.

4 About the other boy: Nobody who follows racing would ever refer to him as the "other boy." No telling how far that kid will go with his track record. Not to be, ahem, critical, but a championship would be a good fit for him right about now.

5 Numbers are important in my sport. I'm not trying to brag, but quite likely you saw my number, as a tribute to me, the last time you were behind the wheel. Or you'll probably see it before the end of the day. It's one of the crooked ones. My highfalutin son has a crooked number, too.

6 Not so fast. That doesn't mean we're crooked. During my career I never was accused of being crooked, but I sure was accused of being just about everything else. And the truth is, most of the time they were right. When competing, my style was *in* … tense. Yes, intense. We'll leave it at that. I have to choose my words carefully. And yes, I had a couple of nicknames. But if you ask me, words like "intimidator" and "ironhead" don't do me justice.

7 The second-most important number involving me is seven, which reflects the number of points championships I won. This might sound petty, but I cherish that number because I share it with another titan of our sport.

8 My career, and my life, came to a screeching halt in 2001. The news sent the NASCAR world into shock. Although I hailed from Carolina, it's probably inevitable that I will be linked forever to the birthplace of our sport, which is on the East Coast of another Southern state that also has West and South coastlines.

CHAPTER 14
ALL SPORTS

—This Day in— Sports

Each of the 10 dates we supply below matches up with three of the major sports events that follow. Test your memory and powers of deduction. Warning: There is one wild-card event that does not match up to any of the dates.

1. June 11

2. January 22

3. September 8

4. October 18

5. April 15

6. May 31

7. July 4

8. December 31

9. February 22

10. March 31

—Events—

◆ Glenn Anderson's goal with 2:24 remaining put the finishing touch on a 3-1 Edmonton victory over Philadelphia and wrapped up the Oilers' third Stanley Cup championship in four years. **(1987)**

◆ The New York Yankees stunned the baseball world by releasing 70-year-old manager Casey

Ben Hogan defied the odds and came back from a near-fatal car crash to win the U.S. Open in 1950.

DID YOU KNOW...

➤ That Gene Sarazen was the first player to win all four of the events that make up today's golf grand slam—the U.S. Open, British Open, PGA Championship and Masters? Sarazen won the first of two U.S. Opens in 1922, the first of three PGA titles in 1922, his only British Open in 1932 and his only Masters in 1935.

➤ That Jack Crawford almost beat out Don Budge for the distinction of completing the first single-season tennis Grand Slam? In 1933, five years before Budge made history, Crawford won the Australian Open, French Open and Wimbledon titles before losing to Fred Perry in the championship match of the U.S. Open.

➤ That Eddie Arcaro is the only jockey to ride two of horse racing's 11 Triple Crown winners? Arcaro made history on Whirlaway in 1941 and Citation in 1948.

John McEnroe won his first Wimbledon title in 1981 and ended Bjorn Borg's five-year reign.

Stengel five days after the Bronx Bombers had lost to Pittsburgh in Game 7 of the World Series. **(1960)**

◆ Edmonton scoring machine Wayne Gretzky set an NHL record when he notched his 61st goal of the season in the Oilers' 50th game. **(1982)**

◆ Michael Chang rallied to defeat Stefan Edberg, 6-1, 3-6, 4-6, 6-4, 6-2, in the final of the French Open, becoming the first American to win the Grand Slam event in 34 years. **(1989)**

◆ Joe Montana fired a 10-yard touchdown pass to John Taylor with 34 seconds remaining in Super Bowl 23 to give the San Francisco 49ers a 20-16 victory over Cincinnati at Miami's Joe Robbie Stadium. **(1989)**

◆ St. Louis first baseman Mark McGwire broke Roger Maris' 37-year-old single-season home run record when he drove a pitch from Chicago righthander Steve Trachsel over the left field fence at Busch Stadium for homer No. 62. **(1998)**

◆ Rod Laver recorded a four-set win over Australian Tony Roche in the final of the U.S. Open and became the first player to achieve two single-season Grand Slams. **(1969)**

◆ In a battle of unbeatens, Notre Dame edged past Alabama, 24-23, in a Sugar Bowl matchup that decided college football's national championship. **(1973)**

◆ Bob Feller, Cleveland's 20-year-old phenom righthander, became the youngest modern-era 20-game winner when he pitched the Indians to a 12-1 victory over the St. Louis Browns. **(1939)**

◆ Reggie Jackson, New York's Mr. October, blasted three

home runs on three swings and powered the Yankees to a World Series-clinching 8-4 victory over Los Angeles and their first championship since 1962. **(1977)**

◆ Richard Washington and Dave Meyers combined for 52 points, and UCLA gave retiring coach John Wooden his record 10th NCAA Tournament title with an inspired 92-85 championship game win over Kentucky at San Diego. **(1975)**

◆ American long jumper Bob Beamon soared an amazing 29 feet, 2½ inches and shattered the world record for the event by almost 2 feet during competition in the Summer Olympic Games at Mexico City. **(1968)**

◆ In a gala pageant attended by 61,808 fans and members of the 1927 championship team between games of a doubleheader at New York's Yankee Stadium, ironman Lou Gehrig, suffering from a debilitating disease that eventually would claim his life, bade an emotional farewell to baseball. **(1939)**

◆ Jackie Robinson became the first black player to set foot on a major league field in more than six decades when he made his long-anticipated debut as a first baseman in Brooklyn's 5-3 victory over the Boston Braves. **(1947)**

◆ Defying predictions he would never swing a golf club again, Ben Hogan completed his amazing comeback from a near-fatal 1949 automobile accident with a play-off-round 69 at the Merion Golf Club in Ardmore, Pa., earning a second U.S. Open championship. **(1950)**

◆ Nebraska running back Jeff Kinney rushed for 174 yards and scored four touchdowns to lead the top-ranked Cornhuskers to a 35-31 win over No. 2 Oklahoma in a Thanksgiving Day shootout billed as the "Game of the Century." **(1971)**

◆ Two expansion teams lost their major league debuts—the Arizona Diamondbacks, 9-2, to Colorado, and the Tampa Bay Devil Rays, 11-6, to Detroit. **(1998)**

◆ Fuzzy Zoeller dropped an 8-foot putt on the second hole of a sudden-death playoff to beat Tom Watson and Ed Sneed for the Masters championship. **(1979)**

◆ Moses Malone scored 24 points and grabbed 23 rebounds, and Julius Erving added 21 points as the Philadelphia 76ers earned their first NBA championship in 16 years with a 115-108 victory that closed out a four-game sweep of the Los Angeles Lakers. **(1983)**

◆ John McEnroe captured his first Wimbledon singles title and ended Bjorn

Roger Maris' 37-year-old home run mark was swept aside in 1998 by Mark McGwire and Sammy Sosa.

DID YOU KNOW...

➤That Louis Meyer became the first three-time winner of the Indianapolis 500 in 1936, 41 years before A.J. Foyt became the prestigious Memorial Day event's first four-time champion?

➤That IBF heavyweight champion *Larry Holmes*, bidding to match *Rocky Marciano*'s record of 49 consecutive professional victories, lost a stunning 15-round decision to light-heavyweight champion Michael Spinks on September 21, 1985—30 years to the day after Marciano had defeated another light-heavyweight champion, Archie Moore, for his 49th straight win?

Marciano

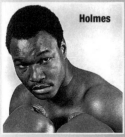

Holmes

Green Bay quarterback Bart Starr brought an emphatic end to the Packers' 1967 Ice Bowl victory over Dallas.

Borg's five-year championship reign with a 4-6, 7-6, 7-6, 6-4 victory at the All-England Tennis Club. **(1981)**

◆ New York lefthander Dave Righetti fired the first Yankee Stadium no-hitter since Don Larsen's 1956 World Series perfect game when he defeated the Boston Red Sox, 4-0. **(1983)**

◆ Four-time N.L. batting champion Roberto Clemente, leading an effort to help Nicaraguan earthquake victims, died when a cargo plane loaded with relief supplies crashed into the ocean shortly after takeoff from San Juan, Puerto Rico. **(1972)**

◆ Mark Johnson scored on a rebound to tie the game, and Mike Eruzione scored on a 30-foot slap shot to give the United States Olympic hockey team a 4-3 victory over the powerful Soviet Union and one of the most stunning upsets in sports history. **(1980)**

◆ George Foreman, a winner of 37 straight professional fights, sent unbeaten heavyweight champion Joe Frazier reeling to the canvas six times and recorded a shocking second-round technical knockout in a title bout at Kingston, Jamaica. **(1973)**

◆ A.J. Foyt posted his record-tying third Indianapolis 500 victory in a Coyote-Ford when Parnelli Jones' STP Oil Treatment Special broke down with three laps remaining. **(1967)**

◆ Quarterback Bart Starr dived into the end zone with 13 seconds remaining and gave Green Bay a 21-17 win over the Dallas Cowboys, ending the "Ice Bowl" and giving the Packers their third straight NFL championship. **(1967)**

◆ Lee Petty, surviving a three-day photo finish investigation, captured the inaugural Daytona 500 with an average speed of 135.42 mph. **(1959)**

◆ Notre Dame coach Knute Rockne died when the plane that was carrying him from Kansas City to Los Angeles crashed into a pasture near Bazaar, Kan. **(1931)**

◆ The San Francisco Giants defeated the Los Angeles Dodgers, 8-0, at Seals Stadium in the first West Coast game in baseball history. **(1958)**

◆ Seattle Slew, attempting to become the first undefeated Triple Crown champion in horse racing history, romped to a four-length win over Run Dusty Run in the 109th running of the Belmont Stakes. **(1977)**

◆ American speed skater Bonnie Blair set a world record (39.10) in the 500-meter sprint and captured the gold medal in the Winter Olympic Games at Calgary. **(1988)**

Championship Connections

Gene Tunney was one of the great pre-World War II heavyweight champions.

Warming up

Each of the following team or individual awards and championships were won in 10-year intervals (i.e., 1950, '60, '70, '80 and '90; 1923, '33, '43, '53 and '63). Identify the five-decade sequences, keeping in mind the final digit always is the same number.

1 Detroit Lions, Jack Nicklaus (Masters), Oakland Athletics, Mike Rozier (Heisman Trophy), Toronto Blue Jays.

2 Detroit Tigers, Detroit Red Wings, UCLA (college basketball), Foolish Pleasure (Kentucky Derby), Chicago Bears.

3 Ray Harroun (Indianapolis 500), Bill Tilden (Wimbledon), St. Louis Cardinals, Boston Bruins, Ben Hogan (U.S. Open).

DID YOU KNOW...

➤That *Dick Button*, the familiar television voice of Olympics figure skating, is credited with introducing the double axel and triple loop maneuvers as a double gold medalist in the 1940s and '50s? Button unveiled his daring double axel in the 1948 Winter Games at St. Moritz, Switzerland. He surprised viewers with the first triple loop in the 1952 Winter Games at Oslo, Norway.

➤That in the 1977-78 through 2003-04 college basketball postseasons, Duke compiled a 69-20 NCAA Tournament record while winning three championships? In that same span, Blue Devil football teams played two bowl games—both losses.

4 New York Yankees, Baltimore Bullets, Baltimore Colts, Arthur Ashe (U.S. Open), Kentucky (college basketball).

5 Pittsburgh Pirates, New York Knicks, Georgia (college football), Hale Irwin (U.S. Open), Juan Montoya (Indianapolis 500).

6 Philadelphia Eagles, California (college basketball), New York Mets, Tracy Austin (U.S. Open), Payne Stewart (PGA Championship).

7 New York Giants (baseball), Boston Celtics, Philadelphia Flyers, Georgetown (college basketball), Nebraska (college football).

8 Chicago White Sox, Gene Tunney (heavyweight champion), Don Budge (Wimbledon), Chicago Cardinals, Boston Celtics.

9 Arnold Palmer (Masters), Miami Dolphins, Herschel Walker (Heisman Trophy), Chicago Bulls, Ward Burton (Daytona 500).

10 Notre Dame (college football), Philadelphia Warriors, Green Bay Packers, Tony Dorsett (Heisman Trophy), New York Mets.

Getting serious

Identify the three missing names from each of the following groups. Hint: Each of the missing last names starts with the same letter.

1 Tiger Woods, winner of the U.S. Open in 2000, plays a round of golf with that year's National League Cy Young winner, NBA championship coach and NHL scoring champion.

2 Tom Watson, winner of the British Open in 1980, plays a round with that year's American League MVP, Wimbledon men's singles champion and Daytona 500 winner.

3 Nick Faldo, winner of the Masters in 1989, plays a round with that year's Wimbledon and U.S. Open women's singles champion, NHL MVP and National League batting champion.

4 Nick Price, winner of the PGA Championship in 1994, plays a round with that year's NFL rushing champion, Heisman Trophy winner and manager of the New York Yankees.

5 Gary Player, winner of the Masters in 1978, plays a round with that year's Triple Crown-winning jockey, U.S. Open men's singles champion and NFL rushing champion.

6 Jack Nicklaus, winner of the British Open in 1966, plays a round with that year's 27-game winner and Cy Young recipient, Wimbledon women's singles champion and coach of the Philadelphia Eagles.

7 Johnny Miller, winner of the U.S. Open in 1973, plays a round with that year's Daytona 500 king, coach of Notre Dame's college football championship team and American League Cy Young winner.

8 Steve Elkington, winner of the PGA Championship in 1995, plays a round with that year's NFL rushing champion, jockey of Kentucky Derby and Belmont winner Thunder Gulch and the Wimbledon and U.S. Open men's singles champion.

9 Billy Casper, winner of the U.S. Open in 1959, plays a round with that year's World Series-winning manager, NBA championship coach and shortstop of the American League pennant-winning team.

10 Fuzzy Zoeller, winner of the Masters in 1979, plays a round with that year's Heisman Trophy winner, NBA championship coach and manager of the American League-champion Baltimore Orioles.

Tiger Woods flashed his championship form when he teed off for the 2000 U.S. Open.

Hale Irwin, a three-time U.S. Open golf champion, has something in common with a former Dolphin.

Linkage

Warming up

1 What do Ray Harroun, Horton Smith, Rene Lacoste, Lee Petty and Jim Barnes have in common?

2 Pete Sampras is the all-time leader in men's Grand Slam singles titles, but he ranks a distant fourth in total singles championships. Name the three tennis players who rank ahead of him.

3 What does Hale Irwin, a three-time U.S. Open golf champion, have in common with Dick Anderson, a starting safety for three Miami Super Bowl teams and member of the "perfect" 17-0 Dolphins of 1972?

4 Annika Sorenstam, Suzie Whaley, Se Ri Pak and Michelle Wie all are successful golfers on the LPGA tour. What distinction do they hold with the great Babe Didrikson?

3 7 11 By the Numbers

The last 10 Triple Crown (baseball and horse racing) and single-season Grand Slam (golf and tennis) winners:

1988–Steffi Graf
Tennis

1978–Affirmed
Horse Racing

1977–Seattle Slew
Horse Racing

1973–Secretariat
Horse Racing

1969–Rod Laver
Tennis

1967–Carl Yastrzemski
Baseball

1966–Frank Robinson
Baseball

1962–Rod Laver
Tennis

1956–Mickey Mantle
Baseball

1948–Citation
Horse Racing

5 These hockey greats, one a Hall of Famer, will forever be linked. They played three seasons (1971-72 to 1973-74) in the WCJHL against each other, one season as baseball teammates for Houston's 1972 Rookie League team in the Appalachian League and 12 seasons as teammates for the four-time NHL-champion New York Islanders (1974-75 to 1985-86). They left the Islanders at the same time, played two more years for different teams and ended their 14-year careers after the 1987-88 season. Name them.

6 This Super Bowl-winning coach fondly remembers his childhood, when he shagged balls and hung out with such Naval Academy heavyweights as Joe Bellino and Roger Staubach, both Heisman Trophy winners. Name the NFL guru whose father coached at Navy for 33 years.

7 This NCAA basketball championship coach was the 1960, '61 and '62 teammate of two future pro basketball greats on a team that played in three straight NCAA Tournament title games, winning one. Name the illustrious threesome.

8 This pro football Hall of Famer, who holds the NFL's single-game scoring record of 40 points, surrendered two of Babe Ruth's record-breaking 60 home runs in 1927 while pitching for the St. Louis Browns. Name him.

9 This NCAA basketball championship coach played in the same Syracuse University backcourt with this former Detroit Pistons great from 1964-66. Name both.

10 Talk about power. Name the future home run champion and the fireballing Cy Young winner who played for the same University of Southern California baseball teams in 1982 and '83.

Getting serious

1 University of Missouri football coach Gary Pinkel, an All-American tight end at Kent State University, shared team captain duties in 1973 with this future pro football Hall of Famer. _____.

2 Former major league pitcher Darrell Jackson (1978-82) was a teammate of these two future Hall of Famers at Locke High School in the Watts section of Los Angeles in the early 1970s. _____, _____.

DID YOU KNOW...

➤That five-time U.S. Open singles champion Jimmy Connors was the first freshman to win the NCAA tennis championship? UCLA freshman Connors defeated Stanford's Roscoe Tanner in a four-set title match on June 19, 1971, at Notre Dame.

3 Former Detroit Lions and Washington Redskins offensive guard Dick Stanfel (1952-58) played on an undefeated 1951 University of San Francisco team that also featured these future Hall of Famers. _____,

_____, _____.

4 NFL Hall of Famer George Musso played football collegiately against these two future U.S. presidents.

_____, _____.

5 To say University of Georgia football coach Mark Richt was overshadowed during his playing career at the University of Miami is an understatement. He was a backup to this Hall of Fame quarterback from 1980-82 and a 1982 teammate of two other prominent quarterbacks—a future Cleveland Browns star and a future Heisman Trophy winner. _____,

_____, _____.

6 Former major league catcher Joe Garagiola never earned election to baseball's Hall of Fame, but two others who lived on Garagiola's childhood street, Elizabeth Avenue in the Hill section of St. Louis, did. One was Garagiola's neighbor and childhood friend; the other lived on Elizabeth Avenue after he had moved away.

_____, _____.

7 In 1918, first-year Notre Dame coach Knute Rockne utilized this fullback, who would go on to Hall of Fame glory as one of the great coaches in NFL history.

_____.

8 Connect the dots for these two pro football Hall of Famers. They were teammates at Jackson State in 1973 and '74. One held the NFL rushing record for 18 years. The other, his primary blocker for two seasons in college, shares an NFL

One of Knute Rockne's prize pupils went on to great coaching success.

This consistent Tom always is a contender, but seldom a champion.

longevity record for most seasons played with one team._____, _____.

9 The Nos. 1 and 2 coaches in career Division I basketball victories were both proteges of legendary Kansas coach Phog Allen. _____, _____.

10 This legendary Olympian and pro football Hall of Famer also was a major league teammate of such Hall of Famers as Christy Mathewson and Edd Roush. _____.

— Tom, Dick and — Harry

Warming up

1 Who is the last person named Tom, Dick or Harry to win a Masters green jacket?

2 Nobody in football history has run for more yards in a single season than this man, who looked at the football world through clear plastic goggles.

3 Tommy Milton won the Indianapolis 500 in 1921 and '23. Since then, only one Tom, Dick or Harry has won the Memorial Day event. Name him.

4 This four-time batting champion was only nine well-placed hits away from being a four-time .400 hitter. Name him.

5 Only four coaches in NFL history have taken two different teams to Super Bowls. One is a Tom, Dick or Harry. Name him.

6 Only two Heisman Trophy winners have been named Tom, Dick or Harry. Name them.

7 Who is the last coach not named Phil Jackson to lead a team to consecutive NBA championships?

8 This trainer, featured in a 2003 hit movie, helped choreograph Seabiscuit's stunning 1937 match race upset of Triple Crown winner War Admiral at Baltimore's Pimlico track. Name him.

9 This point guard was named Outstanding Player of the 1981 NCAA Tournament after leading his team to the championship.

10 This no-nonsense Hit Man has held world titles as a welterweight, junior middleweight, middleweight and light heavyweight boxer. Name him.

Getting serious

1 These two Toms both coached two Super Bowl champions.

2 A golf pioneer, this Harry won a record six British Open titles.

3 This former baseball Harry was best remembered for his colorful nickname: Suitcase.

4 This Dick coached an NBA franchise to its only championship.

5 In 1995, these two Toms, the coach and his Heisman runner-up quarterback, led their team to college football's national championship.

6 This Dick coached the Toronto Maple Leafs to a Stanley Cup title in 1932 and Montreal to titles in 1944, '46 and '53.

7 This Hall of Fame Harry, a baseball pioneer, is considered the "Father of the Professional Game" and organizer of the great Cincinnati Red Stockings team of 1869.

8 This 1973 PGA Rookie of the Year has ranked consistently among leading money winners during his career but has only one major title to his credit. Name the Tom whose biggest victory was the 1992 U.S. Open.

9 This Dick, a three-time PBA Bowler of the Year, won 30 titles in his four-decade career and paved the way for his equally successful son.

10 Holy Cow! This baseball Harry brought life to the broadcast booths in St. Louis, Oakland and Chicago during his Hall of Fame career.

Animal Magnetism

Warming up

1 Name the horse racing Triple Crown winner whose name refers to an animal other than a horse.

2 Birds show up in the nicknames of seven current NFL and NBA teams. How many can you name?

3 If the Golden Jet, the Golden Palomino and the Golden Bear got together for a round of golf, who probably would win?

3 17 7 By the Numbers

Golfers who have won the most career Masters, U.S. Open, British Open and PGA Championship titles through 2003:

Jack Nicklaus..............18
Walter Hagen 11
Ben Hogan................... 9
Gary Player................. 9
Tom Watson................. 8
Tiger Woods 8
Bobby Jones................ 7
Arnold Palmer 7
Gene Sarazen.............. 7
Sam Snead................. 7
Harry Vardon 7

4 If the Thundering Herd played a college basketball game against the Rattlers, what two Division I schools would be represented?

5 This Memphis State guard scored 29 points in an NCAA Tournament championship game loss to a Bill Walton-led UCLA team. Name the Tiger with a birdlike name.

6 When the combatants dramatically entered Houston's Astrodome for the 1973 Battle of the Sexes tennis match, Bobby Riggs and Billie Jean King exchanged symbolic gifts. What did King give Riggs?

7 Name the former football coach at Springfield (Mass.), the University of Chicago and College of the Pacific who held the NCAA record for college victories until 1981.

8 One of the eight Chicago White Sox players banned from baseball for their part in "fixing" the 1919 World Series had a name that reflected an animal. Name him.

9 These two "Geese" never got to face each other, one as a hitter and the other as a pitcher, but they both did

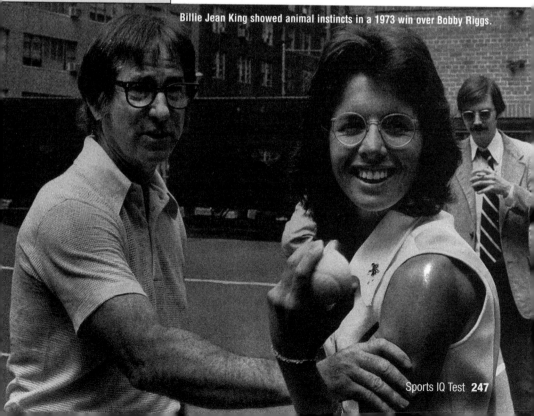

Billie Jean King showed animal instincts in a 1973 win over Bobby Riggs.

justice to their colorful nickname. One is in the baseball Hall of Fame, the other could be someday. Name them.

10 This talented Montreal goalie was co-winner of the Vezina Trophy four times in five years from 1977-81, but he never won it outright. Name him.

Getting serious

1 Combine baseball's first rookie MVP with a graceful waterfowl, and you get a Super Bowl MVP.

2 Combine half of broadcaster Keith Jackson's favorite two-word expression with a major, sports-friendly television network, and get this sly Hall of Fame second baseman.

3 Combine this major college mascot named Mike with a place you might go to commune with nature, and you get a two-time U.S. Open golf champion.

4 An ichthyologist who studies these bewhiskered creatures might combine one with a bow-and-arrow-toting outdoorsman to get this Hall of Fame pitcher.

5 This big, furry, omnivorous carnivore, when combined with a longtime *Today Show* host, gives you a college football legend.

6 Combine the inventor of the elevator, a three-time league MVP for the Boston Celtics and what happens when you put words to music. The result is an NBA guard who played 12 seasons in the 1970s and '80s and averaged 18 points per game.

7 Combine this Easter peeper with boxing's best-known Hit Man, and you have this legendary basketball broadcaster.

8 The Big Unit is no canine carnivore, but other than that difference, only 10 inches and 5 or 6 mph separates him from this current Philadelphia pitcher.

9 Combine a *Monday Night Football* comedian with Elmer, Jim, Harry and a little Irish magic and you get this legendary college football group.

10 Combine the nickname of Arizona's cutting-edge baseball facility with a northern-region deer that sprouts elaborate headgear, and you get the former pitcher whose wild pitch ended the 1972 National League Championship Series.

Famous Numbers

Warming up

1 What was the official time recorded by Roger Bannister when he broke the 4-minute mile in 1954?

2 How many times did George Foreman knock Joe Frazier to the canvas before earning a second-round technical knockout in the January 1973 heavyweight championship fight at Kingston, Jamaica?

3 What did golfer Chip Beck do in the third round of the 1991 Las Vegas Invitational to put his name in the PGA record book alongside Al Geiberger?

4 After Joe DiMaggio's record 56-game hitting streak was stopped by the Cleveland Indians in 1941, the Yankee Clipper immediately started another streak. How many games did it last?

5 What was the final score of the Soviet Union's controversial victory over the United States in the gold medal basketball game at the 1972 Olympic Games at Munich?

6 What was the halftime score of the 1988 NCAA Tournament championship game between Big Eight Conference rivals Kansas and Oklahoma?

7 What was the final score of Super Bowl I—Green Bay's victory over Kansas City?

8 The incredible final-play, five-lateral kickoff runback that gave the University of California a shocking 25-20 victory over Stanford in 1982 covered how many yards—officially?

9 How many laps does the winner of the Daytona 500 have to cover?

10 How many consecutive 400-meter hurdles races did Edwin Moses win before he finally was upset by Danny Harris in 1987?

Getting serious

Identify the sports item, record or event associated with the following numbers:

1. 29 feet, 2½ inches

2. 53⅓ yards

3. 37 feet

4. 6 feet X 3½ feet

5. 222-0

6. 4 inches deep, 4¼ inches wide

7. 78 feet X 27 feet

8. 13½ inches, 25 pounds

9. 483 feet

10. 18 feet, 6 inches

——It Was a Very Good Year——

Warming up

We supply the Heisman Trophy winners, college basketball championship coaches, Kentucky Derby winners, Indianapolis 500 winners, Masters champions and Wimbledon singles champions. You provide the year.

1. Andre Agassi, Fred Couples, Lil E. Tee, Al Unser Jr., Mike Krzyzewski, Gino Torretta.

2. Earl Campbell, A.J. Foyt, Bjorn Borg, Al McGuire, Tom Watson, Seattle Slew.

3. Citation, Louise Brough, Mauri Rose, Claude Harmon, Doak Walker, Adolph Rupp.

Bjorn Borg (left) captured one of his five Wimbledon titles the same year A.J. Foyt (right) won one of his four Indianapolis 500 races.

4. Arie Luyendyk, Unbridled, Nick Faldo, Jerry Tarkanian, Martina Navratilova, Ty Detmer.

5. Bob Knight, Tony Dorsett, Chris Evert, Ray Floyd, Johnny Rutherford, Bold Forbes.

6. Riva Ridge, Stan Smith, Jack Nicklaus, Mark Donohue, Johnny Rodgers, John Wooden.

7. Boris Becker, Rollie Massimino, Spend A Buck, Bo Jackson, Bernhard Langer, Danny Sullivan.

8. Jack Nicklaus, Steve Spurrier, Billie Jean King, Kauai King, Don Haskins, Graham Hill.

9. Venus Williams, Fusaichi Pegusus, Chris Weinke, Vijay Singh, Tom Izzo, Juan Montoya.

10. George Rogers, Evonne Goolagong, Genuine Risk, Denny Crum, Johnny Rutherford, Seve Ballesteros.

Getting serious

1 If you add the last two digits of the inaugural Indianapolis 500 and the first Masters golf tournament years, you will come up with a year in which only two of the majors—the U.S. Open in tennis and PGA Championship in golf—were played.

2 Add the blazing final-round score posted by Johnny Miller in his come-from-behind 1973 U.S. Open victory to Secretariat's victory margin (in lengths) at the 1973 Belmont Stakes, and you come up with the year Arkansas won its first college basketball championship.

3 Subtract the round in which Buster Douglas knocked out heavyweight champion Mike Tyson in 1990 from the last two digits of Dean Smith's record NCAA basketball coaching win total, and you get the year former heavyweight champion Rocky Marciano died in a plane crash.

4 Add the total points scored in Super Bowl 38 to the first two digits of the total laps needed to finish the Indianapolis 500, and you get the year in which Alabama coach Bear Bryant posted his then-record 315th victory.

5 Subtract the number of gold medals won by Mark Spitz in the 1972 Summer Olympic Games from the yardage covered by Doug Flutie's dramatic game-winning touch-down pass in 1984 against Miami, and you get the year Eddie Arcaro rode Whirlaway to a horse racing Triple Crown.

6 Multiply Tracy Austin's age when she won the 1979 U.S. Open singles title by the number of sets played in the Billie Jean King-Bobby Riggs "Battle of the Sexes" tennis match of 1973, and you get the year in which London hosted the Summer Olympic Games for the second time.

7 Add the total score from the Thanksgiving Day showdown between Oklahoma and Nebraska in 1971 to the record number of Masters tournaments won by Jack Nicklaus, and you get the year in which the Soviet Union snapped the United States' 63-game Olympic basketball winning streak.

8 Multiply the number of horse racing Triple Crown winners by the number of male golfers who have won all four major championships in their career, and you get the year two-time-defending Indianapolis 500 winner Bill Vukovich died in a fiery crash during the Memorial Day event.

Tracy Austin became the youngest player to win a U.S. Open singles title in 1979.

9 Add the NCAA-record basketball winning streak compiled by UCLA to the number of PGA Championships won by Tom Watson, and you get the year Canadian sprinter Ben Johnson was sent home from the Olympic Games in disgrace.

10 Multiply the total goals scored in the United States' shocking 1980 Olympic victory over the Soviet Union by the number of championships won by John Wooden-coached UCLA teams, and you get the year Green Bay Packers coaching legend Vince Lombardi died.

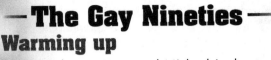

—The Gay Nineties—
Warming up

1 Three players not named Michael Jordan won NBA scoring titles in the 1990s. Name them.

2 Name the coach who lost Super Bowls with different teams in the 1990s—on January 28, 1990, and January 31, 1999.

3 Name the only American League player to win two batting titles in the 1990s.

4 Three horses won the first two legs of the Triple Crown in the 1990s, only to lose in the Belmont Stakes. Name two of them.

5 What NHL player scored the most goals in the 1990s—and, within 30, how many?

6 Mia Hamm dominated women's soccer in the 1990s, helping the United States to two World Cup championships and becoming the leading all-time scorer in international competition. What college did Hamm lead to four national titles?

7 Name the golfer who won two U.S. Open titles in the 1990s and finished second twice—before dying in a tragic accident.

8 Hank Gathers, the national college basketball scoring and rebounding champion for Loyola Marymount in 1988-89, collapsed and died during a March 4, 1990, game in Los Angeles. Name the teammate who went on to lead the nation with a 35.3 scoring average that season.

9 Only four men won U.S. Open tennis titles in the 1990s. Pete Sampras led the way with four. Name two of the other three.

10 What Division I-A college football team recorded the most victories in the 1990s?

Michigan's Desmond Howard was a Heisman Trophy winner in the 1990s.

Getting serious

We supply the yearly 1990s winners in chronological order. You supply the missing piece to the puzzle.

1 Daytona 500: Derrike Cope, Ernie Ivan, Davey Allison, Dale Jarrett, Sterling Marlin, Sterling Marlin, Dale Jarrett, _____, Dale Earnhardt, Jeff Gordon.

2 Stanley Cup champions: Edmonton, Pittsburgh, Pittsburgh, _____, N.Y. Rangers, New Jersey, Colorado, Detroit, Detroit, Dallas.

3 Women's U.S. Open tennis: Gabriela Sabatini, Monica Seles, Monica Seles, Steffi Graf, Arantxa Sanchez Vicario, Steffi Graf, Steffi Graf, _____, Lindsay Davenport, Serena Williams.

4 NBA champions: _____, Chicago, Chicago, Chicago, Houston, Houston, Chicago, Chicago, Chicago, San Antonio.

5 Masters golf tournament: Nick Faldo, Ian Woosnam, Fred Couples, Bernhard Langer, Jose Maria Olazabal, Ben Crenshaw, Nick Faldo, _____, Mark O'Meara, Jose Maria Olazabal.

6 World Series: Cincinnati, Minnesota, Toronto, Toronto, _____, Atlanta, N.Y. Yankees, Florida, N.Y. Yankees, N.Y. Yankees.

7 Kentucky Derby: Unbridled, Strike the Gold, Lil E. Tee, Sea Hero, Go For Gin, Thunder Gulch, Grindstone, Silver Charm, Real Quiet, _____.

8 NCAA basketball champions: UNLV, Duke, Duke, North Carolina, Arkansas, _____, Kentucky, Arizona, Kentucky, Connecticut.

9 Indianapolis 500: Arie Luyendyk, _____, Al Unser Jr., Emerson Fittipaldi, Al Unser Jr., Jacques Villeneuve, Buddy Lazier, Arie Luyendyk, Eddie Cheever Jr., Kenny Brack.

10 Heisman Trophy winners: Ty Detmer, Desmond Howard, Gino Torretta, Charlie Ward, Rashaan Salaam, Eddie George, Danny Wuerffel, Charles Woodson, _____, Ron Dayne.

When national scoring champ Hank Gathers collapsed and died during a 1990 game, a Loyola Marymount teammate went on to claim his title.

——Second Thoughts

Warming up

1 Don Budge became the first player to post a one-season tennis grand slam when he won the 1938 Australian Open, French Open, Wimbledon and U.S. Open tennis titles. Name the second tennis grand slammer.

2 Jack Nicklaus holds the record with 18 victories in the golf grand slam: the Masters, U.S. Open, British Open and PGA Championship. Who holds the record for second-place finishes in those events?

3 Former Montreal great Maurice "Rocket" Richard became the first player in NHL history to score 50 goals in a season in 1944-45. Who was the second player to accomplish that feat—16 years later?

4 Who was the second player to score 20,000 points in his NBA career?

5 Name the first team to finish "second best" in two Super Bowls.

6 Richard Petty holds the record with seven Daytona 500 victories. Who ranks second?

7 When Secretariat completed his Triple Crown romp with a 31-length victory in the 1973 Belmont Stakes, what horse finished second?

8 Beattie Feathers and Cliff Battles are best remembered for their NFL firsts. Feathers was the league's first 1,000-yard rusher in 1934. Battles posted its first 200-yard game in 1933. Name the player who became the second to perform both of those feats.

Chicago right fielder Sammy Sosa always will be remembered for his heroic second-best effort.

9 Former New York Yankees star Babe Ruth was the first 30- , 40- , 50- and 60-homer player in major league baseball. Who was the second to reach 40 home runs?

10 Name the second player to score 50 or more points in a regular-season NBA game.

Getting serious

The following names should trigger flashbacks of memorable second-place finishes. See if you can identify the reasons these non-winners remain locked in our sports conscious.

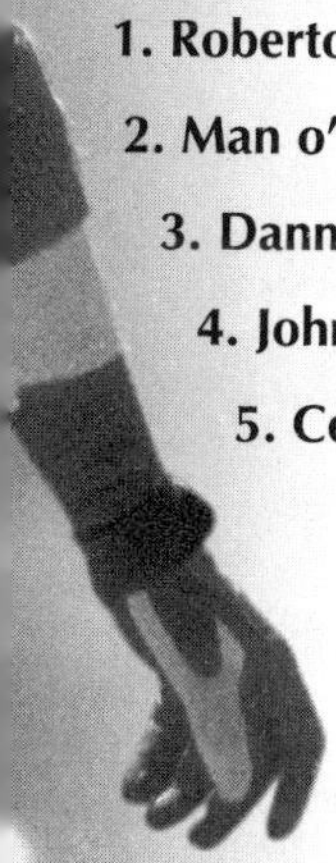

1. Roberto De Vicenzo

2. Man o' War

3. Danny Cater, .290

4. John Landy

5. Cesar Tovar

6. Monk Meyer, Army

7. Alydar

8. Sammy Sosa

9. Finland

10. Georgetown

Chapter 14 answers begin on page 282.

MYSTERY GUESTS

Page 6: Charles Barkley

Page 22: Joe Torre

Page 40: George Brett

Page 58: Tony Stewart

Page 74: Joe Montana

Page 94: Ken Griffey Jr.

Page 110: Bear Bryant

Page 128: Mike Krzyzewski

Page 150: Brett Favre

Page 170: Tim Duncan

Page 184: John Elway

Page 200: Brett Hull

Page 212: Wayne Gretzky

Page 234: Dale Earnhardt

THE ALL-AMERICAN SPORTS IQ TEST
ANSWERS

Where's Yogi?

Chapter 1: Baseball

FIRST TO LAST (WARMING UP): 1. The 1969 Kansas City Royals. 2. The 1993 Colorado Rockies. 3. The 1961 Los Angeles Angels. 4. The 1969 Montreal Expos. 5. The 1993 Florida Marlins. 6. The 1962 Houston Colt .45s. 7. The 1977 Toronto Blue Jays. 8. The 1998 Tampa Bay Devil Rays. 9. The 1962 New York Mets. 10. The 1969 San Diego Padres. 11. The 1998 Arizona Diamondbacks. 12. The 1961 Washington Senators. 13. The 1977 Seattle Mariners. 14. The 1969 Seattle Pilots.

FIRST TO LAST (GETTING SERIOUS): 1. Don Newcombe, the first Cy Young winner. 2. Roberto Clemente, who finished his career with exactly 3,000 hits. 3. Joe Pignatano. 4. Boston's Ted Williams. 5. Pumpsie Green. 6. Mike Shannon. 7. Walter Johnson. 8. The Washington Senators became the Texas Rangers in 1972. 9. Shortstop. 10. Steve Carlton.

THE DRAMA CLUB (WARMING UP): 1. Casey Stengel. 2. Chicago's Harold Baines. 3. Joe Morgan. 4. New York Yankees outfielder Tommy Henrich off Brooklyn's Don Newcombe. 5. Minnesota's Harmon Killebrew and Baltimore's Frank Robinson. 6. Philadelphia's Mike Schmidt against Pittsburgh. 7. Boston's Wade Boggs and Kansas City's Bo Jackson. 8. Jack Reed. 9. Bob Robertson, Pirates, October 3, 1971; George Brett, Royals, October 6, 1978; Adam Kennedy, Angels, October 13, 2002. 10. Dick Drago.

Answers

THE DRAMA CLUB (GETTING SERIOUS): 1. Mitch Williams, Phillies, 1993. 2. Ralph Terry, Yankees, 1960. 3. Catfish Hunter, Athletics, 1967. 4. Mike Torrez, Red Sox, 1978. 5. Claude Passeau, Cubs, 1941. 6. Tom Niedenfuer, Dodgers, 1985. 7. Dick Radatz, Red Sox, 1964. 8. Ralph Branca, Dodgers, 1951. 9. Al Downing, Dodgers, 1974. 10. Dock Ellis, Pirates, 1971. 11. Dennis Eckersley, Athletics, 1988. 12. Tracy Stallard, Red Sox, 1961. 13. Frank Sullivan, Red Sox, 1955. 14. Donnie Moore, Angels, 1986. 15. Steve Rogers, Expos, 1981. 16. Steve Trachsel, Cubs, 1998. 17. Burt Hooton, Elias Sosa, Charlie Hough, Dodgers, 1977. 18. Ted Gray, Tigers, 1950. 19. Chan Ho Park, Dodgers, 2001. 20. Mark Littell, Royals, 1976.

AND THE WINNER IS... (WARMING UP): 1. St. Louis' Bob Gibson and Detroit's Denny McLain were double winners in 1968. 2. Detroit's Charlie Gehringer in 1937, Yankee Joe Gordon in 1942 and Chicago's Nellie Fox in 1959. 3. Gaylord Perry was 24-16 in 1972 for Cleveland. 4. Eric Karros, Mike Piazza, Raul Mondesi, Hideo Nomo and Todd Hollandsworth were consecutive winners for the Dodgers. 5. Boston's Fred Lynn in 1975 and Seattle's Ichiro Suzuki in 2001. 6. Bobby Cox won the award in 1985 with Toronto and 1991 with Atlanta; Tony La Russa won with the Chicago White Sox in 1983, Oakland in 1988 and '92 and St. Louis in 2002. 7. Roger Maris batted .269 in 1961, the same season he hit his record 61 home runs. 8. Frank Robinson. 9. Don Baylor and Joe Torre. 10. The Dodgers have won 9, the Braves 7.

AND THE WINNER IS... (GETTING SERIOUS): 29 A.L. MVPs—Joe DiMaggio, Dick Allen, Al Rosen or Alex Rodriguez, Rod Carew or Roger Clemens, Cal Ripken, Roger Maris, Mickey Mantle, Mo Vaughn, Vida Blue, Boog Powell, Phil Rizzuto, Rollie Fingers, Frank Robinson, Rickey Henderson, Hal Newhouser, Nellie Fox, Fred Lynn, Lefty Grove or Lou Gehrig, George Brett or George Bell, Brooks Robinson, Reggie Jackson, Jackie Jensen, Jose Canseco, Carl Yastrzemski, Yogi Berra, Bobby Shantz, Spud Chandler, Charlie Gehringer, George Brett or George Bell.

33 N.L. MVPs—Jackie Robinson, Ryne Sandberg, Stan Musial, Mike Schmidt, Sammy Sosa, Sandy Koufax, Ken Boyer, Barry Bonds, Bob Elliott, Ernie Banks, Bob Gibson, George Foster, Frank Frisch, Frank Robinson, Roberto Clemente or Roy Campanella, Chipper Jones, Joe Medwick or Joe Morgan, Marty Marion, Mort Cooper, Carl Hubbell, Hank Aaron, Andre Dawson, Dizzy Dean, Dave Parker, Pete Rose, Roberto Clemente or Roy Campanella, Chuck Klein, Kevin Mitchell, Maury Wills, Willie Stargell, Steve Garvey, Gabby Hartnett, Hank Sauer.

26 Cy Young winners—Randy Johnson or Randy Jones, John Denny, Don Drysdale or Doug Drabek, Don Drysdale or Doug Drabek, Denny McLain, Mike Marshall or Mike McCormick, Mark Davis, Dennis Eckersley, Early Wynn, Whitey Ford, Ferguson Jenkins, Jim Palmer or Jim Perry, Pedro Martinez, Mike Marshall or Mike McCormick, Mike Flanagan, Fernando Valenzuela or Frank Viola, Vida Blue, Bob Gibson, Greg Maddux, Mike Scott, Steve Stone, Steve Bedrosian, Bob Welch, Warren Spahn, Steve Carlton, Catfish Hunter.

ROOKIE WATCH (WARMING UP): 1. Jackie Robinson. 2. Bob Grim. 3. Grover Cleveland Alexander. 4. Jerry Grote, Sonny Jackson, Joe Morgan, Rusty Staub and Jim Wynn. 5. Detroit's Mark Fidrych. 6. Oakland's Rickey Henderson stole 130 bases in 1982; St. Louis' Lou Brock stole 118 in 1974; Los Angeles' Maury Wills stole 104 in 1962. 7. Howard broke up Rohr's debut no-hit bid with a two-out, full-count, opposite-field, ninth-inning single. 8. Mark McGwire hit 49 home runs for the Oakland A's in 1987; Wally Berger of the Boston Braves set the N.L. record with 38 in 1930 and was matched in 1956 by Cincinnati's Frank Robinson. 9. Ralph Houk, New York Yankees, 1961. 10. J.D. Drew.

ROOKIE WATCH (GETTING SERIOUS): 1B Willie McCovey, Orlando Cepeda, Eddie Murray; 2B Jackie Robinson, Rod Carew; 3B Pete Rose; SS Luis Aparicio, Cal Ripken; C Johnny Bench, Carlton Fisk; OF Willie Mays, Frank Robinson, Billy Williams; P Tom Seaver.

COMMON LINKS (WARMING UP): 1. Oakland's Henderson was the victim when 42-year-old Texas Rangers righthander Ryan notched his unprecedented 5,000th career strikeout on August 22, 1989. 2. On May 1, 1991, Ryan again grabbed the spotlight by pitching his record seventh no-hitter, beating Toronto, 3-0. Ryan's performance took some of the luster away from Henderson, who stole his record-breaking 939th base on the same day. Henderson's milestone was achieved in a game against the New York Yankees. 3. Oakland's Stewart and Los Angeles' Valenzuela became the first pitchers to throw no-hitters on the same day—June 29, 1990. First Stewart shut out the Blue Jays at Toronto; then Valenzuela shut down St. Louis in a night game at Dodger Stadium. 4. In games played on opposite coasts on August 4, 1985, Tom Seaver posted his 300th career win with a 4-1 victory at New York, and California's Rod Carew collected his 3,000th career hit in a 6-5 victory over the Minnesota Twins at Anaheim Stadium. 5. Joel Youngblood performed an unprecedented feat on August 4, 1982, when he collected hits for two different teams playing games in different cities. Youngblood collected his hits off Jenkins and Carlton, two future Hall of Famers. He singled off Jenkins as a member of the New York Mets in a game at Chicago; after finding out in mid-game about his trade to Montreal, he flew to Philadelphia and singled in his only plate appearance against Carlton. 6. Jeff Maier, a 12-year-old Yankees fan, changed the course of the 1996 ALCS when he reached over the wall and grabbed a Game 1 fly ball by New York shortstop Jeter that might have been caught by Orioles outfielder Tarasco. The ball was ruled a game-tying home run (rather than interference as the Orioles argued) and the Yankees went on to win on an 11th-inning Bernie Williams home run. 7. Game 5 of the 1985 NLCS ended dramatically when veteran St. Louis shortstop Ozzie Smith hit his first-ever lefthanded home run off Dodgers closer Niedenfuer to break a 2-2 tie. Game 6 also ended with ninth-inning dramatics—a three-run Clark home run off Niedenfuer that gave the Cardinals a 7-5 victory and a berth in the World Series. 8. The only players in baseball history to hit home runs in eight consecutive games. Pittsburgh's Long set the record in 1956, Yankees star Mattingly tied it in 1987 and Seattle's Griffey joined the elite club in 1993.

COMMON LINKS (GETTING SERIOUS): 1. The five future Hall of Famers who were consecutive Carl Hubbell strikeout victims in the 1934 All-Star Game. 2. Uniform No. 20s that have been retired. 3. All were Rookie of the Year winners for the Boston, Milwaukee or Atlanta Braves. 4. Members of baseball's exclusive 40-40 club. 5. Chicago White Sox players who have won A.L. MVP awards. 6. Managers who have led the New York Mets to N.L. pennants. 7. The 1969 opening day lineup for the expansion Montreal Expos. 8. A.L. batting champions in the 1990s. 9. The World Series-losing managers each year of the 1980s. 10. Players who have hit walk-off All-Star Game home runs.

NUMBER, PLEASE (WARMING UP): 1. Ron Santo was 10, Ernie Banks 14, Billy Williams 26. 2. Pee Wee Reese was 1, Don Sutton 20, Sandy Koufax 32. 3. Roger Maris was 9, Thurman Munson 15, Reggie Jackson 44. 4. Dale Murphy was 3, Warren Spahn 21, Hank Aaron 44. 5. Stan Musial was 6, Ken Boyer 14, Bob Gibson 45. 6. Paul Molitor was 4, Robin Yount 19, Rollie Fingers 34. 7. Bobby Doerr was 1, Carl Yastrzemski 8, Ted Williams 9. 8. Brooks Robinson was 5, Jim Palmer 22, Eddie Murray 33. 9. Ralph Kiner was 4, Willie Stargell 8, Roberto Clemente 21. 10. Willie Mays was 24, Juan Marichal 27, Willie McCovey 44. 11. Tony Oliva was 6, Kent Hrbek 14, Kirby Puckett 34. 12. George Brett was 5, Dick Howser 10, Frank White 20.

NUMBER, PLEASE (GETTING SERIOUS): 1. The progression of baseball's home run record in the 1900s. 2. Rickey Henderson's stolen base totals in the 1980s. 3. Sammy Sosa's season home run totals from 1998-2003. 4. Sandy Koufax's ERAs during his record five straight N.L.-leading seasons from 1962-66. 5. The career record for hits, home runs, RBIs, wins and saves. 6. Years for baseball's last .400 hitters, 30-game winners. 7. The single-season records for homers, triples, doubles and singles. 8. The season records posted by the 1906 Cubs, 1954 Indians, 1998 Yankees and 2001 Mariners. 9. The height, weight and uniform number of Bill Veeck midget Eddie Gaedel in his one major league appearance. 10. The totals posted by Joe DiMaggio during his 56-game hitting streak in 1941.

GLOVE CONNECTIONS (WARMING UP): 1. Rusty Staub. 2. Tommy John. 3. Charlie Hough. 4. Dennis Eckersley. 5. Phil Niekro. 6. Ted Lyons and Lefty Grove. 7. Dennis Martinez and Mike Morgan. 8. Jim Parque. 9. Satchel Paige. 10. Leo Durocher.

GLOVE CONNECTIONS (GETTING SERIOUS): 1. New York Mets. 2. Kansas City Royals. 3. Philadelphia A's. 4. Baltimore Orioles. 5. Texas Rangers. 6. Chicago White Sox. 7. San Francisco Giants. 8. Philadelphia Phillies. 9. New York Mets. 10. Boston Red Sox.

SECONDARY CONCERNS (WARMING UP): 1. Hack Wilson, Chicago Cubs, 1930. 2. Chuck Klein, Philadelphia Phillies, 1936. 3. Willard Brown, St. Louis Browns, 1947. 4. Orlando Cepeda. 5. Joe DiMaggio, New York Yankees, 1939, '41, '47. 6. Shortstop Mark Koenig. 7. Mike Davis. 8. Oakland A's, 2001. 9. Don Wilson. 10. Boston Red Sox.

SECONDARY CONCERNS (GETTING SERIOUS): 1. These are the second-place homer totals in the four record seasons since 1927. 2. World Series runners-up in the 21st century. 3. All are Hall of Fame second basemen. 4. Years the Dodgers finished second to the Yankees in World Series play. 5. Aaron and Abbey are the second player and pitcher listed in the Baseball Encyclopedia. 6. The players who rank second all-time in hits, homers, wins and saves. 7. Second stops for franchises that have moved twice. 8. The second Hall of Fame class. 9. Opening day second basemen for N.L. expansion teams. 10. The name of the second baseman in the "Who's on First?" Abbott and Costello comedy routine.

INITIAL REACTION (WARMING UP): 1. E.P. (Eddie Plank, Athletics). 2. B.F. (Bob Feller, Indians). 3. S.C. (Steve Carlton, Phillies). 4. W.S. (Warren Spahn, Braves). 5 P.S. (Paul Splittorff, Royals). 6. C.R. (Charlie Root, Cubs). 7. E.R. (Eppa Rixey, Reds). 8. H.D. (Hooks Dauss, Tigers). 9. J.S. (Jim Slaton, Brewers). 10. R.C. and C.Y. (Roger Clemens and Cy Young, Red Sox). 11. C.H. (Charlie Hough, Senators/Rangers). 12. B.G. (Bob Gibson, Cardinals). 13. T.S. (Tom Seaver, Mets). 14. R.J. (Randy Johnson, Mariners). 15. D.S. (Don Sutton, Dodgers). 16. S.R. (Steve Rogers, Expos). 17. C.F. (Chuck Finley, Angels). 18. C.M. (Christy Mathewson, Giants). 19. W.F. (Whitey Ford, Yankees). 20. J.N. (Joe Niekro, Astros). 21. W.C. (Wilbur Cooper, Pirates). 22. W.J. (Walter Johnson, Senators/Twins). 23. D.S. (Dave Stieb, Blue Jays). 24. E.S. (Eric Show, Padres). 25. T.L. (Ted Lyons, White Sox). 26. J.P. (Jim Palmer, Browns/Orioles).

INITIAL REACTION (GETTING SERIOUS): 1. J.G. (Juan Gonzalez, Rangers). 2. J.B. (Johnny Bench, Reds). 3. J.B. (Jeff Bagwell, Astros). 4. D.S. (Duke Snider, Dodgers). 5. H.A. (Hank Aaron, Braves). 6. V.G. (Vladimir Guerrero, Expos). 7. F.T. (Frank Thomas, White Sox). 8. W.M. (Willie Mays, Giants). 9. J.T. (Jim Thome, Indians). 10. L.G. (Luis Gonzalez, Diamondbacks). 11. D.S. (Darryl Strawberry, Mets). 12. R.Y. (Robin Yount, Brewers). 13. T.W. (Ted Williams, Red Sox). 14. N.C. (Nate Colbert, Padres). 15. W.S. (Willie Stargell, Pirates). 16. B.R. (Babe Ruth, Yankees). 17. M.S. (Mike Schmidt, Phillies). 18. H.K. (Harmon Killebrew, Senators/Twins). 19. A.K. (Al Kaline, Tigers). 20. L.W. (Larry Walker, Rockies). 21. G.B. (George Brett, Royals). 22. C.R. (Cal Ripken, Browns/Orioles). 23. D.L. (Derrek Lee, Marlins). 24. M.M. (Mark McGwire, A's). 25. S.S. (Sammy Sosa, Cubs). 26. C.D. (Carlos Delgado, Blue Jays). 27. T.S. (Tim Salmon, Angels). 28. F.M. (Fred McGriff, Devil Rays). 29. K.G. (Ken Griffey, Mariners). 30. S.M. (Stan Musial, Cardinals).

Chapter 2: College Mascots

1. Florida State, Chief Osceola. 2. DePaul, Blue Demon. 3. Alabama's Elephant, Big Al. 4. Dayton, Rudy Flyer. 5. Clemson, Howard's Rock. 6. Auburn's War Eagle, Tiger. 7. Arizona, Wilbur Wildcat. 8. Florida, Florida Gator. 9. Colorado, Ralphie. 10. Syracuse, Otto Orange. 11. Duke, the Duke Blue Devil. 12. Georgia, Uga. 13. Georgia Tech, Buzz the Yellow Jacket. 14. Kansas, the Jayhawk. 15. LSU, Mike the Tiger. 16. Louisville, the Cardinal. 17. Maryland, Testudo Terrapin. 18. Miami (Fla.), Sebastian the Ibis. 19. Marquette, the Golden Eagle. 20. Missouri, Truman Tiger. 21. Oregon, the Oregon Duck. 22. Oklahoma State, Pistol Pete. 23. Notre Dame, the Leprechaun. 24. Michigan State, Sparty. 25. North Carolina, Rameses. 26. Purdue, Purdue Pete. 27. Oklahoma, the Sooner Schooner. 28. Wake Forest, Demon Decon. 29. Virginia Tech, Gobblers the Turkey. 30. Illinois, Chief Illiniwek. 31. Vanderbilt, Mr. Commodore. 32. South Carolina, Cocky the Gamecock. 33. Texas, Bevo. 34. Murray State, Dunker the Horse. 35. Seton Hall, Pirate. 36. Ohio State, Brutus Buckeye. 37. Tennessee, Smokey. 38. Texas Tech, Raider Red. 39. Oregon State, Benny Beaver. 40. Virginia, the Cavalier. 41. Stanford's tree, Stanford. 42. Nebraska, Lil' Red. 43. Air Force, the Falcon. 44. Washington, King Redoubt. 45. Texas-El Paso, Paydirt Pete. 46. Texas A&M, Reveille. 47. Xavier, the Musketeer. 48. N.C. State, Mr. and Mrs. Wulf. 49. Wisconsin, Bucky Badger. 50. USC, Tommy Trojan.

Chapter 3: Pro Football

YEAR IN REVIEW: 1. 1965. 2. 1978. 3. 1984. 4. 1966. 5. 1996. 6. 1988. 7. 1954. 8. 1992. 9. 1970. 10. 1959.

COMMON LINKS (WARMING UP): 1. Terry Bradshaw and Chuck Noll spent 14 seasons together with the Pittsburgh Steelers (1970-83). 2. Dallas Cowboys star Emmitt Smith rushed for 2,434 yards in 25 MNF appearances; Tony Dorsett ran for 1,897 yards. 3. Former tackle Jackie Slater blocked for Walter Payton at Jackson State and Eric Dickerson for the Los Angeles Rams. 4. Buffalo's Jim Kelly. 5. Danny

White. 6. Brett Favre caught his own pass (for minus-7 yards) after it deflected off a Tampa Bay defender. 7. Denver's John Elway fired 180 TDs at Mile High Stadium from 1983-98. 8. Jack Pardee (three years), Neill Armstrong (four) and Mike Ditka (six). 9. Rookie Joe Ferguson quarterbacked Buffalo in 1973 and Jeff Kemp called signals for the Rams in 1984. 10. Tight end Shannon Sharpe caught 42 John Elway TD passes; WR Sterling Sharpe caught 41 Brett Favre TD throws.

COMMON LINKS (GETTING SERIOUS): 1. All are lefthanders. 2. All are University of Miami players selected in the first round of the 2002 draft. 3. All are former No. 1 draft picks by the Colts. 4. All are teams that have never won a Super Bowl. 5. Players who have kicked an NFL-record seven field goals in a game. 6. The first and last players listed in a football encyclopedia. 7. Players who have held the NFL's all-time rushing record. 8. Coaches who preceded and succeeded Don Shula at Miami. 9. Players who have won Super Bowl MVPs. 10. Quarterbacks who have thrown seven TD passes in a game.

JACKS AND JOHNS (WARMING UP): The nickname of former Raiders defensive back Jack Tatum. 2. The nickname of 10-year Dallas Cowboys fullback Daryl Johnston. 3. The nickname of former defensive end John Matuszak. 4. Tom Jackson, the former linebacker who turned to broadcasting after a 14-year NFL career with Denver. 5. John David Crow at Texas A&M in 1957. 6. Pepper Johnson played alongside LT during the New York Giants' victory over Buffalo. 7. The real first and middle name of Bo Jackson. 8. Jack Pardee was Payton's coach when he played his first season for the Chicago Bears in 1975. 9. Mark Jackson and Vance Johnson formed two-thirds of John Elway's "Three Amigos" receiving tandem in the late 1980s and early '90s. 10. Hall of Fame running back John Henry Johnson.

JACKS AND JOHNS (GETTING SERIOUS): 1. John Elway and Charley Johnson. 2. Jon Gruden and John Fox. 3. Norm Johnson and Chris Jacke. 4. John Taylor and Jackie Smith. 5. John Rauch and John Madden. 6. Jack Christiansen and Billy "White Shoes" Johnson. 7. John Hannah and Jackie Slater. 8. Jack Lambert and Jack Ham. 9. John Brockington and John Riggins. 10. Jimmy Johnson and Jimmy Johnson.

A LICENSE TO KILL (WARMING UP): 1. QB Peyton Manning, WR Marvin Harrison, RB Dominic Rhodes. 2. QB Jeff Garcia, WR Terrell Owens, RB Charlie Garner. 3. QB Peyton Manning, WR Marvin Harrison, RB Edgerrin James. 4. QB Scott Mitchell, WR Herman Moore, RB Barry Sanders. 5. QB Brett Favre, WR Robert Brooks, RB Edgar Bennett. 6. QB Neil Lomax, WR Roy Green, RB O.J. Anderson. 7. QB Kurt Warner, WRs Torry Holt and Isaac Bruce, RB Marshall Faulk, who scored 21 touchdowns. 8. Kevin Mack and Earnest Byner. 9. Franco Harris and Rocky Bleier. 10. Larry Csonka and Mercury Morris.

A LICENSE TO KILL (GETTING SERIOUS): 1. Steve Young to Jerry Rice, 49ers (1987-99). 2. Dan Marino to Mark Clayton, Dolphins (1983-92). 3. Jim Kelly to Andre Reed, Bills (1986-96). 4. Johnny Unitas to Raymond Berry, Colts (1955-67). 5. Brett Favre to Antonio Freeman, Packers (1995-2001). 6. John Hadl to Lance Alworth, Chargers (1962-70). 7. Dan Marino to Mark Duper, Dolphins (1983-92). 8. Joe Montana to Jerry Rice, 49ers (1985-92). 9. Sonny Jurgensen to Charley Taylor, Redskins (1964-74). 10. Ken Anderson to Isaac Curtis, Bengals (1973-84).

MISSING IN ACTION (WARMING UP): 1. Todd Blackledge. 2. Vance Johnson. 3. Marshall Faulk. 4. Warren Moon. 5. Lamar Lundy. 6. Priest Holmes. 7. Russ Grimm. 8. Reggie McKenzie. 9. Cris Carter. 10. Roosevelt Brown and Willie Brown.

MISSING IN ACTION (GETTING SERIOUS): 1. Bill Parcells has appeared in three Super Bowls. 2. Len Dawson threw for 28,711 career yards. 3. Steve Largent had 819 career receptions. 4. Green Bay has played in four Super Bowls. 5. Dorsett carried the ball 2,936 times. 6. Troy Aikman passed for 689 Super Bowl yards. 7. Lynn Swann. 8. Parcells has never coached the Buffalo Bills. 9. Rison never played for the Dallas Cowboys. 10. Stabler is not a member of the Hall of Fame.

STATUESQUE (WARMING UP): 1. Vinny Testaverde. 2. Angelo Bertelli. 3. Billy Cannon. 4. O.J. Simpson. 5. George Rogers. 6. Jay Berwanger. 7. Leon Hart. 8. Jim Plunkett. 9. Terry Baker. 10. Tom Harmon. 11. Paul Hornung. 12. Bo Jackson. 13. Frank Sinkwich. 14. Ernie Davis. 15. Earl Campbell. 16. Billy Sims.

STATUESQUE (GETTING SERIOUS): 1. O.J. Simpson and Roger Staubach were inducted in 1985. 2. Barry Sanders rushed for 15,269 yards in 10 NFL seasons, third on the all-time list, before retiring in

1998. 3. Paul Hornung, a versatile runner passer and kicker, scored an NFL-record 176 points in 1960 for the Green Bay Packers. 4. Former Texas A&M star John David Crow rushed for 1,071 yards in 1960 for the St. Louis Cardinals. 5. Former Notre Dame quarterback Johnny Lujack threw for 2,658 yards and 23 touchdowns in 1949 for the Chicago Bears. 6. Roger Staubach was MVP of Super Bowl 6 for Dallas; Jim Plunkett was MVP of Super Bowl 15 for Oakland; Marcus Allen was MVP of Super Bowl 18 for the Los Angeles Raiders; Desmond Howard was MVP of Super Bowl 31 for Green Bay. 7. Through the 2003 season, Doug Flutie, a six-time Most Outstanding Player in the Canadian Football League, had thrown for 368 touchdowns in the CFL, USFL and NFL combined. 8. Steve Spurrier played 10 NFL seasons before coaching the University of Florida, his alma mater, and the NFL's Washington Redskins. 9. Charles White ran for 1,374 yards in 1987 for the Los Angeles Rams. 10. O.J. Simpson scored 23 in 1975 for the Buffalo Bills.

SEQUENTIAL (WARMING UP): 1. Walter Payton, Jamal Lewis—players who have held the NFL's single-game rushing record. 2. Sam Wyche—men who have coached the Tampa Bay Buccaneers. 3. Keyshawn Johnson—No. 1 overall draft picks in the 1990s. 4. Redskins—the first seven Super Bowl losers. 5. Tom Brady—the last seven Super Bowl MVPs. 6. Tony Dorsett—the top six players on the NFL's all-time rushing chart. 7. Elmer Layden—the four men who have served as NFL commissioner. 8. Chuck Noll—the top five names on the NFL's all-time coaching victory list. 9. Broncos—the last six Super Bowl winners. 10. Dallas Texans—the original eight teams in the American Football League that began play in 1960.

SEQUENTIAL (GETTING SERIOUS): 1. Dallas Cowboys, 1989-93. 2. Miami Dolphins, 1970-74. 3. Cleveland Browns, 1950-54. 4. Tampa Bay Bucs, 1976-80—their first five NFL seasons. 5. Chicago Bears, 1983-87. 6. Buffalo Bills, 1990-94. 7. Green Bay Packers, 1961-65. 8. Indianapolis Colts, 1998-2002. 9. Pittsburgh Steelers, 1975-79. 10. Tennessee Titans, 1996-2000.

SUPER STARS (WARMING UP): 1. Green Bay's Herb Adderley scored his touchdown against Oakland in Super Bowl 2. 2. Mike Ditka scored on a 7-yard pass from Dallas quarterback Roger Staubach in Super Bowl 6, and he coached the Chicago Bears to victory in Super Bowl 20. 3. Pittsburgh's Terry Bradshaw hit John Stallworth for 75 yards in Super Bowl 13 against Dallas and for 73 yards in Super Bowl 14 against Los Angeles. 4. Fulton Walker. 5. Timmy Smith's big effort in Super Bowl 22 was overshadowed by the four-touchdown passing effort of Washington quarterback Doug Williams. 6. San Francisco's Jerry Rice enjoyed his big day against the Cincinnati Bengals. 7. Defensive lineman Mike Lodish played in four Super Bowls with Buffalo (25 through 28) and two with Denver (32 and 33). 8. Defensive end Charles Haley played for two Super Bowl winners (23 and 24) with San Francisco; three Super Bowl winners (27, 28 and 30) with Dallas. 9. Green Bay quarterback Brett Favre and receiver Antonio Freeman against New England. 10. Marcus Allen ran 74 yards for a touchdown in the Raiders' Super Bowl 18 win over Washington.

SUPER STARS (GETTING SERIOUS): 1-2. Jake Scott, Dolphins; Dexter Jackson, Buccaneers. 3. Larry Brown, Cowboys. 4-5. Chuck Howley, Cowboys; Ray Lewis, Ravens. 6-7. Harvey Martin, Cowboys; Richard Dent, Bears. 8. Randy White, Cowboys. 9-15. Larry Csonka, Dolphins; Franco Harris, Steelers; John Riggins, Redskins; Marcus Allen, Raiders; Ottis Anderson, Giants; Emmitt Smith, Cowboys; Terrell Davis, Broncos. 16-18. Lynn Swann, Steelers; Fred Biletnikoff, Raiders; Jerry Rice, 49ers. 19. Desmond Howard, Packers.

INITIAL REACTION (WARMING UP): 1. S.G. (Sid Gillman, Chargers). 2. G.H. (George Halas, Bears). 3. T.L. (Tom Landry, Cowboys). 4. D.R. (Dan Reeves, Broncos or Falcons). 5. B.G. (Bud Grant, Vikings). 6. D.S. (Don Shula, Dolphins or Colts). 7. M.H. (Mike Holovak, Patriots). 8. C.L. (Curly Lambeau, Packers). 9. D.C. (Dom Capers, Panthers or Texans, or Don Coryell, Cardinals). 10. W.E. (Weeb Ewbank, Jets). 11. T.D. (Tony Dungy, Buccaneers). 12. J.R. (John Robinson, Rams). 13. G.N. (Greasy Neale, Eagles). 14. B.B. (Brian Billick, Ravens). 15. J.M. (John Madden, Raiders, or Jim Mora, Saints). 16. D.S. (Don Shula, Dolphins or Colts). 17. H.S. (Hank Stram, Chiefs). 18. J.M. (John Madden, Raiders, or Jim Mora, Saints). 19. S.O. (Steve Owen, Giants). 20. C.K. (Chuck Knox, Seahawks). 21. D.C. (Dom Capers, Panthers or Texans, or Don Coryell, Cardinals). 22. J.F. (Jeff Fisher, Titans). 23. C.N. (Chuck Noll, Steelers). 24. D.R. (Dan Reeves, Broncos or Falcons). 25. W.F. (Wayne Fontes, Lions). 26. M.L. (Marv Levy, Bills). 27. P.B. (Paul Brown, Browns). 28. D.C. (Dom Capers, Panthers or Texans, or Don Coryell, Cardinals). 29. S.W. (Sam Wyche, Bengals). 30. J.G. (Joe Gibbs, Redskins). 31. G.S. (George Seifert, 49ers). 32. T.C. (Tom Coughlin, Jaguars).

INITIAL REACTION (GETTING SERIOUS): 1. O.A. (Ottis Anderson, Cardinals). 2. J.T. (Jim Taylor,

Packers). 3. C.O. (Christian Okoye, Chiefs). 4. L.C. (Larry Csonka, Dolphins). 5. J.P. (Joe Perry, 49ers). 6. T.T. (Thurman Thomas, Bills). 7. J.R. (John Riggins, Redskins). 8. F.M. (Freeman McNeil, Jets). 9. W.P. (Walter Payton, Bears). 10. G.R. (George Rogers, Saints, or Gerald Riggs, Falcons). 11. W.M. (Wilbert Montgomery, Eagles). 12. F.H. (Franco Harris, Steelers). 13. J.W. (James Wilder, Buccaneers). 14. B.S. (Barry Sanders, Lions). 15. E.S. (Emmitt Smith, Cowboys). 16. S.C. (Sam Cunningham, Patriots). 17. J.B. (Jim Brown, Browns). 18. C.W. (Chris Warren, Seahawks). 19. M.A. (Marcus Allen, Raiders). 20. D.D. (Domanick Davis, Texans). 21. R.H. (Rodney Hampton, Giants). 22. E.D. (Eric Dickerson, Rams). 23. F.T. (Fred Taylor, Jaguars). 24. C.D. (Corey Dillon, Bengals). 25. T.B. (Tshimanga Biakabutuka, Panthers). 26. P.L. (Paul Lowe, Chargers). 27. E.J. (Edgerrin James, Colts). 28. T.D. (Terrell Davis, Broncos). 29. J.L. (Jamal Lewis, Ravens). 30. R.S. (Robert Smith, Vikings). 31. E.G. (Eddie George, Titans). 32. G.R. (George Rogers, Saints, or Gerald Riggs, Falcons).

Chapter 4: Faces From the Past

1. Buddy Reynolds, who changed his name to Burt when he began his long and successful acting career, earned varsity letters as a part-time running back for the 1955 and 1957 Florida State football teams. 2. Actor/comedian Bill Cosby was a Temple running back in the early 1960s. 3. Colorado Rockies first baseman Todd Helton, who owns the highest career batting average among active players, is a former University of Tennessee quarterback. 4. Cal Ripken played the 1981 season for Rochester of the International League before beginning his record-breaking career with the Baltimore Orioles. 5. Paul "Bear" Bryant coached University of Kentucky football from 1946-53 before gaining more lasting fame at Alabama. 6. Mark Harmon, the son of Heisman Trophy winner Tom Harmon, quarterbacked the UCLA football team in 1972 and '73 before embarking on his successful acting career. 7. Jon Stewart, a former college soccer player at William & Mary, is a comedian and actor who has hosted Comedy Central's *The Daily Show* since 1999. 8. Baseball home run king Hank Aaron was a 19-year-old prospect in 1953 when he played second base for Jacksonville in the Class A South Atlantic League. 9. Arnold "Red" Auerbach won his first NBA championship in 1956-57, his seventh season as coach of the Boston Celtics. 10. Gerald Ford, who was named the outstanding player of the 1934 Michigan team and played for the College All-Stars against the Chicago Bears in 1935, later served for 24 years in the U.S. House of Representatives before becoming vice president of the United States in 1973 and president in 1974. 11. A young George Steinbrenner had not yet acquired the powerful bearing that gives him status as a ship-building tycoon and owner of the New York Yankees. 12. Don Shula, a defensive back for the Baltimore Colts from 1953-56, went on to win more games as an NFL coach (Baltimore and Miami) than anyone in history. 13. This photo of basketball giant Wilt Chamberlain was taken between his final season at Kansas (1957-58) and his first season with the NBA's Philadelphia Warriors (1959-60). 14. Longtime Los Angeles Dodgers manager Tommy Lasorda pitched in 26 games from 1954-56 with Brooklyn and the Kansas City Athletics. 15. Baseball Hall of Famer Carl Yastrzemski played for Raleigh of the Carolina League in 1959, two years before reaching the major leagues with the Boston Red Sox. 16. Actor Tommy Lee Jones was an All-Ivy League offensive guard for Harvard in 1968. 17. Richard Nixon was a reserve player for Whittier College in California in the early 1930s before beginning a political career that eventually vaulted him to the U.S. presidency. 18. Merlin Olsen, a Hall of Fame defensive tackle for the Los Angeles Rams, later gained acting fame in the television series *Father Murphy* and *Little House on the Prairie*. 19. Known during his football-playing days at USC (1925 and 1926) as Marion Morrison, he went on to greater fame as actor John Wayne. 20. Phil Jackson, a bearded 6-8 forward for the New York Knicks in 1975-76, went on to greater success as a nine-time championship coach with the Chicago Bulls and Los Angeles Lakers. 21. Ed Marinaro, the Cornell running back who finished second in the 1971 Heisman Trophy voting to Auburn's Pat Sullivan, went on to play briefly in the NFL before finding acting fame in the hit television series *Hill Street Blues*. 22. Former Arizona State baseball star Reggie Jackson, who went on to hit 563 major league home runs and earn Hall of Fame election, was the New York Yankees' reputed Mr. October. 23. Craig Kilborn, a former college basketball player at Montana State University, has reached greater fame as a *SportsCenter* anchor, the host of Comedy Central's *The Daily Show* and Tom Snyder's replacement as host of *The Late Show*. 24. Tony La Russa, an infielder for the Oakland A's in 1971, has posted more than 2,000 wins as manager of the Chicago White Sox, Oakland A's and St. Louis Cardinals. 25. George "Sparky" Anderson, pictured as an American Legion player in 1951, is the only major league manager to guide teams (Cincinnati and Detroit) to championships in both leagues. 26. Jennifer Capriati's high school senior photograph did not foretell the heights she would reach as a professional tennis champion. 27. Charles Barkley, pictured as a high school senior, went on to an outstanding career in the NBA. 28. Jackie Robinson was a four-sport star at

UCLA in the early 1940s before gaining prominence as the Brooklyn Dodgers player who broke baseball's color barrier. 29. Lenny Wilkens was a star guard at Providence before starring in the NBA and later breaking the NBA record for coaching wins. 30. George Clooney was a high school basketball player before embarking on a successful acting career. 31. Kansas City Chiefs All-Pro tight end Tony Gonzalez played 82 games for the University of California's basketball team in the mid-1990s. 32. Nolan Ryan made a brief stop at Jacksonville of the International League in 1967 before joining the New York Mets and beginning his legendary big-league career. 33. Former Boston Red Sox great Ted Williams played for Hoover High School in the early 1930s. 34. Mike Ditka, pictured as a high school senior, went on to a Hall of Fame career as an NFL tight end and later coached the Chicago Bears to a 1985 championship. 35. Few suspected in high school that Jeff Gordon would go on to become a championship NASCAR driver. 36. Even in high school, Joe Namath had that smug look that would carry him to Hall of Fame heights as an NFL quarterback. 37. Orel Hershiser might have passed for a bookworm in high school, but major league hitters got to know him later as a star major league pitcher and World Series hero. 38. Arnold Palmer's championship golf career started as a high school phenom in Latrobe, Pa. 39. Fred Dryer, recognized by television fans as *Hunter*, was a Pro Bowl defensive end for the Los Angeles Rams in the 1970s. 40. Young Bob Feller looked more like a hitter than a Hall of Fame pitcher in this early 1930s photo taken at his home in Van Meter, Iowa. 41. Women's soccer star Mia Hamm was far from her World Cup championship form when this high school photo was taken. 42. Jim Brown, a lacrosse, basketball and football star at Syracuse University, was a Hall of Fame NFL running back and actor. 43. From high school star to Olympic champion, Carl Lewis became one of the most heralded track stars in American history. 44. Mike Schmidt played for Ohio University in 1971 before becoming a Hall of Fame third baseman for the Philadelphia Phillies and a three-time National League MVP.

Chapter 5: Pro Basketball

FINAL THOUGHTS (WARMING UP): 1. The San Antonio Spurs in 1999. 2. Those same 1998-99 Spurs completed the ABA/NBA double by defeating the New York Knicks. 3. Magic Johnson, doing his best imitation of teammate Kareem Abdul-Jabbar, connected on what he called his "junior, junior sky-hook." 4. Four. 5. Alex Hannum coached the ABA's Oakland Oaks to a 1969 title and the NBA's St. Louis Hawks and Philadelphia 76ers to NBA titles in 1958 and 1967, respectively; Bill Sharman guided the ABA's Utah Stars to a 1971 championship and the NBA's Los Angeles Lakers to a 1972 title. 6. The Lakers have lost 14 times. 7. Buddy Jeannette was both coach and player for the champion Baltimore Bullets in 1948; Bill Russell performed the double for Boston in 1968 and 1969. 8. The Baltimore/Washington Bullets were 1-3 during the decade. 9. Pat Riley. 10. James Worthy scored 36 points, grabbed 16 rebounds and handed out 10 assists.

FINAL THOUGHTS (GETTING SERIOUS): 1. Cedric Maxwell. 2. Vernon Maxwell. 3. Byron Scott. 4. Bill Cartwright. 5. Rick Fox. 6. Sean Elliott. 7. Bob Cousy. 8. Maurice Lucas. 9. Joe Dumars. 10. Ed Macauley.

AND THE WINNER IS ... (WARMING UP): 1. Moses Malone won the award in 1981-82 for Houston and in 1982-83 for Philadelphia. 2. Malone did it for Houston and Philadelphia; Wilt Chamberlain did it while playing for the Philadelphia Warriors and 76ers; Kareem Abdul-Jabbar won for the Milwaukee Bucks and Los Angeles Lakers. 3. Bob Pettit's St. Louis Hawks were 33-39 in 1955-56; Kareem Abdul-Jabbar's Los Angeles Lakers were 40-42 in 1975-76. 4. Hubie Brown was honored in 1977-78 when he coached Atlanta to a 41-41 record, and in 2003-04 when he guided the Memphis Grizzlies to a 50-32 record and playoff berth at age 71. 5. Chicago's Michael Jordan in 1988 and Houston's Hakeem Olajuwon in 1994. 6. Willis Reed, the 1964-65 top rookie, was the New York Knicks' first pick of the second round. 7. Dikembe Mutombo is the award's only four-time winner. 8. Willis Reed made the triple sweep in 1970, Michael Jordan matched it in 1996 and '98 and Shaquille O'Neal did it in 2000, although he shared the All-Star award with Tim Duncan. 9. Pat Riley won in 1989-90 for the Lakers, in 1992-93 for the Knicks and in 1996-97 for the Heat. 10. No Boston player, despite the team's incredible success, has ever led the NBA in scoring.

AND THE WINNER IS ... (GETTING SERIOUS): 1. W.R. (Willis Reed), K.A. (Kareem Abdul-Jabbar), M.M. (Moses Malone), L.B. (Larry Bird), E.J. (Earvin "Magic" Johnson), M.J. (Michael Jordan), H.O. (Hakeem Olajuwon), S.O. (Shaquille O'Neal), T.D. (Tim Duncan). 2. M.J. (Michael Jordan), G.P. (Gary

Payton), S.P. (Scottie Pippen), B.J. (Bobby Jones). 3. R.S. (Ralph Sampson), P.E. (Patrick Ewing), D.R. (David Robinson). 4. K.M. (Kevin McHale), R.P. (Ricky Pierce), D.S. (Detlef Schrempf). 5. St. Louis' Bob Pettit (B.P.) won the first league MVP in 1955-56; Lakers guard Jerry West (J.W.) was the first NBA Finals MVP in 1969 while playing for the losing team; Boston's Ed Macauley (E.M.) was the first All-Star Game MVP in 1951; Fort Worth's Don Meineke (D.M.) was the first Rookie of the Year in 1952-53. 6. W.C. (Wilt Chamberlain), W.U. (Wes Unseld). 7. K.M. (Karl Malone), K.A. (Kareem Abdul-Jabbar), E.B. (Elgin Baylor), B.C. (Bob Cousy), M.J. (Michael Jordan), B.P. (Bob Pettit), J.W. (Jerry West). 8. S.O. (Shaquille O'Neal, Orlando), A.M. (Alonzo Mourning, Charlotte), C.L. (Christian Laettner, Minnesota), T.G. (Tom Gugliotta, Washington), L.E. (LaPhonso Ellis, Denver). 9. D.D. (Dave DeBusschere, Knicks), N.T. (Nate Thurmond, Warriors), B.R. (Bill Russell, Celtics), W.F. (Walt Frazier, Knicks), J.S. (Jerry Sloan, Bulls). 10. B.F. (Bill Fitch), G.S. (Gene Shue), D.N. (Don Nelson), C.F. (Cotton Fitzsimmons), P.R. (Pat Riley), H.B. (Hubie Brown).

ON THE REBOUND (WARMING UP): 1. Buck Williams (Nets) and Shaquille O'Neal (Magic). 2. Bill Russell (Celtics) and Alvan Adams (Suns). 3. Hakeem Olajuwon (Rockets) and Dolph Schayes (76ers). 4. Kareem Abdul-Jabbar (Bucks) and Elgin Baylor (Lakers). 5. Dan Issel (Nuggets) and James Donaldson (Mavericks). 6. Wes Unseld (Wizards) and Karl Malone (Jazz). 7. Sam Lacey (Kings) and Patrick Ewing (Knicks). 8. Bob Pettit (Hawks) and Rony Seikaly (Heat). 9. Michael Jordan (Bulls) and Larry Johnson (Hornets). 10. David Robinson (Spurs) and Kevin Garnett (Timberwolves). 11. Bill Laimbeer (Pistons) and Jack Sikma (SuperSonics). 12. Nate Thurmond (Warriors) and Mel Daniels (Pacers).

ON THE REBOUND (GETTING SERIOUS): 1. Neil Johnston of the Philadelphia Warriors in 1954-55 and Bob Pettit of the St. Louis Hawks in 1955-56. 2. Wilt Chamberlain in 1967-68 for the Philadelphia 76ers. 3. San Francisco's Nate Thurmond pulled down 42 rebounds in a 1965 game against Detroit and Cincinnati's Jerry Lucas grabbed 40 in a 1964 contest at Philadelphia. 4. Dennis Rodman won consecutive titles from 1991-92 through 1997-98 while playing for Detroit, San Antonio and Chicago. 5. Charles Barkley. 6. Swen Nater won in 1974-75 for the ABA's San Antonio Spurs and 1979-80 for the NBA's San Diego Clippers. 7. None. In fact, Ewing never led the NBA in any major statistical category. 8. Houston's Hakeem Olajuwon did it in 1989-90; Detroit's Ben Wallace did it in 2001-02. 9. Dennis Rodman averaged 18.7 for the Detroit Pistons. 10. Chamberlain finished the historic night with 25 rebounds.

GO FIGURE (WARMING UP): 1. Wilt Chamberlain's scoring averages in his first five NBA seasons. 2. The Fort Wayne Pistons beat the Minneapolis Lakers, 19-18, in the lowest-scoring game in NBA history in 1950; the Detroit Pistons beat the Denver Nuggets, 186-184, in the highest-scoring game in NBA history in 1983. 3. Wilt Chamberlain's field goals, free throws, rebounds and assist totals during his 100-point game on March 2, 1962. 4. The five highest single-game scoring totals for Michael Jordan. 5. The career records through 2003-04 of the NBA's three winningest coaches—Lenny Wilkens, Don Nelson and Pat Riley. 6. The Chicago Bulls posted an all-time best 72-10 regular-season record in 1995-96; the Philadelphia 76ers posted an all-time worst 9-73 mark in 1972-73. 7. The incredible home record compiled by the 1985-86 Boston Celtics en route to an NBA championship. 8. The length and width of a regulation NBA court. 9. The career records for points (Kareem Abdul-Jabbar), rebounds (Wilt Chamberlain) and assists (John Stockton). 10. Years in which the Chicago Bulls won NBA championships.

GO FIGURE (GETTING SERIOUS): 1. 13 (Wilt Chamberlain), 24 (Rick Barry), 42 (Nate Thurmond). 2. 4 (Joe Dumars), 11 (Isiah Thomas), 16 (Bob Lanier). 3. 6 (Julius Erving), 10 (Maurice Cheeks), 34 (Charles Barkley). 4. 22 (Clyde Drexler), 32 (Bill Walton). 5. 7 (Pete Maravich), 12 (John Stockton), 32 (Karl Malone). 6. 22 (Elgin Baylor), 32 (Magic Johnson), 42 (James Worthy). 7. 23 (Calvin Murphy), 24 (Moses Malone), 34 (Hakeem Olajuwon). 8. 4 (Jerry Sloan), 23 (Michael Jordan), 33 (Scottie Pippen). 9. 10 (Walt Frazier), 19 (Willis Reed), 33 (Patrick Ewing). 10. 21 (Tim Duncan), 44 (George Gervin).

FEELING A DRAFT (WARMING UP): 1. Jay Williams was picked No. 2 by Chicago; Mike Dunleavy was tabbed No. 3 by Golden State. 2. Darius Miles of East St. Louis High School was picked No. 3 overall by the Los Angeles Clippers in the 2000 draft. Garnett was the No. 5 pick in 1995, Bryant was No. 13 in 1996 and McGrady was No. 9 in 1997. 3. John Stockton was selected out of Gonzaga by the Utah Jazz. 4. St. Louis got local favorite Ed Macauley and the draft rights to Cliff Hagan. 5. The Philadelphia Warriors picked Wilt Chamberlain out of Kansas in 1959; the Cincinnati Royals grabbed University of Cincinnati star Oscar Robertson in 1960. 6. Maurice Cheeks. 7. Kareem Abdul-Jabbar and

Glenn Robinson. 8. The Houston Rockets picked Twin Towers Ralph Sampson (Virginia) and Akeem Olajuwon (Houston) with the No. 1 picks in 1983 and 1984. 9. Reggie Williams (Clippers), Muggsy Bogues (Bullets) and Reggie Lewis (Celtics). 10. Scott Burrell in 1993.

FEELING A DRAFT (GETTING SERIOUS): 1. Milwaukee Bucks. 2. 1990. 3. Wake Forest. 4. Los Angeles Clippers. 5. Brad Daugherty. 6. 2001. 7. UNLV. 8. Pervis Ellison. 9. Pacific. 10. 1985. 11. Dallas Mavericks. 12. Joe Barry Carroll. 13. Georgetown. 14. Mychal Thompson. 15. Golden State Warriors. 16. 1987. 17. Cincinnati. 18. Orlando Magic. 19. 1983. 20. Yao Ming.

ALIAS SMITH, JONES AND JOHNSON (WARMING UP): 1. Boston Celtics guard Sam Jones played for 10 title winners in an NBA career that stretched from 1957-58 through 1968-69. 2. Magic Johnson was picked by the Los Angeles Lakers in 1979; Larry Johnson was picked by the Charlotte Hornets in 1991; Joe Smith was picked by Golden State in 1995. 3. Philadelphia's Bobby Jones. 4. Phil Johnson. 5. Randy Smith and Eddie Johnson. 6. Adrian Smith. 7. Avery Johnson. 8. Caldwell Jones. 9. Larry Smith. 10. Vinnie Johnson.

ALIAS SMITH, JONES AND JOHNSON (GETTING SERIOUS): 1. Eddie Johnson. 2. Phil Smith. 3. Steve Smith. 4. Eddie Jones. 5. Dennis Johnson. 6. Sam Jones. 7. Derek Smith (23.5) and Marques Johnson. 8. Kevin Johnson. 9. Kenny Smith. 10. Gus Johnson.

BIG MAN, LITTLE MAN: 1. M (7-6) and KK (Manute Bol). 2. A (5-3) and NN (Muggsy Bogues). 3. C (5-6) and BB (Spud Webb). 4. N (7-7) and II (Gheorghe Muresan). 5. F (5-9) and HH (Calvin Murphy). 6. L (7-5) and AA (Shawn Bradley). 7. K (7-4) and CC (Rik Smits). 8. B (5-5) and JJ (Earl Boykins). 9. E (5-8) and FF (Charlie Criss). 10. J (7-3) and EE (Mark Eaton). 11. G (5-10) and DD (Avery Johnson). 12. D (5-7) and LL (Monty Towe). 13. H (7-1) and MM (Sam Bowie). 14. I (7-2) and GG (Greg Ostertag).

MISCELLANEOUS (WARMING UP): 1. Former ABA star Moses Malone played in the NBA through the 1994-95 season. 2. Alvin Robertson (20 points, 11 rebounds, 10 assists, 10 steals) against Phoenix in 1986; Hakeem Olajuwon (18 points, 16 rebounds, 11 blocks, 10 assists) against Milwaukee in 1990; David Robinson (34 points, 10 rebounds, 10 assists, 10 blocks) against Detroit in 1994. 3. Los Angeles Lakers forward Elgin Baylor. 4. Guard Micheal Williams. 5. The Indiana Pacers and Kentucky Colonels. 6. Connie Hawkins. 7. Karl Malone was second to Jordan four times, Dominique Wilkins three times. 8. Walt Bellamy. 9. San Antonio's David Robinson led the league with a 29.8 average in 1993-94. 10. Julius Erving.

MISCELLANEOUS (GETTING SERIOUS): 1. Clyde Drexler. 2. Patrick Ewing. 3. Charles Barkley. 4. David Robinson. 5. John Stockton. 6. Larry Bird. 7. Chris Mullin. 8. Michael Jordan. 9. Karl Malone. 10. Magic Johnson. 11. Scottie Pippen. 12. Christian Laettner. 13. All were members of the Dream Team at the Barcelona Summer Olympic Games in 1992.

FINGER POINTING (WARMING UP): 1. D.C. (Dell Curry, Hornets). 2. K.A. (Kareem Abdul-Jabbar, Bucks). 3. O.R. (Oscar Robertson, Royals/Kings). 4. H.G. (Hal Greer, 76ers). 5. V.C. (Vince Carter, Raptors). 6. A.E. (Alex English, Nuggets). 7. J.H. (John Havlicek, Celtics). 8. K.M. (Karl Malone, Jazz). 9. B.W. (Buck Williams, Nets). 10. W.C. (Wilt Chamberlain, Warriors). 11. H.O. (Hakeem Olajuwon, Rockets). 12. G.P. (Gary Payton, SuperSonics). 13. G.R. (Glen Rice, Heat). 14. B.D. (Brad Daugherty, Cavaliers). 15. D.W. (Dominique Wilkins, Hawks). 16. J.W. (Jerry West, Lakers). 17. R.B. (Rolando Blackman, Mavericks). 18. E.H. (Elvin Hayes, Bullets/Wizards). 19. P.E. (Patrick Ewing, Knicks). 20. M.J. (Michael Jordan, Bulls). 21. R.M. (Reggie Miller, Pacers). 22. W.D. (Walter Davis, Suns). 23. I.T. (Isiah Thomas, Pistons). 24. C.D. (Clyde Drexler, Trail Blazers). 25. S.A. (Shareef Abdur-Rahim, Grizzlies). 26. R.S. (Randy Smith, Braves/Clippers). 27. D.R. (David Robinson, Spurs). 28. K.G. (Kevin Garnett, Timberwolves). 29. N.A. (Nick Anderson, Magic).

FINGER POINTING (GETTING SERIOUS): 1. Karl Malone scored a single-franchise record 36,374 points for the Utah Jazz. 2. Malone, 36,374 for the Jazz; Michael Jordan, 29,277 for the Bulls; Hakeem Olajuwon, 26,511 for the Rockets; John Havlicek, 26,395 for the Celtics; Jerry West, 25,192 for the Lakers. 3. Kareem Abdul-Jabbar, the Milwaukee Bucks' career scoring leader with 14,211 points, scored 24,176 for the Los Angeles Lakers, second only to Jerry West. 4. Jerry West scored 1,679 points in NBA Finals play, Kareem Abdul-Jabbar was second with 1,317 and Michael Jordan third with 1,176. 5. Moses Malone ranks fifth all-time with 27,409 career points. 6. Denver's David Thompson scored 73 points in a game at Detroit in 1978; Elgin Baylor of the L.A. Lakers scored 71 in a game at New York in 1960. 7. George Gervin, who won four scoring titles, finished second to David Robinson on the San Antonio career points list. 8. Wilt Chamberlain scored 17,783 points for the Warriors, 7,651 for the 76ers and 5,985 for the Lakers. 9. John Havlicek, Celtics; Brad Daugherty, Cavaliers; Isiah Thomas, Pistons; Reggie Miller, Pacers; Jerry West, Lakers; Kevin Garnett, Timberwolves; Hal Greer, Nationals/76ers; David Robinson, Spurs; Vince Carter, Raptors. 10. The Hornets' Dell Curry.

Chapter 6: Pro Team Logos

1. NFL: Dolphins

2. NFL: Ravens

3. NHL: Avalanche

4. NBA: Nuggets

5. MLB: Diamondbacks

6. NBA: Bulls

7. NFL: Bills

8. MLB: Cardinals

9. MLB: Marlins

10. NHL: Mighty Ducks

11. NHL: Coyotes

12. NFL: Cardinals

13. NBA: Warriors

14. MLB: Pirates

15. MLB: Astros

16. MLB: Expos

17. NHL: Thrashers

18. NFL: Broncos

19. MLB: Braves

20. NBA: Rockets

21. MLB: Tigers

22. NBA: Timberwolves

23. NHL: Blackhawks

24. NFL: Texans

25. NHL: Hurricanes

26. MLB: Twins

27. NFL: Eagles

28. NBA: Wizards

Answers

 29. MLB: Indians

 30. NFL: Buccaneers

 31. NBA: Celtics

 32. NHL: Sabres

 33. NHL: Flyers

 34. MLB: Rockies

 35. NBA: Pacers

 36. NFL: Jaguars

 37. MLB: White Sox

 38. NBA: Hawks

 39. NFL: Chargers

 40. NHL: Flames

 41. NHL: Stars

 42. NFL: Jets

 43. MLB: Brewers

 44. NBA: Grizzlies

 45. MLB: Phillies

 46. NFL: Chiefs

 47. NHL: Panthers

 48. NBA: Clippers

 49. NBA: Lakers

 50. NFL: Bears

 51. NHL: Capitals

 52. MLB: Dodgers

 53. MLB: Reds

 54. NHL: Red Wings

 55. NBA: Heat

 56. NFL: Bengals

 57. NHL: Canucks

 58. MLB: Yankees

 59. NBA: Bucks

 60. NFL: Falcons

 61. NHL: Maple Leafs

 62. MLB: Royals

 63. NBA: Jazz

 64. NFL: Patriots

65. NHL: Predators
66. NBA: SuperSonics
67. MLB: Mets
68. NBA: Nets

69. NFL: 49ers
70. NHL: Blues
71. NBA: Magic
72. NFL: Rams

73. NHL: Islanders
74. NHL: Penguins
75. MLB: Giants
76. NFL: Vikings

Chapter 7: Hockey

ELITE COMPANY (WARMING UP): 1. Mike Bossy. 2. Detroit great Gordie Howe scored a career-best 49 goals in 1952-53. 3. Pittsburgh's Bob Johnson in 1991. 4. Mike Gartner enjoyed his convergence of milestones in 1991-92. 5. Maurice "Rocket" Richard. 6. Florida's Pavel Bure in 1999-2000 and 2000-01, Colorado's Joe Sakic in 2000-01, Pittsburgh's Jaromir Jagr in 2000-01, Calgary's Jarome Iginla in 2001-02 and Colorado's Milan Hejduk in 2002-03. 7. Pittsburgh's Mario Lemieux and Jaromir Jagr. 8. 14. 9. Tkachuk scored into an empty net. 10. Patrick Roy.

ELITE COMPANY (GETTING SERIOUS): 1. Gilbert Perreault. 2. Lanny McDonald. 3. Dino Ciccarelli. 4. Mark Messier. 5. Brett Hull. 6. Joe Mullen. 7. Dave Andreychuk. 8. Luc Robitaille. 9. Ron Francis. 10. Brendan Shanahan.

GAME WINNERS (WARMING UP): 1. Nikolai Khabibulin. 2. Martin Brodeur. 3. Patrick Roy. 4. Mike Richter. 5. Grant Fuhr. 6. Ken Dryden. 7. Gump Worsley. 8. Johnny Bower. 9. Terry Sawchuk. 10. Terry Sawchuk. 11. Harry Lumley. 12. Frank McCool. 13. Turk Broda.

GAME WINNERS (GETTING SERIOUS): 1. Pete Babando. 2. Tony Leswick. 3. Jason Arnott. 4. Brett Hull. 5. Bob Nystrom. 6. Henri Richard. 7. Bill Barilko. 8. Bobby Orr. 9. Uwe Krupp. 10. Jacques Lemaire.

ROOKIES, THE DRAFT AND OTHER THINGS (WARMING UP): 1. Jaromir Jagr. 2. Bobby Hull. 3. Brett Hull. 4. Mario Lemieux. 5. Patrick Roy. 6. Mike Bossy. 7. Roger Neilson. 8. Derian Hatcher. 9. Pavel Bure. 10. Marcel Dionne.

ROOKIES, THE DRAFT AND OTHER THINGS (GETTING SERIOUS): 1. Gilbert Perreault, Buffalo (1970); Denis Potvin, N.Y. Islanders (1973); Bobby Smith, Minnesota (1978); Dale Hawerchuk, Winnipeg (1981); Mario Lemieux, Pittsburgh (1984); Bryan Berard, Ottawa (1995). 2. Bernie Geoffrion, Montreal; Bobby Orr, Boston; Bryan Trottier, N.Y. Islanders; Mario Lemieux, Pittsburgh; Peter Forsberg, Quebec/Colorado. 3. Frank Brimsek, Boston; Terry Sawchuk, Detroit; Gump Worsley, N.Y. Rangers/Montreal; Glenn Hall, Detroit/Chicago/St. Louis; Tony Esposito, Chicago; Ken Dryden, Montreal; Tom Barrasso, Buffalo; Ed Belfour, Chicago; Martin Brodeur, New Jersey. 4. Bobby Orr; Bryan Trottier; Mario Lemieux. 5. Anton and Peter Stastny. 6. Winnipeg's Teemu Selanne scored 76 in 1992-93, New York Islander Mike Bossy scored 53 in 1977-78 and Calgary's Joe Nieuwendyk scored 51 in 1987-88. 7. Winnipeg's Teemu Selanne (132) in 1992-93, Quebec's Peter Stastny (109) in 1980-81, Winnipeg's Dale Hawerchuk (103) in 1981-82, Boston's Joe Juneau (102) in 1992-93 and Pittsburgh's Mario Lemieux (100) in 1984-85. 8. Brian Leetch, N.Y. Rangers, 23 in 1988-89; Barry Beck, Colorado Rockies, 22 in 1977-78. 9. Minnesota's Dino Ciccarelli in 1981. 10. Montreal's Jean Perron.

THE PUCK STOPS HERE (WARMING UP): 1. Montreal's Ken Dryden. 2. Ed Belfour. 3. Philadelphia's Bernie Parent. 4. Billy Smith of the New York Islanders in 1979. 5. Terry Sawchuk. 6. Patrick Roy. 7. Philadelphia's Pelle Lindbergh. 8. Bill Ranford. 9. Montreal great Jacques Plante. 10. Gump Worsley.

THE PUCK STOPS HERE (GETTING SERIOUS): 1. Fuhr (Edmonton Oilers). 2. Belfour (Dallas Stars). 3. Lalime (Ottawa Senators). 4. Khabibulin (Tampa Bay Lightning). 5. Roy (Colorado Avalanche/Quebec Nordiques). 6. Sawchuk (Detroit Red Wings). 7. Liut (St. Louis Blues). 8. Esposito (Chicago Blackhawks). 9. Barrasso (Pittsburgh Penguins). 10. Essensa (Phoenix Coyotes/Winnipeg Jets). 11. Richter (New York Rangers). 12. Broda (Toronto Maple Leafs). 13. Smith (New York Islanders). 14. Hextall (Philadelphia Flyers). 15. Brodeur (New Jersey Devils/Colorado Rockies/Kansas City Scouts). 16. Vachon (Los Angeles Kings). 17. Plante (Montreal Canadiens). 18. Nabokov (San Jose Sharks). 19. Hasek (Buffalo Sabres). 20. Irbe (Carolina Hurricanes/Hartford Whalers/New England Whalers). 21. Vernon (Calgary Flames). 22. Hebert (Anaheim Mighty Ducks). 23. Thompson (Boston Bruins). 24. Vanbiesbrouck (Florida Panthers). 25. McLean (Vancouver Canucks). 26. Kolzig (Washington Capitals).

FIRST IMPRESSIONS (WARMING UP): 1. H. 2. I. 3. D. 4. J. 5. F. 6. E. 7. C. 8. A. 9. G. 10. B.

FIRST IMPRESSIONS (GETTING SERIOUS): 1. Bobby Carpenter. 2. The Washington Capitals. 3. Montreal's Ken Dryden in 1970-71. 4. Colorado center Peter Forsberg, who hails from Sweden. 5. Jacques Lemaire, who played for eight Montreal winners and coached one for New Jersey. 6. Calgary right wing Jarome Iginla. 7. Brent and Ron Sutter. 8. Scotty Bowman. 9. Roger Neilson. 10. St. Louis' Brendan Shanahan and Dallas' Mike Modano.

PUBLIC RELATIONS (WARMING UP): 1. Gretzky married actress Janet Jones. 2. Hedican married former Olympic figure skating gold medalist Kristi Yamaguchi. 3. Manon Rheaume, a player for Canada's silver medal-winning women's hockey team in the 1998 Winter Olympics. 4. Cammi Granato, captain for the American women's team that won a gold medal at the 1998 Nagano Olympics. 5. Mark Rypien, a Super Bowl MVP quarterback for the Washington Redskins. 6. Former NHL players Joe Kocur and Barry Melrose, who later coached the Los Angeles Kings. 7. Former NHL goaltender Mike Liut. 8. 10-year NHL defenseman Kea is the uncle of 500-goal man Joe Nieuwendyk and former defenseman Jeff Beukeboom. 9. Former Philadelphia great Clarke is the father-in-law of current NHL center Peter White. 10. Left wing Corson and right wing Darcy Tucker were Toronto teammates from 2000-01 through 2003-04.

PUBLIC RELATIONS (GETTING SERIOUS): 1. Peter and Anton Stastny. 2. Geoff and Russ Courtnall. 3. Dale and Mark Hunter. 4. Brian, Brent, Darryl and Duane Sutter. 5. Dennis Hull. 6. Henri Richard. 7. Joey and Brian Mullen. 8. Neal and Paul Broten. 9. Charlie Conacher. 10. Frank and Pete Mahovlich. 11. Pavel and Valeri Bure. 12. Marcel Dionne. Rankings by goals: Sutters (1,320), Hulls (913), Richards (902), Stastnys (823), Mahovliches (821), Dionnes (792), Mullens (762), Hunters (669), Courtnalls (664), Bures (611), Conachers (531), Brotens (521).

COACH SPEAK (WARMING UP): 1. D. 2. G. 3. J. 4. B. 5. I. 6. C. 7. F. 8. A. 9. H. 10. E.

COACH SPEAK (GETTING SERIOUS): 1. New York Rangers. 2. Vancouver Canucks. 3. Chicago Blackhawks. 4. Detroit Red Wings. 5. Toronto Maple Leafs. 6. Calgary Flames. 7. Buffalo Sabres. 8. Boston Bruins. 9. Philadelphia Flyers. 10. Pittsburgh Penguins.

BEST OF TEAMS, WORST OF TEAMS (WARMING UP): 1. E. 2. F. 3. C. 4. A. 5. J. 6. G. 7. B. 8. I. 9. H. 10. D.

BEST OF TEAMS, WORST OF TEAMS (GETTING SERIOUS): 1. The Boston Bruins. 2. The second-year New York Rangers in 1928. 3. The Montreal Maroons played from 1924-25 through 1937-38; the Montreal Wanderers were an NHL charter member in 1917-18. 4. Los Angeles Kings, St. Louis Blues, Philadelphia Flyers, Pittsburgh Penguins, Minnesota North Stars, California Golden Seals. 5. New England (Hartford) Whalers, Winnipeg Jets, Quebec Nordiques, Edmonton Oilers. 6. The Quebec Nordiques became the Colorado Avalanche and the Winnipeg Jets became the Phoenix Coyotes. 7. The New York Islanders from 1979-80 to 1982-83. 8. The Philadelphia Flyers in 1974. 9. Toronto was previously called the Arenas and the St. Patricks. 10. The Americans.

GOAL ORIENTED (WARMING UP): 1. J.B. (John Bucyk, Bruins). 2. W.G. (Wayne Gretzky, Oilers). 3. R.F. (Ron Francis, Hurricanes/Whalers). 4. B.B. (Bill Barber, Flyers). 5. O.N. (Owen Nolan, Sharks). 6. M.D. (Marcel Dionne, Kings). 7. M.R. (Maurice Richard, Canadiens). 8. B.H. (Bobby Hull, Blackhawks, or Brett Hull, Blues). 9. M.M. (Mike Modano, Stars/North Stars). 10. M.B. (Mike Bossy, Islanders). 11. P.K. (Paul Kariya, Mighty Ducks). 12. D.S. (Darryl Sittler, Maple Leafs). 13. V.L. (Vincent Lecavalier, Lightning). 14. D.H. (Dale Hawerchuk, Coyotes/Jets). 15. M.L. (Mario Lemieux, Penguins). 16. P.B. (Peter Bondra, Capitals). 17. T.L. (Trevor Linden, Canucks). 18. B.H. (Bobby Hull, Blackhawks, or Brett Hull, Blues). 19. R.G. (Rod Gilbert, Rangers). 20. S.M. (Scott Mellanby, Panthers). 21. G.H. (Gordie Howe, Red Wings). 22. A.Y. (Alexei Yashin, Senators). 23. G.P. (Gilbert Perreault, Sabres). 24. J.S. (Joe Sakic, Avalanche/Nordiques). 25. T.F. (Theo Fleury, Flames). 26. J.M. (John MacLean, Devils/Rockies/Scouts).

GOAL ORIENTED (GETTING SERIOUS): 1. Ray Bourque, Bruins; Stan Mikita, Blackhawks; Guy Lafleur, Canadiens; Bryan Trottier, Islanders; Bobby Clarke, Flyers; Bernie Federko, Blues; Brian Bradley, Lightning. 2. Phil Esposito (717) and Mike Gartner (708). 3. Mark Messier. 4. Toronto's Darryl Sittler scored 389 goals and 916 points. 5. Montreal with Rocket Richard (544), Guy Lafleur (518) and Jean Beliveau (507). 6. Pittsburgh's Mario Lemieux has scored 683 goals in 889 games. 7. Former Chicago great Bobby Hull scored his 610 goals in 1,063 games. 8. Philadelphia's Reggie Leach scored 61 goals in 1975-76. 9. Wayne Gretzky, Mario Lemieux and Brett Hull. 10. Edmonton's Paul Coffey.

Chapter 8: Sports Movies

Field of Dreams—1. Archibald "Moonlight" Graham. 2. Terence Mann was the author played by James Earl Jones. 3. Dyersville, Iowa. 4. The Godfather. **Hoosiers**—1. The Hickory Huskers. 2. Shooter, played by Dennis Hopper. 3. Jimmy Chitwood. 4. Myra Fleener. **A League of Their Own**—1. Jimmy Dugan. 2. Dottie and Kit were milking cows. 3. Madonna. 4. Third base. **Rudy**—1. Ruettiger. 2. 27 seconds. 3. Sean Astin. 4. Dan Devine. **Slap Shot**—1. Steve and Jeff Carlson. 2. Reggie Dunlop. 3. Tin foil. 4. Jack was No. 16, Steve was 17 and Jeff was 18. **The Bad News Bears**—1. A pool cleaner. 2. Tanner Boyle. 3. Amanda Whurlitzer. 4. The Yankees. **Rocky**—1. Butkus. 2. Link and Cuff. 3. Talia Shire. 4. Joe Frazier. **Major League**—1. Miami, Fla. 2. Wild Thing. 3. Bob Uecker was the colorful Indians play-by-play man. 4. Pete Vuckovich. **The Mighty Ducks**—1. Gordon Bombay. 2. Gerald Ducksworth. 3. "Quack, Quack! Quack, Quack!" 4. Hawks. **Tin Cup**—1. Roy McAvoy. 2. Big Dog. 3. He runs a dusty driving range in the West Texas town of Salome. 4. He took a seven-over-par 12. **Brian's Song**—1. James Caan was Brian Piccolo and Billy Dee Williams was Gale Sayers. 2. They were the Bears' first interracial roommates. 3. Bears linebacker Dick Butkus played himself. 4. It was the same house used by Samantha and Darrin Stephens in *Bewitched*. **Eight Men Out**—1. Charles Comiskey was owner of the Chicago White Sox. 2. D.B. Sweeney. 3. Cicotte, who started the Series opener, hit Cincinnati leadoff batter Morrie Rath with a pitch to signal the fix was on. 4. Baseball commissioner Kenesaw Mountain Landis. **The Longest Yard**—1. Crewe was a former NFL superstar. 2. Actor Richard Kiel played Jaws. 3. Former Green Bay Packers linebacker Ray Nitschke. 4. Actor Eddie Albert. **Semi-Tough**—1. Reynolds played Billy Clyde Puckett and Kristofferson was Shake Tiller. 2. Barbara Jane Bookman or B.J. 3. Carl Weathers. 4. Miami. **Space Jam**—1. Jordan, while playing golf, was sucked through a golf hole and into Looney Tunes-land. 2. Actor Danny DeVito is the voice of Swackhammer. 3. Charles Barkley, Patrick Ewing, Muggsy Bogues, Larry Johnson and Shawn Bradley are victims of the talent theft. 4. Lola Bunny. **Everybody's All-American**—1. He was called "The Grey Ghost." 2. LSU. 3. Miss Magnolia. 4. The Washington Redskins. **Raging Bull**—1. Robert De Niro. 2. Joe Pesci. 3. De Niro was quoting Marlon Brando's memorable line from On the Waterfront—"I coulda been a contender." 4. Scorsese used Hershey's chocolate as blood. **North Dallas Forty**—1. The North Dallas Bulls. 2. Nick Nolte played Elliott and Mac Davis was Maxwell. 3. After Elliott caught a touchdown pass with time expired to pull the Bulls within one point of forcing overtime, Hartman fumbled the snap on the extra point attempt and Chicago won. 4. John Matuszak. **The Rookie**—1. Morris tested his fastball speed by throwing past a speed monitor on the side of the road. 2. The Owls played in Big Lake, Texas. 3. Morris made his debut for Tampa Bay against the Texas Rangers at The Ballpark in Arlington. 4. Texas' Royce Clayton struck out on three pitches in the movie, four in real life. ***61**—1. Mark McGwire's record-breaking 62nd home run was the first one seen in the movie. 2. Tiger Stadium in Detroit, no longer being used in August 2000, was dressed up to look like Yankee Stadium. 3. Bob Cerv was a roommate of Maris and Mantle. 4. Saving Private Ryan. **Remember the Titans**—1. The team gathered to attend Bertier's funeral. 2. T.C. Williams High School in Alexandria, Va. 3. Coach Herman Boone. 4. The Gettysburg Civil War battlefield. **Caddyshack**—1. Chuck Rodent. 2. It was hole No. 14. 3. He was holding a pitchfork. 4. A Baby Ruth. **Miracle**—1. Herb Brooks died tragically in an automobile accident just as the primary photography for the film was completed. 2. In the movie, Craig said he was playing to honor his recently deceased mother. 3. Bill Ranford transformed into Jim Craig for the hockey scenes. 4. Former NHL goaltender Ken Dryden. **Ali**—1. Will Smith played the role of Ali. 2. Jon Voight. 3. Floating behind Ali momentarily was a lone white butterfly, an obvious allusion to his "Float like a butterfly, sting like a bee" mantra. 4. Ali told Sonji that he is prettier than she is. **The Natural**—1. Roy's bat was named Wonderboy. 2. The Whammer. 3. Bartholomew "Bump" Bailey. 4. Harriet Bird. **Bull Durham**—1. Annie Savoy. 2. Ebby Calvin LaLoosh. 3. Crash is approaching the record for most minor league home runs. 4. The Asheville Tourists. **White Men Can't Jump**—1. Sidney Deane. 2. Ron Shelton. 3. Gary Payton. 4. "Foods that being with the letter Q." **Breaking Away**—1. Bloomington, Ind. 2. "Cutters." 3. Dave shaves his legs. 4. A truck. **Seabiscuit**—1. Red Pollard. 2. Gary Stevens. 3. War Admiral. 4. Tom Smith. **Jerry Maguire**—1. Bob Sugar. 2. Frank Cushman. 3. Dennis Wilburn. 4. Leigh Steinberg.

Sports Movies Photos: Pages 130-131: Joe Gordon. Pages 132-133: William Bendix was the fictional Babe Ruth. Pages 134-135: Bill Mazeroski. Pages 136-137: Stratton continued his baseball career after losing his leg in a hunting accident. Pages 138-139: De Niro and Moriarty played for the New York Mammoths. Pages 140-141: Richard Crenna was Paul; Dan Dailey was Dizzy. Pages 142-143: Mickey Mantle (left) and Roger Maris. Pages 144-145: Edward G. Robinson played Hans Lobert. Pages 146-147: Baseball action in *The Natural* was filmed at War Memorial Stadium in Buffalo, N.Y. Pages 148-149: Gwen Verdon played Lola.

Chapter 9: College Football

CAUGHT IN A DRAFT (WARMING UP): 1. Southern California (63). 2. Texas. 3. Irving Fryar and Dean Steinkuhler. 4. The St. Louis Cardinals. 5. Herschel Walker. 6. Len Dawson (Purdue), Jim Brown (Syracuse) and Jim Parker (Ohio State). 7. Paul Hornung (Notre Dame), O.J. Simpson (USC), Earl Campbell (Texas). 8. The Minnesota Vikings. 9. Ohio State (15). 10. Clinton Portis.

CAUGHT IN A DRAFT (GETTING SERIOUS): 1. Leon Hart (1950), Paul Hornung (1957), Walt Patulski (1972). 2. Ron Yary (1968), O.J. Simpson (1969), Ricky Bell (1977), Keyshawn Johnson (1996), Carson Palmer (2003). 3. Tom Cousineau (1979), Dan Wilkinson (1994), Orlando Pace (1997). 4. Tommy Nobis (1966), Earl Campbell (1978), Kenneth Sims (1982). 5. Bobby Garrett (1954), Jim Plunkett (1971), John Elway (1983). 6. Tucker Frederickson (1965), Bo Jackson (1986), Aundray Bruce (1988). 7. Bruce Smith (1985), Michael Vick (2001). 8. Ki-Jana Carter (1995), Courtney Brown (2000). 9. Lee Roy Selmon (1976), Billy Sims (1980). 10. Vinny Testaverde (1987), Russell Maryland (1991).

HEISMEN (WARMING UP): 1. Pittsburgh's Tony Dorsett. 2. Doc Blanchard beat out teammate Glenn Davis for the 1945 Heisman. 3. Nebraska's Johnny Rodgers and Rich Glover performed that double in 1972; Mike Rozier and Dean Steinkuhler matched that feat in 1983. 4. Archie Griffin won the award in 1974 and '75 for Ohio State. 5. Michigan defensive back/receiver Charles Woodson in 1997. 6. BYU's Ty Detmer in 1990. 7. Wisconsin's Ron Dayne is the all-time Division I-A rushing champion with 6,397 yards; Oklahoma State's Barry Sanders ran for a single-season record 2,628 yards in 1988. 8. Ed Smith. 9. John Hicks. 10. Brian Bosworth.

HEISMEN (GETTING SERIOUS): 1. Ron Dayne. 2. Gino Torretta. 3. Marshall Faulk. 4. Roger Staubach's 1,356-vote margin was the second highest ever when he won in 1963. 5. Bo Jackson won by a 45-vote margin in 1985. 6. Anthony Davis. 7. Alan Ameche was from Wisconsin, the same school that later produced Ron Dayne. 8. BYU's Ty Detmer passed for 15,031 career yards, the highest total in NCAA history. 9. Texas' Ricky Williams ran for 350 yards in a 1998 game against Iowa State. 10. Charlie Ward, who chose to pursue a professional basketball career.

SEASONAL OFFERINGS: 1. 1972. 2. 1983. 3. 1991. 4. 1969. 5. 1988. 6. 1963. 7. 1979. 8. 1999. 9. 1951. 10. 1984.

BOWL SESSIONS (WARMING UP): 1. Former Texas coach Darrell Royal was 5-5 in Cotton Bowl games. 2. Oklahoma's Barry Switzer. 3. Georgia Tech was the first of four, completing that feat with a win over Tulsa in the 1944 Sugar Bowl. 4. Alabama. 5. Ohio State, Penn State and Notre Dame. 6. Hugo Bezdek in 1923; Bob Higgins in 1948; Rip Engle in 1959, '60, '61 and '62. 7. Rockne made his only postseason appearance on January 1, 1925, when he watched his Irish beat Stanford in the Rose Bowl. No other Notre Dame team appeared in a bowl until 1970, primarily because of a self-imposed ban on postseason play. 8. Akron, Alabama-Birmingham, Arkansas State, Central Florida, Connecticut, Louisiana-Lafayette, Louisiana-Monroe, Middle Tennessee State, South Florida and Troy State. 9. Through the 2003 bowl season, Alabama teams had posted 29 postseason wins—two more than USC. 10. Nebraska, Tennessee and Texas all had 21 bowl losses.

BOWL SESSIONS (GETTING SERIOUS): 1. C. 2. F. 3. H. 4. A. 5. E. 6. D. 7. I. 8. J. 9. G. 10. B.

WHO'S THE BOSS? (WARMING UP): 1. Arkansas. 2. Kentucky. 3. West Virginia. 4. Wyoming. 5. TCU. 6. Miami of Ohio. 7. Iowa State. 8. Washington. 9. Georgia Tech. 10. Pittsburgh.

WHO'S THE BOSS? (GETTING SERIOUS): 1. John Cappelletti (Penn State). 2. John David Crow (Texas A&M). 3. Billy Vessels (Oklahoma). 4. Danny Wuerffel (Florida). 5. Herschel Walker (Georgia). 6. John Huarte (Notre Dame). 7. Ty Detmer (BYU). 8. Pat Sullivan (Auburn). 9. Billy Sims (Oklahoma). 10. Tim Brown (Notre Dame).

THE NAME GAME (WARMING UP): 1. North Texas (Mean Green) vs. Demon Deacons (Wake Forest). 2. Middle Tennessee (Blue Raiders) vs. Texas Tech (Red Raiders). 3. Ohio University (Bobcats) vs. Penn State (Nittany Lions). 4. Akron (Zips) vs. Kent State (Golden Flashes). 5. Central Michigan (Chippewas) vs. Florida State (Seminoles). 6. Wisconsin (Badgers) vs. Minnesota (Gophers). 7. Colorado (Buffaloes) vs. Marshall (Thundering Herd). 8. Maryland (Terrapins) vs. TCU (Horned Frogs). 9. N.C. State (Wolfpack) vs. New Mexico (Lobos). 10. Temple (Owls) vs. Rice (Owls).

THE NAME GAME (GETTING SERIOUS): 1. LSU, Auburn and Clemson, all Tigers. 2. Army, Auburn, Alabama and Arkansas. 3. TCU, Texas A&M and Texas. 4. The Georgia Tech Yellow Jackets, Alabama Crimson Tide and Syracuse Orangemen. 5. Five—Ohio State, Michigan State, Louisiana State, Penn State and Florida State. 6. The Georgia Bulldogs and Washington Huskies. 7. Minnesota, Michigan, Michigan State, Maryland, Mississippi and Miami (Fla.). 8. UCLA, USC, Brigham Young, Colorado and Washington. 9. Tennessee and Washington. 10. Ohio State, Oklahoma, Notre Dame and Nebraska.

RUSH, RUSH, RUSH: 1. Kevin Faulk (LSU). 2. George Rogers (South Carolina). 3. Bo Jackson (Auburn). 4. Herschel Walker (Georgia). 5. Deuce McAllister (Mississippi). 6. Errict Rhett (Florida) 7. Anthony Thompson (Indiana). 8. Archie Griffin (Ohio State). 9. Curt Warner (Penn State). 10. Darrell Thompson (Minnesota). 11. Ron Dayne (Wisconsin). 12. Eric Bieniemy (Colorado). 13. Mike Rozier (Nebraska). 14. Thurman Thomas (Oklahoma State). 15. Billy Sims (Oklahoma). 16. Troy Davis (Iowa State). 17. Charles White (USC). 18. Darrin Nelson (Stanford). 19. Woody Green (Arizona State). 20. Rueben Mayes (Washington State). 21. Ken Simonton (Oregon State).

FAMOUS PAIRS (WARMING UP): 1. USC and Ohio State have met seven times in the Rose Bowl. 2. Nebraska has played Miami (Fla.) four times in the Orange Bowl. 3. Vanderbilt and South Carolina. 4. Minnesota and Oklahoma. 5. Big 12 members Missouri and Kansas had played 112 times through the 2003 season. 6. Minnesota and Wisconsin have been playing for the axe trophy since 1948. 7. Michigan pounded Stanford, 49-0. 8. Woodrow Danzler of Clemson performed the feat in 2001 and Missouri's Brad Smith followed suit in 2002. 9. Oklahoma State in 1988 (Barry Sanders 2,628 rushing yards, Mike Gundy 2,163 passing and Hart Lee Dykes 1,278 receiving); Texas in 1998 (Ricky Williams 2,124 rushing, Major Applewhite 2,453 passing and Wane McGarity 1,087 receiving). 10. Michigan's Rick Leach (1975-78) scored 204 and passed for 270; Indiana's Antaan Randle-El (1988-01) scored 264 and passed for 258.

FAMOUS PAIRS (GETTING SERIOUS): 1. I—Hayes, the Ohio State coach, punched Clemson defender Bauman after he had intercepted a late-game pass to preserve a 17-15 Tigers victory in the 1978 Gator Bowl. The incident cost Hayes his job. 2. R—Penn State linebacker Giftopoulos secured a national championship by picking off a late-game pass from Heisman Trophy-winning quarterback Testaverde at the Lions' 1-yard line to preserve a win over Miami in the 1987 Fiesta Bowl. 3. B—Colorado receiver Westbrook caught a tipped 64-yard Hail Mary pass from Stewart as time expired, beating Michigan in a 1994 game that will forever be remembered for "The Catch." 4. G—Texas receiver Speyrer and quarterback Street connected on a fourth-and-2 pass that set up the winning touchdown in a 1970 Cotton Bowl win over Notre Dame. 5. O—Lewis was an Alabama player who jumped off the bench to tackle Rice's Moegle, who had broken free for an apparent 95-yard touchdown run in the 1954 Cotton Bowl. 6. L—Phelan was on the receiving end of college football's most celebrated Hail Mary pass, the 48-yard toss by Boston College's Flutie in a shocking 1984 win over Miami (Fla.). 7. A—Snow was Huarte's go-to receiver in a Cinderella 1964 season in which Huarte earned a Heisman Trophy and came within a few minutes of leading Notre Dame to an undefeated season. 8. C—Nebraska QB Frost threw the pass and Davison made a diving end zone catch after it had been deflected to cap a miracle 1997 comeback that forced an overtime at Missouri and led to ultimate victory. 9. F—Houston QB Klingler (563) and TCU QB Vogler (690) combined for 1,253 passing yards in a 56-35 TCU win in 1990. 10. P—Davis and Blanchard were Army's Mr. Inside and Mr. Outside running tandem and consecutive winners of the Heisman Trophy (1945 and '46). 11. T—Thomas, the leading rusher in Oklahoma State history, was the reason Sanders saw limited playing time until 1988, his junior season. 12. E—Bryant was Namath's coach at Alabama from 1962-64. 13. S—Parseghian and Daugherty are the former Notre Dame and Michigan State coaches whose teams played to a controversial 10-10 tie in a 1966 national championship-influencing game. 14. J—When Notre Dame QB Dorais put on college football's first real passing display in a 1913 game against Army, Rockne caught a touchdown pass. 15. Q—When Tomlinson ran for a Division I-A record 406 yards in a 1999 game against TCU, he bested the former mark of 396 held by Kansas back Sands. 16. D—The Tensi-to-Biletnikoff passing combination clicked for Florida State often from 1962-64. 17. H—Chicago's Berwanger was the 1935 recipient of the first Heisman Trophy, the statue contemporary New York University star Smith posed for. 18. K—Brown and Davis were legendary stars who followed each other at Syracuse University. 19. N—Pittsburgh's Brown hauled in a 33-yard TD pass from Marino in the final 35 seconds of the 1982 Sugar Bowl to give the Panthers a 24-20 win over Georgia. 20. M—Nebraska's Tagge and Oklahoma's Mildren were the opposing quarterbacks in the so-called "Game of the Century" won by the Cornhuskers in 1971.

PLACES OF THE HEART (WARMING UP): 1. Bobby Dodd Stadium at Grant Field has been used by Georgia Tech teams since 1913. 2. Harvard students have been attending games at Harvard Stadium since 1903. 3. The Mountain West. War Memorial is home of Wyoming football, Rice-Eccles is Utah, Qualcomm is San Diego State, University is New Mexico and Hughes is Colorado State. 4. It was the first indoor game in college football history. 5. All of them have an animal in their name: Air Force (Falcon), Arkansas (Razorback), Boise State (Bronco), Fresno State (Bulldog), Louisville (Cardinal), LSU (Tiger), Northern Illinois (Huskie), Penn State (Beaver) and Washington (Husky). 6. UCLA (Rose), Texas-El Paso (Sun), Toledo (Glass), Miami-Florida (Orange), Memphis (Liberty) and Akron (Rubber). 7. The game, played at Houston's Astrodome, was the first on artificial turf. 8. Michigan Stadium (107,501), Penn State's Beaver Stadium (106,537), Tennessee's Neyland Stadium (104,079) and Ohio Stadium (101,568). 9. Iowa's Kinnick Stadium was named after 1939 Heisman winner Nile Kinnick. 10. Auburn's Cliff Hare Stadium honored coach Ralph "Shug" Jordan in 1973 by renaming its facility Jordan-Hare Stadium.

PLACES OF THE HEART (GETTING SERIOUS): 1. Army's Michie Stadium. 2. Wisconsin's Camp Randall Stadium. 3. Clemson's Memorial Stadium. 4. Florida's Ben Hill Griffin Stadium, a k a The Swamp. 5. Tennessee's Neyland Stadium. 6. Florida's State's Doak Campbell Stadium. 7. Texas' Memorial Stadium. 8. Georgia's Sanford Stadium. 9. Auburn's Jordan-Hare Stadium. 10. Nebraska's Memorial Stadium.

Chapter 10: Game Faces

1. Yao Ming

2. Terry Bradshaw

3. Tim Duncan

4. Dale Earnhardt

5. Julius Erving

6. Kevin Garnett

7. Jeff Gordon

8. Wayne Gretzky

9. Howie Long

10. Al Davis

11. Dick Butkus

12. Larry Bird

13. Alex Rodriguez

14. Hale Irwin

15. Barry Bonds

16. Brett Hull

17. Ichiro Suzuki

18. Kareem Abdul-Jabbar

19. Derek Jeter

20. Randy Johnson

21. Lebron James

22. John Madden

23. Magic Johnson

24. Mark McGwire

25. Joe Montana

26. Jack Nicklaus

27. Richard Petty

28. David Robinson

29. Dennis Rodman

30. Rollie Fingers

31. Tiger Woods

32. Michael Jordan

33. Peyton Manning

34. Sammy Sosa

35. Joe Torre

36. Yogi Berra

37. Dick Vermeil

Chapter 11: College Basketball

MATCHUPS (WARMING UP): 1. Houston's Astrodome. 2. Notre Dame's Athletic and Convocation Center, now known as the Edmund P. Joyce Center. 3. St. Louis' Checkerdome. 4. Munich, Germany. 5. Assembly Hall in Bloomington, Ind. 6. New York's Madison Square Garden. 7. Gersten Pavilion in Los Angeles. 8. The Spectrum in Philadelphia. 9. The St. Louis Arena. 10. San Diego Sports Arena.

MATCHUPS (GETTING SERIOUS): 1. Ohio State's Lucas-Havlicek defeated California's Imhoff-McClintock. 2. Georgetown's Wingate-Williams defeated Houston's Olajuwon-Franklin. 3. North Carolina's Montross-Williams defeated Michigan's Howard-Rose. 4. Duke's Hill-Hill defeated Kansas' Randall-Jordan. 5. UCLA's Alcindor-Wicks defeated Purdue's Mount-Gilliam. 6. N.C. State's Thompson-Burleson defeated Marquette's Lucas-Ellis. 7. Kentucky's Macy-Robey defeated Duke's Spanarkel-Banks. 8. Maryland's Dixon-Baxter defeated Indiana's Jeffries-Coverdale. 9. Louisville's Thompson-Wagner defeated Duke's Dawkins-Henderson. 10. Kentucky's Mercer-Walker defeated Syracuse's Wallace-Burgan.

FOLLOW THE LEADER (WARMING UP): 1. Michigan, 1989. 2. UCLA, 1965. 3. Kentucky, 1996. 4. N.C. State, 1983. 5. Indiana, 1976. 6. California, 1959. 7. Cincinnati, 1962. 8. Duke, 2001. 9. Georgetown, 1984. 10. Kentucky, 1949.

FOLLOW THE LEADER (GETTING SERIOUS): 1. Duke (Dawkins). 2. Tennessee (Houston). 3. Arkansas (Day). 4. Wisconsin (Finley). 5. Iowa State (Grayer). 6. Georgia (Green). 7. Georgia Tech (Yunkus). 8. Arizona State (House). 9. Missouri (Chievous). 10. Iowa (Marble). 11. Kentucky (Issel). 12. North Carolina (Ford). 13. Baylor (Teagle). 14. Stanford (Lichti). 15. Florida State (Sura). 16. UCLA (MacLean). 17. Mississippi State (Malone). 18. Virginia (Stith). 19. Purdue (Mount). 20. Indiana (Cheaney). 21. Nebraska (Hoppen). 22. Oregon State (Payton). 23. Illinois (Thomas). 24. Clemson (Campbell). 25. Auburn (Person).

FIRST THINGS FIRST (WARMING UP): 1. Oklahoma A&M (now Oklahoma State) won in 1945 and '46. 2. Kentucky won the NIT title in 1946, the NCAA title in 1948. 3. Bradshaw became the first player to break the 70-point barrier in an all-Division I game when he scored 72 against Loyola Marymount. 4. LSU guard Chris Jackson averaged 30.2 in 1988-89. 5. Pete Maravich still holds the NCAA career record with 3,667 points, despite playing only three seasons. 6. Tom Gola finished his career in 1955 with 2,462 points and 2,201 rebounds. 7. Duke finished 37-3 after losing the title game to Louisville. 8. The University of San Francisco posted 60 straight wins from 1955-57. 9. UCLA's Gail Goodrich scored 42 points against Michigan in 1965. 10. UNLV beat Duke, 103-73, in 1990.

FIRST THINGS FIRST (GETTING SERIOUS): 1. James Worthy, 15.6 points per game. 2. Scott May, 23.5. 3. Corliss Williamson, 20.4. 4. Greg Kelser, 18.8. 5. Jerry Lucas, 26.3. 6. Glen Rice, 25.6. 7. Richard Hamilton, 21.5. 8. Sidney Wicks, 18.6. 9. Alex Groza, 20.5. 10. Bob Kurland, 19.5.

THE WINNING TOUCH (WARMING UP): 1. Oscar Robertson. 2. George Mikan. 3. Elgin Baylor. 4. Wayman Tisdale. 5. Phil Ford. 6. Cazzie Russell. 7. Jerry West. 8. Walter Davis. 9. Loren Woods. 10. Chris Webber.

THE WINNING TOUCH (GETTING SERIOUS): 1. Indiana. 2. North Carolina. 3. Connecticut. 4. Louisville. 5. Kentucky. 6. Michigan. 7. N.C. State. 8. Kansas. 9. Duke. 10. Loyola of Chicago.

AND THEN THERE WERE FOUR (WARMING UP): 1. Arizona achieved that feat in 1997. 2. Both North Carolina and Wisconsin were 22-13 when they reached the Final Four. 3. Tubby Smith (Tulsa, Georgia and Kentucky), Eddie Sutton (Arkansas, Kentucky and Oklahoma State) and Bill Self (Tulsa, Illinois and Kansas). 4. Bill Self performed that feat with Tulsa in 2000 and Illinois in 2001. 5. Connecticut performed that unique double in 2004. 6. Bob Bender played for Indiana's 1976 national champions and the 1978 Duke team that lost to Kentucky. 7. Ohio State (1961-62), Houston (1983-84) and Michigan (1992-93). 8. Marques (1975) and Kris (1995) Johnson did it with UCLA; Henry (1970, '71, '72) and Mike (1997) Bibby did it for UCLA and Arizona, respectively. 9. One—Texas Western (UTEP) in 1966. 10. Duke and North Carolina.

AND THEN THERE WERE FOUR (GETTING SERIOUS): 1. UNLV (Tarkanian and Hunt) defeated Duke (Krzyzewski and Hurley), 103-73. 2. Villanova (Massimino and McClain) defeated Georgetown (Thompson and Williams), 66-64. 3. Kentucky (Hall and Macy) defeated Duke (Foster and Gminski), 94-88. 4. Texas Western (Haskins and Hill) defeated Kentucky (Rupp and Riley), 72-65. 5. Indiana (Knight and Benson) defeated Michigan (Orr and Green), 86-68. 6. Arkansas (Richardson and Thurman) defeated Duke (Krzyzewski and Hill), 76-72. 7. Cincinnati (Jucker and Hogue) defeated Ohio State (Taylor and Havlicek), 71-59. 8. Indiana (Knight and Wittman) defeated North Carolina (Smith and Perkins), 63-50. 9. UCLA (Wooden and Wicks) defeated Jacksonville (Williams and Gilmore), 80-69. 10. San Francisco (Woolpert and Russell) defeated La Salle (Loeffler and Gola), 77-63.

SIGNAL-CALLERS (WARMING UP): 1. Knight—Kent Benson and Andre Emmett. 2. Tarkanian—Larry Johnson and Melvin Ely. 3. Bartow—Larry Kenon and Marques Johnson. 4. Harrick—Tyus Edney and Jarvis Hayes. 5. Williams—Dennis Hopson and Steve Francis. 6. Olson—Ronnie Lester and Mike Bibby. 7. Pitino—Billy Donovan and Jamal Mashburn. 8. Sutton—Sidney Moncrief and Bryant Reeves. 9. Tubbs—Wayman Tisdale and Brent Price. 10. Orr—Rickey Green and Jeff Grayer.

SIGNAL-CALLERS (GETTING SERIOUS): 1. UCLA—Gene Bartow, Larry Brown, Gary Cunningham. 2. Kansas—Dick Harp, Larry Brown, Ted Owens. 3. Kentucky—Eddie Sutton, Joe B. Hall, Rick Pitino. 4. Memphis—Dana Kirk, Gene Bartow, John Calipari. 5. Illinois—Lou Henson, Gene Bartow, Lon Kruger. 6. Florida—Norm Sloan, Lon Kruger, Billy Donovan. 7. Kansas State—Tex Winter, Lon Kruger, Jack Hartman. 8. Marquette—Al McGuire, Hank Raymonds, Tex Winter. 9. N.C. State—Norm Sloan, Jim Valvano, Les Robinson. 10. Creighton—Eddie Sutton, Willis Reed, Tony Barone.

WHAT'S IN A NAME? (WARMING UP): 1. F. 2. A. 3. B. 4. H. 5. E. 6. I. 7. G. 8. C. 9. J. 10. D.

WHAT'S IN A NAME? (GETTING SERIOUS): 1. The "Fab Five" of Michigan in the early 1990s. 2. The former Oklahoma State star (1992-95) known as "Big Country." 3. The "Cameron Crazies," so-called because Duke plays its home games at Cameron Indoor Stadium. 4. The nickname given to Purdue star Glenn Robinson (1993-94). 5. The primary supporting cast for UCLA's "Walton Gang," named for star center Bill Walton, from 1971-72 through 1973-74. 6. The "Wizard of Westwood" led UCLA to 10 national championships from 1949-75. 7. New Mexico's home arena is known affectionately as "The Pit." 8. "Zeke from Cabin Creek" was the moniker given to the quick-shooting West Virginia guard, who hailed from the mountainous backwoods of the state he represented. 9. The nickname given to Jerry Tarkanian, who coached UNLV to a national championship in 1989-90. 10. Phi Slama Jama, the nickname bestowed on Houston's high-flying dunking fraternity in the early 1980s.

POLL CLIMBING (WARMING UP): 1. St. Louis University. 2. The 1991-92 Duke Blue Devils. 3. UNLV in 1989-90 and 1990-91. 4. UCLA. 5. Ohio State. The Buckeyes, the national champion in 1960, were upset in the title game each of the next two seasons by Cincinnati. 6. Duke held that distinction from 1999 through 2002. 7. Kentucky. 8. Duke and Kansas. 9. In each case, the AP's No. 2 team upset its No. 1. 10. The Bruins were not ranked in either of the first two polls that season.

POLL CLIMBING (GETTING SERIOUS): 1. F. 2. I. 3. B. 4. E. 5. G. 6. A. 7. H. 8. J. 9. D. 10. C.

——— Chapter 12: Baseball Silhouettes ———

1. St. Louis Cardinals center fielder Jim Edmonds. 2. Houston Astros first baseman Jeff Bagwell. 3. Cincinnati Reds center fielder Ken Griffey Jr. 4. San Francisco Giants left fielder Barry Bonds. 5. Seattle Mariners right fielder Ichiro Suzuki. 6. Chicago Cubs left fielder Moises Alou. 7. Boston Red Sox pitcher Byung-Hyun Kim. 8. Florida Marlins pitcher Dontrelle Willis. 9. Arizona Diamondbacks first baseman Richie Sexson. 10. Houston Astros pitcher Roger Clemens. 11. Milwaukee Brewers infielder Craig Counsell. 12. Chicago White Sox first baseman Frank Thomas. 13. New York Yankees shortstop Derek Jeter. 14. Houston Astros pitcher Andy Pettitte. 15. Boston Red Sox pitcher Tim Wakefield. 16. Chicago Cubs right fielder Sammy Sosa. 17. Philadelphia Phillies first baseman Jim Thome. 18. Texas Rangers second baseman Alfonso Soriano. 19. Arizona Diamondbacks pitcher Randy Johnson. 20. Los Angeles Dodgers pitcher Hideo Nomo. 21. Seattle Mariners designated hitter Edgar Martinez. 22. Boston Red Sox left fielder Manny Ramirez. 23. Atlanta Braves first baseman Julio Franco. 24. Los Angeles Dodgers closer Eric Gagne.

Chapter 13: Pro Sports

A 10-YEAR ITCH: 1. Wagner won his first batting title in 1900; the first World Series was played in 1903; the Giants refused to play the Red Sox in a 1904 World Series; Merkle made his infamous baserunning blunder in 1908; Shibe Park opened in 1909. 2. Alexander was a rookie pitcher in 1911; Fenway Park opened in 1912; Ruth hit his first home run in 1915; the Toney-Vaughn double no-hitter occurred in 1917; the NHL played its first season in 1918. 3. The NFL was founded in 1920; Yankee Stadium opened in 1923; the Boston Bruins were added to the NFL roster in 1924; Johnson won his 400th game in 1926; Ruth hit his 60 home runs in 1927. 4. Wilson enjoyed his record binge for the Cubs in 1930; baseball's first All-Star Game was played in 1933; the NFL's "Sneakers Game" was played in 1934; baseball's first Hall of Fame class was announced in 1936; Lou Gehrig Day was celebrated in 1939. 5. DiMaggio's streak ended in 1941; the Maple Leafs pulled off their amazing comeback in 1942; the Rams became football's first West Coast franchise in 1945; the Warriors won the NBA's first championship in 1947; Ruth died in 1948. 6. Thomson hit his pennant-winning homer in 1951; the Lions won their second straight NFL title in 1953; the NBA adopted the 24-second clock in 1955; Mantle captured the Triple Crown in 1956; Haddix's dazzling pitching effort occurred in 1959. 7. Williams retired in 1960; Wills set his stolen base record in 1962; the Astrodome opened in 1965; the Celtics won their eighth straight title in 1966; the first Super Bowl was played in 1967. 8. The WHA organized in 1971; Clemente died on New Year's Eve in 1972; Simpson set his rushing record in 1973; the Flyers won their second straight Cup title in 1975; the Pirates "Family" won the World Series in 1979. 9. The Islanders won their first Stanley Cup in 1980; Henderson stole his 130 bases in 1982; Rose collected his record hit in 1985; the Lakers won their fourth 1980s title in 1987; Gretzky was traded to the Kings in 1988. 10. The Bulls won their first NBA title in 1991; the World Series was cancelled in 1994; the Avs won their first Cup title in 1996; McGwire became baseball's single-season home run king in 1998; Elway played his final game in 1999.

UNIFORMITY (WARMING UP): 1. Abdul Jabbar (33) + Mattingly (23) + Brock (20) ÷ Orr (4) = 19 (Johnny Unitas); 2. Butkus (51) + Havlicek (17) + Aaron (44) — (Esposito (7) + Kaline (6)) = 99 (George Mikan); 3. Gretzky (99) — Russell (6) — Carlton (32) + Harvey (2) = 63 (Willie Lanier); 4. (Robinson (42) X Killebrew (3)) — West 44 ÷ Seaver (41) + Fouts (14) = 16 (Frank Gifford); 5. Ryan (34) + Elway (7) —Unseld (41) + Thompson = 33 (Larry Bird); 6. (Berry (82) + Bossy (22)) ÷ Berra (8) = 13 (Wilt Chamberlain); 7. (Jackson (44) + Parent (1) + Munson (15)) X Moncrief (4) ÷ Murphy (3) = 80 (Steve Largent); 8. (Sutton (20) X Ruth (3)) X English (2) — Page (88) + Bradley (24) = 56 (Lawrence Taylor); 9. (Maravich (7) ÷ Beliveau (4)) X Molitor (4) + Lasorda (2) = 9 (Gordie Howe); 10. Frazier (10) + Sayers (40) — Dionne (16) = 34 (Earl Campbell).

UNIFORMITY (GETTING SERIOUS): No. 4—Lou Gehrig (baseball), Brett Favre (football), Chris Webber (basketball), Bobby Orr (hockey); No. 5—George Brett (baseball), Paul Hornung (football), Jason Kidd (basketball), Denis Potvin (hockey); No. 33—Eddie Murray (baseball), Sammy Baugh (football), Larry Bird (basketball), Patrick Roy (hockey); No. 22—Jim Palmer (baseball), Emmitt Smith (football), Elgin Baylor (basketball), Mike Bossy (hockey); No. 10—Ron Santo (baseball), Fran Tarkenton (football), Mike Bibby (basketball), Guy Lafleur (hockey); No. 16—Whitey Ford (baseball), Joe Montana (football), Bob Lanier (basketball), Bobby Clarke (hockey); No. 11—Barry Larkin (baseball), Phil Simms (football), Isiah Thomas (basketball), Mark Messier (hockey); No. 19—Tony Gwynn (baseball), Johnny Unitas (football), Willis Reed (basketball), Steve Yzerman (hockey); No. 31—Mike Piazza (baseball), Jim Taylor (football), Reggie Miller (basketball), Grant Fuhr (hockey); No. 21—Sammy Sosa (baseball), Deion Sanders (football), Kevin Garnett (basketball), Stan Mikita (hockey). Note: Joe Morgan, the extra, wore No. 8.

ROOTS (WARMING UP): 1. Minnesota North Stars. 2. Decatur Staleys. 3. Baltimore Orioles. 4. Rochester Royals. 5. Toronto Arenas. 6. Milwaukee Brewers. 7. Houston Oilers. 8. Syracuse Nationals. 9. Winnipeg Jets. 10. Cleveland Rams.

ROOTS (GETTING SERIOUS): 1. The American Basketball Association, which existed from 1967-76. 2. The World Football League, 1974-75. 3. The World Hockey Association, 1972-79. 4. The United States Football League, 1983-85. 5. The Federal League (baseball), 1914-15. 6. The ABA. 7. The All-America Football Conference, 1946-49. 8. The American Football League, 1960-69. 9. The WHA. 10. The Xtreme Football League, 2001.

MIXED RESULTS (WARMING UP): 1. The 1972 Miami Dolphins were 14-0 (1.000) in the regular season en route to a victory in Super Bowl 7; the 1995-96 Chicago Bulls were 72-10 (.878) en route to an NBA championship; the 1906 Chicago Cubs finished 116-36 (.763) before losing in the World Series to the Chicago White Sox. 2. Orioles first baseman Boog Powell was A.L. MVP. 3. Scotty Bowman coached the Montreal Canadiens to five Stanley Cup titles, the Pittsburgh Penguins to one and the Detroit Red Wings to three. 4. Auburn's Bo Jackson enjoyed his best professional success with the Kansas City Royals and Chicago White Sox, although he did raise a few eyebrows on the football field as well; Florida State's Charlie Ward completed his 10th season with the New York Knicks in 2003-04. 5. Wayne Gretzky (Edmonton, Los Angeles) and Mark Messier (Edmonton, N.Y. Rangers) in hockey; Kareem Abdul-Jabbar (Milwaukee, Los Angeles), Wilt Chamberlain (Philadelphia Warriors and 76ers), Moses Malone (Houston, Philadelphia) in basketball; Barry Bonds (Pittsburgh, San Francisco), Jimmie Foxx (Philadelphia A's, Boston Red Sox), Frank Robinson (Cincinnati, Baltimore) in baseball. 6. Gordie Howe played 1,767 games in the NHL, Robert Parish played 1,611 in the NBA, George Blanda played 340 in the NFL and Pete Rose played 3,562 in baseball. 7. Phillies third baseman Scott Rolen was the National League's top rookie and 76ers guard Allen Iverson won in the NBA. 8. Abdul-Jabbar had 38,387 points, Gretzky had 2,857 points, Anderson had 2,346 points and Henderson had 2,295 runs. 9. Thurman Thomas, 1991 in the NFL; Dominik Hasek, 1997-98 in the NHL, and Bob McAdoo, 1974-75 in the NBA. 10. California—three by the NBA's Los Angeles Lakers and one by baseball's Anaheim Angels. Florida teams had three.

MIXED RESULTS (GETTING SERIOUS): 1. Tom Lasorda, Dodgers; Tom Flores, Raiders; Bill Walsh, 49ers; Joe Gibbs, Redskins; Pat Riley, Lakers; K.C. Jones, Celtics; Al Arbour, Islanders; Glen Sather, Oilers. 2. Steve Garvey, 1974 Dodgers; Roman Gabriel, 1969 Rams; Wayne Gretzky, 1988-89 Kings; Magic Johnson, 1989-90 Lakers, and Shaquille O'Neal, 1999-2000 Lakers. 3. Ray Bourque, 1,506 points for the Bruins; Gino Cappelletti, 1,130 points for the Patriots; Larry Bird, 21,791 points for the Celtics; Carl Yastrzemski, 1,816 runs scored for the Red Sox. 4. Jacques Demers led the Montreal Canadiens to a 1993 championship; Cito Gaston led the Toronto Blue Jays to titles in 1992 and '93; John Muckler led the Edmonton Oilers to a title in 1990; Terry Crisp guided the Calgary Flames to a title in 1989; Glen Sather led the Oilers to a title in 1988. 5. Michael Jordan is a 10-time NBA scoring champion; Wayne Gretzky a 10-time NHL scoring champion; Wilt Chamberlain a seven-time NBA scoring champion; Babe Ruth a six-time MLB RBI champion; Gordie Howe a six-time NHL scoring champion; Mario Lemieux a six-time NHL scoring champion; Lou Gehrig a five-time MLB RBI champion; Phil Esposito a five-time NHL scoring champion; Don Hutson a five-time NFL scoring champion; Jaromir Jagr a five-time NHL scoring champion. 6. Ken Griffey Jr., baseball; Vinny Testaverde, NFL; David Robinson, NBA; Pierre Turgeon, NHL. 7. Derek Jeter, Yankees; Kurt Warner, Rams; Shaquille O'Neal, Lakers; Scott Stevens, Devils. 8. George Allen, NFL; Felipe Alou, baseball; Rick Adelman, NBA; Sid Abel, NHL. 9. Jim Marshall, NFL, 282 games; Cal Ripken, baseball, 2,632; A.C. Green, NBA, 1,192; Doug Jarvis, NHL, 964. 10. Michael Vick, Atlanta Falcons; Yao Ming, Houston Rockets; Rick Nash, Columbus Blue Jackets; Bryan Bullington, Pittsburgh Pirates.

NICKNAMES (WARMING UP): 1. Mr. Cub is baseball's Ernie Banks; Mr. Goalie is hockey's Glenn Hall; Mr. October is baseball's Reggie Jackson; Mr. Hockey is hockey's Gordie Howe. 2. The Big Train is baseball's Walter Johnson; Big Dog is basketball's Glenn Robinson; Big Bird is hockey's Don Saleski; The Big Unit is baseball's Randy Johnson. 3. The Pearl is basketball's Earl Monroe; The Flower is hockey's Guy Lafleur; Silk is basketball's Jamaal Wilkes; Twinkle Toes is baseball's George Selkirk. 4. White Shoes is football's Billy Johnson; Le Grande Orange is baseball's Rusty Staub, The Golden Jet is hockey's Bobby Hull, Greyhound is basketball's Walter Davis. 5. Kong is baseball's Dave Kingman; Manimal is football's Randy White; Cujo is hockey's Curtis Joseph; The Beast is baseball's Jimmie Foxx. 6. Moose is baseball's Bill Skowron; Bambi is football's Lance Alworth; Ducky is baseball's Joe Medwick; Snake is football's Ken Stabler. 7. Shoeless Joe is baseball's Joe Jackson; Broadway Joe is football's Joe Namath; Jumpin' Joe is basketball's Joe Fulks; Mean Joe is football's Joe Greene. 8. The Hawk is baseball's Andre Dawson; The Stork is football's Ted Hendricks; The Worm is basketball's Dennis Rodman; The Cobra is baseball's Dave Parker. 9. Boom Boom is hockey's Bernie Geoffrion; Bye-Bye is baseball's Steve Balboni; Choo Choo is football's Charlie Justice; Say Hey is baseball's Willie Mays. 10. The Russian Rocket is hockey's Pavel Bure; The Reading Rifle is baseball's Carl Furillo; The Commerce Comet is baseball's Mickey Mantle; The Tyler Rose is football's Earl Campbell.

NICKNAMES (GETTING SERIOUS): 1. Chicago—The Stags, Packers, Zephyrs and Bulls all have competed in the NBA; the Tigers, Cardinals and Bears in the NFL; the Cubs in MLB. 2. Detroit—The Falcons and Pistons have competed in the NBA; the Heralds, Panthers, Wolverines and Lions in the NFL;

the Cougars and Falcons in the NHL; the Tigers in MLB. 3. St. Louis—The Hawks and Bombers have competed in the NBA; the Cardinals and Rams in the NFL; the Eagles and Blues in the NHL; the Cardinals and Browns in MLB. 4. Cleveland—The Rebels have competed in the NBA; the Tigers, Indians, Bulldogs and Browns in the NFL; the Barons in the NHL; the Naps (a commonly used nickname when Nap Lajoie played for Cleveland) and Indians in MLB. 5. Kansas City—The Kings have competed in the NBA; the Scouts in the NHL; the Cowboys and Chiefs in the NFL; the Athletics in MLB. 6. Boston—The Celtics have competed in the NBA; the Bulldogs, Braves and Patriots in the NFL; the Bruins in the NHL; the Braves and Pilgrims in MLB. 7. New York—The Nets have competed in the NBA; the Giants and Jets in the NFL; the Americans, Rangers and Islanders in the NHL; the Highlanders and Mets in MLB. 8. Toronto—The Huskies and Raptors have competed in the NBA; the Arenas, St. Patricks and Maple Leafs in the NHL; the Blue Jays in MLB. 9. Philadelphia—The Warriors and 76ers have competed in the NBA; the Eagles in the NFL; the Quakers and Flyers in the NHL; the Athletics in MLB. 10. Brooklyn—The Lions, Tigers and Dodgers have competed in the NFL; the Americans in the NHL; the Robins (a commonly used nickname when Wilbert Robinson managed the team) and Dodgers in MLB.

RICH MAN, JOE MAN (WARMING UP): 1. Joe Medwick (1937), Joe Torre (1971) and Joe Morgan (1975, '76) in the N.L.; Joe DiMaggio (1939, '41, '47) and Joe Gordon (1942) in the A.L. 2. Mitch Richmond played for the 2001-02 NBA-champion Los Angeles Lakers. 3. "Toe" Blake, who went on to coach eight Montreal Stanley Cup champions, was a member of the Punch Line. 4. Longtime San Francisco 49ers star Joe Perry. 5. Philadelphia Phillies third baseman Richie Allen was N.L. Rookie of the Year. 6. Former Buffalo and Cleveland offensive guard Joe DeLamielleure. 7. Curtis Joseph trailed only Ed Belfour and Martin Brodeur. 8. All three were Heisman Trophy runners-up in college—Penn State's Lucas to Billy Cannon in 1959; Notre Dame's Theismann to Jim Plunkett in 1970; Georgia Tech's Hamilton to Ron Dayne in 1999. 9. Joe Sakic finished the 2003-04 season with 542 career goals. 10. Gail Goodrich averaged 25.9 points in 1971-72.

RICH MAN, JOE MAN (GETTING SERIOUS): 1. New York Jets quarterback Joe Namath. 2. Former Kansas guard Kirk Hinrich. 3. The nickname of former Montreal Canadiens star Henri Richard. 4. Oakland quarterback Rich Gannon completed a record 418 passes in the 2002 season. 5. Hall of Fame center fielder Richie Ashburn wore uniform No. 1 in his long Philadelphia career. 6. Toronto's Joe Carter hit a World Series-clinching home run against Phillies pitcher Williams in 1993. 7. Jo Jo White played in the backcourt for Boston championship teams in 1974 and 1976. 8. New York Yankees manager Joe Torre has been all three in his distinguished baseball career. 9. The career numbers of Hall of Fame quarterback Joe Montana. 10. Tarkenton was born in Richmond.

RELATIVELY SPEAKING (WARMING UP): 1. Randy Moffitt and Billie Jean King. 2. Boxer Ken Norton and football player Ken Norton Jr. 3. Hall of Fame golfer Nancy Lopez and former baseball player Ray Knight. 4. Basketball stars Reggie and Cheryl Miller are the brother and sister of former major leaguer Darrell Miller. 5. Frank Tripucka and son Kelly Tripucka. 6. Todd Zeile and Julianne McNamara. 7. Jack Snow and J.T. Snow. 8. Bill Walton and Bruce Walton. 9. Don Drysdale and Ann Meyers. 10. Calvin Hill and Grant Hill.

RELATIVELY SPEAKING (GETTING SERIOUS): 1. Major league pitcher Jamie Moyer. 2. NFL quarterback Chris Chandler. 3. Former major league player and manager Bobby Valentine. 4. Former major league pitcher Denny McLain. 5. NHL Hall of Famer and former right wing Boom Boom Geoffrion. 6. Former major league pitcher Greg Booker. 7. Former NBA coach Jim O'Brien. 8. 1937 horse racing Triple Crown winner War Admiral. 9. Former major league first baseman Pete LaCock. 10. NFL linebacker Ryan Nece. 11. Former NFL quarterback Bobby Hoying. 12. Major league infielders Bret Boone and Aaron Boone. 13. NHL goaltender Brent Johnson. 14. Major league outfielder Gary Sheffield. 15. NHL winger Brett Hull. 16. NFL wide receiver Jake Reed. 17. Former major league outfielder Jose Cardenal.

CALLING THE SHOTS (WARMING UP): 1. In 1997 and 1998, Mike Shanahan guided the NFL's Denver Broncos to consecutive titles, Phil Jackson led the NBA's Chicago Bulls to their second and third straight titles and Scotty Bowman directed the NHL's Detroit Red Wings to consecutive championships. 2. The NBA's Phil Jackson. 3. Joe McCarthy, Casey Stengel, Joe Torre. 4. Red Auerbach led the Boston Celtics to eight straight titles from 1959 through 1966. 5. Vince Lombardi, 1965 through 1967. 6. Al Arbour guided the New York Islanders to four straight Stanley Cup championships from 1980 through

1983. 7. Billy Cunningham, 1983 Philadelphia 76ers. 8. The top five coaches in NHL history have produced 30 championships, one more than the top five in NBA history and four more than the top five baseball managers. 9. It's a three-way tie. Scotty Bowman in the NHL, Red Auerbach in the NBA and Phil Jackson in the NBA all have nine titles. 10. Ralph Houk, New York Yankees, 1961 and 1962.

CALLING THE SHOTS (GETTING SERIOUS):: 1. 1989. 2. 1979. 3. 1969. 4. 1986. 5. 1957. 6. 1993. 7. 1974. 8. 1967. 9. 1948. 10. 1999.

CITY SLICKERS (WARMING UP):: 1. New York has celebrated 20 title-winning teams. 2. Boston has 17, Los Angeles 14 and Montreal 13. 3. 1968. 4. 1983. 5. Boston had 9 in the 1960s, Los Angeles 8 in the 1980s. 6. The 1990s. 7. San Francisco and Edmonton, 1980s. 8. Anaheim, Atlanta, Calgary, Cleveland, Milwaukee, Phoenix, Portland, Seattle and Tampa. 9. Philadelphia and New York. 10. Baltimore in 1970, Pittsburgh in 1979, New York in 1986 and Los Angeles in 1988.

CITY SLICKERS (GETTING SERIOUS):: 1. 13. 2. Six. 3. Nine. 4. Four. 5. Six. 6.Nine. 7. Six. 8. Five. 9. Zero. 10. One.

Four's a Crowd

Chapter 14: All Sports

THIS DAY IN SPORTS: 1. Seattle Slew completed the 1977 Triple Crown, Ben Hogan won the 1950 U.S. Open and Michael Chang won the 1989 French Open on June 11. 2. Wayne Gretzky set his 50-game scoring record, Joe Montana orchestrated a Super Bowl 23 victory for the 49ers and George Foreman stunned Joe Frazier in a 1973 championship bout on January 22. 3. Mark McGwire became baseball's single-season home run champion, Rod Laver completed his second career grand slam and Bob Feller became the youngest no-hit pitcher in baseball history on September 8. 4. Reggie Jackson hit three Game 6 home runs to wrap up the Yankees' 1977 World Series win over the Dodgers, Bob Beamon leaped into the record books during the 1968 Summer Olympic Games at Mexico City and Casey Stengel was fired by the Yankees on October 18. 5. Jackie Robinson broke baseball's color barrier by playing in a 1947 game for the Dodgers, the transplanted Giants and Dodgers played the first game on the West Coast and

Fuzzy Zoeller won a 1979 Masters playoff on April 15. 6. Moses Malone and Julius Erving led the Philadelphia 76ers to their first NBA title in 16 years, Glenn Anderson's goal gave the Edmonton Oilers their third Stanley Cup championship in four years and A.J. Foyt won his record-tying third Indianapolis 500 on May 31. 7. Baseball said an emotional farewell to the Iron Horse during "Lou Gehrig Day" ceremonies at Yankee Stadium, John McEnroe ended Bjorn Borg's five-year championship reign at Wimbledon and Yankees lefthander Dave Righetti fired a holiday no-hitter at the Red Sox on July 4. 8. Roberto Clemente died when a cargo plane carrying relief supplies to Nicaraguan earthquake victims crashed into the ocean, Bart Starr scored the winning touchdown in the 1967 "Ice Bowl" game against Dallas and Notre Dame beat Alabama, 24-23, in the Sugar Bowl to win a national championship on December 31. 9. The U.S. Olympic hockey team shocked the powerful Soviets at Lake Placid, N.Y., Lee Petty won the first Daytona 500 and Bonnie Blair won the speed skating 500-meter gold medal in world-record time at the 1988 Winter Olympic Games on February 22. 10. Notre Dame coach Knute Rockne died in a plane crash at Bazaar, Kan., UCLA defeated Kentucky to give retirement-bound John Wooden his 10th NCAA championship and expansion teams Arizona and Tampa Bay lost their major league debut games on March 31. 11. The Thanksgiving Day Nebraska-Oklahoma football shootout is the extra event.

CHAMPIONSHIP CONNECTIONS (WARMING UP): 1. 1953, '63, '73, '83, '93. 2. 1945, '55, '65, '75, '85. 3. 1911, '21, '31, '41, '51. 4. 1938, '48, '58, '68, '78. 5. 1960, '70, '80, '90, 2000. 6. 1949, '59, '69, '79, '89. 7. 1954, '64, '74, '84, '94. 8. 1917, '27, '37, '47, '57. 9. 1962, '72, '82, '92, 2002. 10. 1946, '56, '66, '76, '86.

CHAMPIONSHIP CONNECTIONS (GETTING SERIOUS): 1. Cy Young winner Randy Johnson; NBA championship coach Phil Jackson; NHL scoring leader Jaromir Jagr. 2. A.L. MVP George Brett; Wimbledon champion Bjorn Borg; Daytona champion Buddy Baker. 3. Women's tennis champion Steffi Graf; Hart Trophy winner Wayne Gretzky; N.L. batting champion Tony Gwynn. 4. NFL rushing champion Barry Sanders; Heisman winner Rashaan Salaam; Yankees manager Buck Showalter. 5. Affirmed jockey Steve Cauthen; U.S. Open champion Jimmy Connors; NFL rushing champion Earl Campbell. 6. Cy Young winner Sandy Koufax; Wimbledon champ Billie Jean King; Eagles coach Joe Kuharich. 7. Daytona winner Richard Petty; Notre Dame coach Ara Parseghian; A.L. Cy Young winner Jim Palmer. 8. NFL rushing champion Emmitt Smith; Thunder Gulch jockey Gary Stevens; Wimbledon and U.S. Open champion Pete Sampras. 9. Los Angeles Dodgers manager Walter Alston; Boston Celtics coach Red Auerbach; Chicago White Sox shortstop Luis Aparicio. 10. Heisman winner Charles White; Seattle SuperSonics coach Lenny Wilkens; Orioles manager Earl Weaver.

LINKAGE (WARMING UP): 1. All were the inaugural winners of major sports events—Harroun won the first Indianapolis 500 in 1911; Smith the first Masters in 1934; Lacoste the first French Open in 1925; Petty the first Daytona 500 in 1959; Barnes the first PGA Championship in 1916. 2. Jimmy Connors (109), Ivan Lendl (94) and John McEnroe (77) rank ahead of Sampras (64). 3. Irwin and Anderson were members of the same defensive backfield for the University of Colorado in 1965 and '66. 4. All competed in events on the men's golf tour. 5. Bob Bourne and Clark Gillies. 6. New England Patriots coach Bill Belichick. 7. Bob Knight won three championships while coaching at Indiana University; John Havlicek and Jerry Lucas both are members of the basketball Hall of Fame. All played together for Ohio State teams that won a national title (1960) and lost two others in the championship game. 8. Ernie Nevers. 9. Current Syracuse coach Jim Boeheim and Hall of Famer Dave Bing once were Orangemen backcourt mates. 10. Mark McGwire and Randy Johnson.

LINKAGE (GETTING SERIOUS): 1. Jack Lambert. 2. Ozzie Smith and Eddie Murray. 3. Ollie Matson, Gino Marchetti and Bob St. Clair. 4. Gerald Ford and Ronald Reagan. 5. Richt backed up Jim Kelly for three seasons. He also was a one-year teammate of Bernie Kosar and future Heisman winner Vinny Testaverde. 6. Yogi Berra and Garagiola lived across the street from each other. Longtime Cardinals broadcaster Jack Buck lived on the street after Berra and Garagiola had left. 7. Green Bay Packers organizer and coach Curly Lambeau. 8. Walter Payton and Jackie Slater. 9. Dean Smith and Adolph Rupp. 10. Jim Thorpe.

TOM, DICK AND HARRY (WARMING UP): 1. Tom Watson, 1981. 2. Rams running back Eric Dickerson ran for a single-season record 2,105 yards in 1984. 3. Tom Sneva won the Indy 500 in 1983. 4. Detroit's Harry Heilmann won batting titles in 1921, '23, '25 and '27 with averages of .394, .403, .393 and .398. 5. Dick

Vermeil guided the 1980 Philadelphia Eagles to Super Bowl 15, where they lost; he directed the 1999 St. Louis Rams to Super Bowl 34, where they won. 6. Tom Harmon, a halfback from Michigan, won the Heisman in 1940; Dick Kazmaier, a Princeton tailback, won in 1951. 7. Rudy Tomjanovich guided the Houston Rockets to consecutive titles in 1994 and '95. 8. Tom Smith. 9. Isiah Thomas of Indiana. 10. Thomas Hearns.

TOM, DICK AND HARRY (GETTING SERIOUS): 1. Tom Landry's Cowboys won Super Bowls 6 and 12; Tom Flores' Raiders won Super Bowls 15 and 18. 2. Harry Vardon, after whom golf's Vardon Trophy is named. 3. Harry "Suitcase" Simpson was a major league outfielder from 1951-59. 4. Dick Motta guided the 1977-78 Washington Bullets to a seven-game Finals win over Seattle. 5. Coach Tom Osborne and quarterback Tommie Frazier performed their magic for the Nebraska Cornhuskers. 6. Dick Irvin. 7. Harry Wright. 8. Tom Kite. 9. Dick Weber. 10. Harry Caray.

ANIMAL MAGNETISM (WARMING UP): 1. Gallant Fox, 1930. 2. The Atlanta Hawks and Toronto Raptors of the NBA; the Arizona Cardinals, Atlanta Falcons, Baltimore Ravens, Philadelphia Eagles and Seattle Seahawks of the NFL. 3. Golf great Jack Nicklaus, the Golden Bear, would have little trouble dispatching hockey's Bobby Hull, the Golden Jet, and football's Donnie Anderson, the Golden Palomino. 4. The Thundering Herd of Marshall vs. the Rattlers of Florida A&M. 5. Larry Finch. 6. A baby pig, a fitting gift for the king of chauvinists. 7. Amos Alonzo Stagg. 8. Chick Gandil. 9. Outfielder Goose Goslin and relief ace Goose Gossage. 10. Bunny Larocque.

ANIMAL MAGNETISM (GETTING SERIOUS): 1. Lynn Swann. 2. Nellie Fox. 3. Tiger Woods. 4. Catfish Hunter. 5. Bear Bryant. 6. Otis Birdsong. 7. Chick Hearn. 8. Randy Wolf. 9. Notre Dame's Four Horsemen. 10. Bob Moose.

FAMOUS NUMBERS (WARMING UP): 1. 3:59.4. 2. Six times. 3. Beck shot the second 59 in a sanctioned PGA tournament event. 4. DiMaggio followed his 56-game streak with a 16-game streak. 5. 51-50. 6. 50-50. 7. 35-10. 8. It went into the books as a 57-yard kickoff return. 9. 200. 10. 122.

FAMOUS NUMBERS (GETTING SERIOUS): 1. The record long jump distance covered by Bob Beamon in the 1968 Summer Olympic Games at Mexico City. 2. The width of a football field. 3. The height of Fenway Park's Green Monster left field wall. 4. The width and height of an NBA backboard. 5. The score by which Georgia Tech defeated Cumberland College in 1916. 6. The depth and diameter of a regulation golf hole. 7. The length and width of a tennis court. 8. The height and weight of the Heisman Trophy. 9. The most distant point of the center field wall at New York's Polo Grounds. 10. The distance between the uprights on NFL goalposts.

IT WAS A VERY GOOD YEAR (WARMING UP): 1. 1992. 2. 1977. 3. 1948. 4. 1990. 5. 1976. 6. 1972. 7. 1985. 8. 1966. 9. 2000. 10. 1980.

IT WAS A VERY GOOD YEAR (GETTING SERIOUS): 1. 11 + 34 = (19)45. 2. 63 + 31 = (19)94. 3. 79 — 10 = (19)69. 4. 61 + 20 = (19)81. 5. 48 — 7 = (19)41. 6. 16 x 3 = (19)48. 7. 66 + 6 = (19)72. 8. 11 x 5 = (19)55. 9. 88 + 0 = (19)88. 10. 7 x 10 = (19)70.

THE GAY NINETIES (WARMING UP): 1. San Antonio's David Robinson won in 1993-94, Orlando's Shaquille O'Neal won in 1994-95 and Philadelphia's Allen Iverson won in 1998-99. 2. Dan Reeves lost while coaching Denver against San Francisco and Atlanta against Denver. 3. Seattle DH Edgar Martinez won in 1992 and '95. 4. Silver Charm finished second in the Belmont in 1997, Real Quiet finished second in the Belmont in 1998 and Charismatic finished third in the Belmont in 1999. 5. Brett Hull scored 512 goals in the decade. 6. North Carolina. 7. Payne Stewart won in 1991 and 1999; he finished second to Lee Janzen in 1993 and 1998. 8. Bo Kimble. 9. Andre Agassi, Stefan Edberg and Patrick Rafter won two apiece. 10. Marshall won 114 games, including bowls. Florida State's .890 winning percentage (109-13-1) was tops.

THE GAY NINETIES (GETTING SERIOUS): 1. Jeff Gordon. 2. Montreal. 3. Martina Hingis. 4. Detroit. 5. Tiger Woods. 6. No World Series was played in 1994. 7. Charismatic. 8. UCLA. 9. Rick Mears. 10. Ricky Williams.

SECOND THOUGHTS (WARMING UP): 1.Maureen Connolly won all four women's titles in 1953.

2. Nicklaus finished second or tied for second in grand slam events 19 times over his illustrious career. 3. Another Montreal star, Boom Boom Geoffrion, scored 50 goals in 1960-61. 4. Wilt Chamberlain reached the 20,000 plateau in 1965-66, two years after Bob Pettit did it for the St. Louis Hawks. 5. The Minnesota Vikings lost in Super Bowl 4 and Super Bowl 8. 6. Cale Yarborough won at Daytona four times. 7. Twice a Prince. 8. Philadelphia's Steve Van Buren ran for 1,008 yards in 1947 and enjoyed a 205-yard game two years later. 9. St. Louis second baseman Rogers Hornsby hit 42 homers in 1922. 10. George Mikan scored 61 points in a double-overtime game for Minneapolis in 1952, almost three years after Joe Fulks had scored 63 in a regulation game for Philadelphia.

SECOND THOUGHTS (GETTING SERIOUS): 1. The Venezuelan golfer who signed an incorrect score-card on the final day of the 1968 Masters, costing himself a first-place tie and a shot at a playoff. A distraught De Vicenzo finished second to Bob Goalby. 2. The great racehorse that was pushed to second-place status for the first time in his storied career when he was upset, appropriately, by Upset in a 1919 race at Saratoga, N.Y. 3. The American League's second-best hitter in 1968, the year Carl Yastrzemski won a batting title with a .301 average. 4. The second man to break the 4-minute mile barrier in 1954. Roger Bannister was first. 5. Minnesota's Tovar is the second player to play all nine positions in a single game, following the 1965 lead of Kansas City shortstop Bert Campaneris. 6. Meyer finished second to Jay Berwanger in the first Heisman Trophy vote in 1935. 7. A close second in all three 1978 Triple Crown races—the Kentucky Derby, Preakness and Belmont—when Affirmed won his Triple Crown. 8. When St. Louis first baseman Mark McGwire hit his single-season record 70 home runs in 1998, Chicago Cubs right fielder Sosa finished second with 66—four more than the previous single-season record. 9. Finland lost to the United States in the 1980 Olympic gold medal hockey game at Lake Placid, N.Y., and claimed the silver medal. The Soviet Union finished third, not second as is commonly believed. 10. The school that suffered what many consider the biggest upset loss in NCAA Tournament championship game history when it fell in 1985 to Villanova. The powerful Hoyas had to settle for second.

Photo Credits

Photographers

Albert Dickson/Sporting News: Pages 16, 16-17, 28 (No. 15), 30 (No. 22), 31 (Nos. 23, 24), 32 (No. 27), 35 (No. 36), 37 (No. 42), 121, 158 (Manning), 175, 177 (No. 17), 178 (No. 20), 179 (Nos. 24, 26), 182, 203 (No. 7), 211 (No. 22).

Bob Leverone/Sporting News: Pages 23 (top right, Blue Devil), 23 (No. 1), 25 (Nos. 5, 7), 27 (Nos. 11, 12, 13), 29 (Nos. 17, 18, 19), 31 (No. 25), 32 (Nos. 26, 28), 33 (No. 29), 34 (Nos. 32, 35), 35 (No. 37), 36 (No. 40), 38 (No. 47), 39 (No. 48), 54, 56, 118 (Hasek), 152-153, 156 (Bowden), 166, 172 (No. 4), 173 (No. 7), 174 (No. 12), 178 (No. 21), 179 (No. 27), 180 (No. 31), 181, 206 (No. 13), 218 (Glavine), 222 (Anderson), 241, 256 (Duncan), 256 (Hull).

Paul Nisely/Sporting News: Pages 33 (No. 30), 35 (No. 38), 154 (Penn State).

Robert Seale/Sporting News: Pages 24 (No. 3), 26 (Nos. 8, 10), 34 (No. 33), 36 (Nos. 39, 41), 37 (No. 44), 38 (No. 46), 39 (No. 50), 50-51, 76 (Olajuwon), 77, 152 , 171, 172 (No. 3), 173 (No. 6), 174 (No. 13), 176, 177 (No. 19), 180 (Nos. 28, 29), 192, 202 (Nos. 2, 3), 211 (No. 24), 256 (Torre).

John Cordes for Sporting News: Page 30 (No. 21).

Dave Darnell for Sporting News: Page 33 (No. 31).

David Durochik for Sporting News: Pages 232-233 (crowd).

Garrett W. Ellwood for Sporting News: Pages 37 (No. 43), 38 (No. 45).

Chris Grassmick for Sporting News: Page 26 (No. 9).

Fernando Medina for Sporting News: Page 28 (No. 16).

Craig Melvin for Sporting News: Page 24 (Nos. 2, 4).

John Reed for Sporting News: Page 25 (No. 6).

Jamie Sabau for Sporting News: Page 34 (No. 34).

Associated Press: Page 129.

Classmates Media, Inc.: Pages 63 (Steinbrenner), 68 (Hamm, Barkley), 70 (Ditka, Gordon), Page 71 (Namath, Palmer, Hershiser), 72 (Hamm), 73 (Lewis).

College and Universities: California—Page 69 (Gonzalez); Harvard—Page 64 (Tommy Lee Jones); Montana State—Page 67 (Kilborn); Syracuse—Page 73 (Brown); Temple—Page 60 (Cosby); Tennessee—Pages 60-61 (Helton); UCLA—Pages 61 (Harmon), 68 (Robinson); William & Mary—Page 61 (Stewart).

Augusta High School: Page 69 (Clooney).

Sporting News Archives: Pages 4-5 (crowd), 4-5 (Berra), 7, 8 (Thomas), 8 (Bagwell), 8 (Ainge), 9, 10 (Hassey), 10 (DiMaggio), 10-11, 12 (Drysdale), 12 (Banks), 12 (Ruppert-Gordon), 13, 14 (Aaron), 14 (Reese), 14 (McGwire), 17 (Wilhelm), 17 (Nen), 18, 19, 20, 23 (top right, Jayhawk), 28 (No. 14), 30 (No. 20), 39 (No. 49), 41, 42 (Taylor), 42 (Sayers), 43, 44 (Mora), 44 (Mularkey), 44 (Simpson), 44-45, 46 (Watters), 46 (Elway), 47, 48 (Reed), 48 (Morris), 49, 50 (Favre), 50 (Marino), 52-53. 55, 59, 60 (Ripken), 61 (Bryant), 62 (Aaron), 62 (Auerbach), 62 (Ford), 63 (Chamberlain), 63 (Shula), 64 (Lasorda), 64 (Yastrzemski), 65 (Nixon), 65 (Olsen), 65 (Wayne), 66 (P. Jackson), 66 (Marinaro), 66-67, 67 (Anderson), 67 (La Russa), 69 (Wilkens), 69 (Ryan), 70 (Williams), 72 (Dryer), 72 (Feller), 73 (Schmidt), 75, 76 (Roberts), 76 (Wilkins), 78, 78-79, 80 (Bird), 80 (Walton), 81, 82 (West), 82 (Baylor), 82-83, 84 (Malone), 84 (Hardaway), 86, 86-87, 88, 89, 90-91, 111, 112 (Robinson), 112 (Yzerman), 113, 114 (Richard), 114 (Bowman), 114 (Arbour), 114-115, 115, 116 (Shore), 116 (Messier), 117, 118 (Roy), 119, 120, 120-121, 122, 123, 124, 126-127, 130-131, 132-133, 134-135, 136-137, 138-139, 140-141, 142-143, 144-145, 146-147, 148-149, 151, 154 (Rice), 154 (Cappelletti), 155, 156 (Griffin), 156-157, 158 (Davis), 158-159, 160 (Marinaro), 160 (Dooley), 161 (Heisman), 161 (Edwards), 162, 163 (Holtz), 163 (Terrapin),

164, 165, 167 (Bryant), 167 (Hayes), 168-169, 172 (Nos. 2, 5), 173 (Nos. 8, 9),174 (Nos. 10, 11), 177 (Nos. 16, 18), 178 (Nos. 22, 23), 179 (No. 25), 180 (No. 30), 183 (Nos. 34, 35, 36, 37), 185, 186, 186-187, 188, 188-189, 189, 190, 191 (Maravich), 191 (Robertson), 193, 194, 194-195, 196 (Calipari), 196 (Reeves), 198, 201, 202 (No. 4), 203 (Nos. 5, 6), 204 (Nos. 8, 9, 10), 205, 206 (Nos. 12, 14), 207 (Nos. 15, 16), 208 (Nos. 17, 18, 19), 209, 210, 211 (No. 23), 213, 214 (Bezdek), 214 (Jefferies), 214-215, 216, 216-217, 218 (J. Robinson), 220 (Russell), 220 (F. Robinson), 220 (Twyman), 221, 222 (Sosa), 222 (Jagr), 222-223, 224, 225, 226, 228, 229, 230 (Lombardi), 230 (Hannum), 232-233 (Elway, Knight, Rodman, Torre), 235, 236, 237, 238 (Marciano), 238 (Holmes), 238 (Starr), 239, 240, 242 (Louis), 242 (Irwin), 244, 245, 247, 250 (Borg), 250 (Foyt), 251, 252, 253, 254, 256 (Barkley), 256 (Brett), 256 (Stewart), 256 (Montana), 256 (Griffey), 256 (Bryant), 256 (Krzyzewski), 256 (Favre), 256 (Elway), 256 (Gretzky), 256 (Earnhardt).